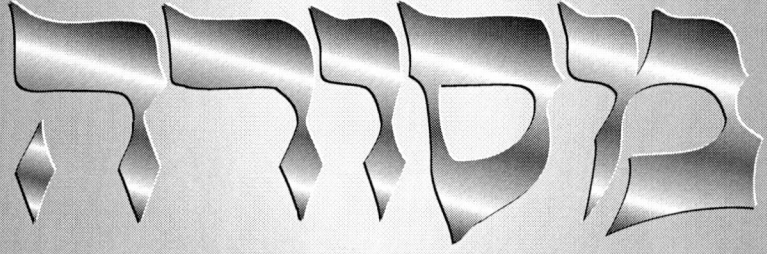

ArtScroll Series™

Rabbi Nosson Scherman / Rabbi Meir Zlotowitz
General Editors

Shlomo Gross
A life of growth and achievement

Published by
Mesorah Publications, ltd

SHLOMIE!

by
Rabbi Shimon Finkelman

FIRST EDITION
First Impression ... March 2013

Published and Distributed by
MESORAH PUBLICATIONS, LTD.
4401 Second Avenue / Brooklyn, N.Y 11232

Distributed in Europe by
LEHMANNS
Unit E, Viking Business Park
Rolling Mill Road
Jarow, Tyne & Wear, NE32 3DP
England

Distributed in Australia and New Zealand
by **GOLDS WORLDS OF JUDAICA**
3-13 William Street
Balaclava, Melbourne 3183
Victoria, Australia

Distributed in Israel by
SIFRIATI / A. GITLER — BOOKS
6 Hayarkon Street
Bnei Brak 51127

Distributed in South Africa by
KOLLEL BOOKSHOP
Northfield Centre, 17 Northfield Avenue
Glenhazel 2192, Johannesburg, South Africa

ARTSCROLL SERIES™
SHLOMIE!
© Copyright 2013, by MESORAH PUBLICATIONS, Ltd.
4401 Second Avenue / Brooklyn, N.Y. 11232 / (718) 921-9000 / www.artscroll.com

---

Photo Credits:
Mirrer Yeshivah (of Brooklyn)   Envogue Studios
Tsemach Glenn   Mendel Meyers Studios
The Visual Image Studios   Nechomas Yisroel

ALL RIGHTS RESERVED
The text, prefatory and associated textual contents and introductions
— including the typographic layout, cover artwork and ornamental graphics —
have been designed, edited and revised as to content, form and style.

No part of this book may be reproduced
IN ANY FORM, PHOTOCOPYING, OR COMPUTER RETRIEVAL SYSTEMS
— even for personal use without written permission from
the copyright holder, Mesorah Publications Ltd.
except by a reviewer who wishes to quote brief passages
in connection with a review written for inclusion in magazines or newspapers.

THE RIGHTS OF THE COPYRIGHT HOLDER WILL BE STRICTLY ENFORCED.

ISBN 10: 1-4226-1372-0 / ISBN 13: 978-1-4226-1372-6

Typography by CompuScribe at ArtScroll Studios, Ltd.
Printed in the United States of America
Bound by Sefercraft, Quality Bookbinders, Ltd., Brooklyn N.Y. 11232

Table of Contents

	A Letter to the Reader	7
	Author's Preface	9
Chapter 1	Man With a Mission	13
Chapter 2	Turbulent Beginnings	31
Chapter 3	Marriage	48
Chapter 4	Reaching Higher	62
Chapter 5	The 'Great Connector'	83
Chapter 6	His Great Heart	104
Chapter 7	The Ultimate Baal Tzedakah	144
Chapter 8	A Man of Action	177
Chapter 9	For Love of Torah	201
Chapter 10	A (Not So) "Regular Guy"	234
Chapter 11	Helping Our Youth	263
Chapter 12	Family Man	277
Chapter 13	Final Days	298
Chapter 14	Mourning the Loss	309

A Letter to the Reader

DEAR READER,

It is hard to believe that a year has passed since our world was suddenly, irrevocably, turned upside down. The pain is still fresh, the tears still flow freely. While *Klal Yisrael* has come to terms with the loss of its *Amud HaChesed,* we still mourn the loss of our loving husband and father.

Over the last year many stories of Shlomie's selfless acts of *chesed* have come to light. We, Shlomie's family, knew he gave *tzedakah* and helped people, yet we were never aware of how far his acts of kindness went, of how great his generosity was — for he was always very careful to keep his accomplishments private.

He ingrained this sense of privacy within all of us. Therefore, publishing a book about his accomplishments is the antithesis of his, as well as our, very nature. Yet, we still approached ArtScroll to undertake this publication because our only *nechamah* lies in the countless acts of *chesed,* and the hours of *limud haTorah,* that are done *l'iluy nishmaso.* It is when we hear how an individual is improving or overcoming his natural tendencies because "that's what Shlomie would have done!" that our pain eases just a bit.

Shlomie was not born the legend he became. His greatest traits did not come to him naturally. His story is a story of transformation, of personal growth, of constantly working on himself to improve, striving to become a better husband, a better father, a better *eved Hashem*. It was with this goal in mind that he placed himself in surroundings that would nurture his growth, that he befriended those who would prod him along on his chosen path, and that he attached himself to *gedolei Yisrael* to learn from their ways.

In publishing this book we are hoping that you, the reader, will be inspired to improve, to grow, to realize that no matter what your natural tendencies may be, you too can achieve greatness. That inspiration and growth will be a *zechus* for Shlomie's *neshamah*.

We are eternally grateful to Rabbi Shimon Finkelman for the professionalism and sensitivity he brought to this project. Shlomie meant so much to so many people. The author dedicated much time and effort to get a complete picture of who Shlomie was, and blended it together with a mastery that has resulted in this final product which, we hope, will do justice to Shlomie's legacy.

Mrs. Mimi Gross and Family

Author's Preface

"As I join the ranks of thousands who feel the indescribable loss, I'm reminded of all the inspiration that I've been privileged to attain over the years from R' Shlomie.

"...He taught the world how to give, give, and then give some more.

"...The last time I saw him, he was in the middle of learning. He smiled and waved but would not interrupt his learning ... that's how he valued his time for limud haTorah.

"...His way of doing things — the right way — inspired all those who were privileged to know him.

"Perhaps a small nechamah comes from the knowledge that his memory and zest for chesed will continue to inspire others."

THE ABOVE IS DRAWN FROM ONE OF THE MANY LETTERS the family of Shlomo Yehudah Gross ע"ה received following his sudden passing one year ago. Shlomie viewed himself as a "regular guy" and, as his family wrote in their "Letter to the Reader," did his best to keep his countless good deeds a secret. There is no doubt that many of his acts of *tzedakah* and *chesed* will remain hidden forever. That is what he wanted.

This book is not intended to be a complete biography like books on *gedolei Yisrael*. Only a small percentage of it is devoted to biographical material, and even that is intended to contrast how Shlomie was in his younger years with the change he underwent later in life. The book's purpose is to inspire, to tell of a man whose great accomplishments can be summed up this way: He changed himself and he changed the world around him by "giving and then giving some more" — not just money, but giving of himself with his great heart that overflowed with *ahavas Yisrael*.

Writing this book has been an emotional experience. Scores of interviews were conducted, with rabbanim and roshei yeshivah, with friends, relatives, and acquaintances of Shlomie. It happened a number of times that the same interviewee laughed and cried — laughed as he recalled Shlomie's fun-loving nature, his scintillating humor, his antics; and cried for the pain of the loss of this great man of kindness and compassion who, in the words of Rabbi Elya Ber Wachtfogel, "would have given the shirt off his back for someone else."

My only personal memories of Shlomie were from his days as a sweet but wild teenager in Camp Torah Vodaath, and later of his warm handshake when we met at *simchos* over the years. In essence, I did not know him. But I have gotten to know him during the past half-year, and I must confess that I have cried a number of times in the privacy of my home as I sat listening to recordings of *hespeidim* and reviewing photos for this book.

Through this book you too, dear reader, will come to know Shlomie — and a very special experience it is.

It is a privilege to have worked with the Gross family on this book, and I cannot thank them enough for having entrusted me with the sacred task of writing about Shlomie.

While I am grateful to the entire extended family, I am especially grateful to Shlomie's wife, Mrs. Mimi Gross תחי׳, and members of her family for granting me this privilege and for investing so much time and effort into ensuring that this project be done right.

The primary letters of the word אֱמוּנָה, *faith,* spell אֵם, *mother.* This alludes to a mother's crucial role in instilling *emunah* in her offspring. Shlomie's mother, Mrs. Rivka Gross תחי׳, embodies this truth. I thank her for allowing me to interview her. I know that it was not easy.

I was privileged to interview Shlomie's mother-in-law, Mrs. Sarah Cyperstein תחי׳, who also expressed a deep-rooted faith in Hashem. May Hashem grant these great women good health and much *nachas* from their beautiful families.

I thank all those who gave of their time to share their recollections. I sincerely apologize to the many friends and others who would have liked to share their recollections of Shlomie but were not contacted. With any biography it is simply impossible to contact everyone, and such was especially the case with this book. Shlomie had many close friends, of varying ages and walks of life.

Rabbi Meir Zlotowitz recognized the importance of a book about a *"balabos,"* someone who was neither a rav or rosh yeshivah, but who accomplished great things in his allotted time on this earth. I am indebted to him for having arranged the *"shidduch"* between me and the Gross family to collaborate on this book.

As always, Rabbi Nosson Scherman, my *rebbi*, mentor, and constructive critic, has made himself available whenever I sought his input — including his editing of three chapters. And he has done this kindness at a difficult time, for his *eishes chayil*, Mrs. Chana Scherman ע״ה, passed away less than two months ago.

Chazal tell us, אֵשֶׁת חָבֵר הֲרֵי הִיא כְּחָבֵר, *The wife of a scholar is like a scholar.* I owe an eternal debt of gratitude to Mrs. Scherman for all that I have gained from Rabbi Scherman over the years. And I will never forget the warmth with which she welcomed me and my family into their home on Purim and other occasions. May Hashem grant her family *nechamah*. Surely, she intercedes in *Shamayim* on behalf of her family and all of *Klal Yisrael*.

This book is yet another testimony to the talents of Rabbi Sheah Brander, whose ground-breaking graphics artistry continues to enhance *kevod Shamayim*.

Rabbi Avrohom Biderman always finds time in his busy schedule to respond to my questions and assist me whenever needed.

Mendy Herzberg has the perfect temperament to be a project coordinator; it is a pleasure to work with him. My thanks to him; to Reb Eli Kroen for the beautiful cover; to Sury England for her expert pagination; and to the rest of the ArtScroll staff.

Some vignettes were culled from articles in *Yated Ne'eman* that appeared during the *shivah* and at the conclusion of *sheloshim*.

Tsemach Glenn was among Shlomie's friends and over the years photographed Shlomie with *gedolei Yisrael* and friends. Many of his photos appear in this book. I thank him and the others who contributed photos.

My wife Tova 'תחי is an equal partner in whatever I accomplish. יהי רצון שימלא ה' משאלות לבה לטובה.

I offer thanks to the *Ribono shel Olam* for His having allowed me to undertake and complete this project. My *tefillah* is that this book accomplish its intended purpose — to inspire its readers to strengthen their relationship with Hashem and with their fellow Jew. And may this inspiration be a source of *nechamah* to Shlomie's family and bring his lofty *neshamah* to an even higher place in *Gan Eden*.

Shimon Finkelman
Adar 5773

1

Man With a Mission

IT WAS ABOUT TWO WEEKS BEFORE PESACH, A VERY BUSY time. A family in Boro Park had fallen upon hard times, and could not make their Yom Tov purchases without financial assistance. A *chesed* organization in Williamsburg was providing them with their basic Yom Tov needs — boxes, sacks and cases of food, and food-related items.

The family did not own a car, and the merchandise had to be picked up from the warehouse. How would they get it? It was no problem. Shlomie[1] Gross, who helped this family in other ways, was happy to serve as delivery boy.

On the surface this seems strange. Why would a successful, charismatic, extremely busy *askan* (community activist) bother with such a thing? If he wanted to help out the family, he could have easily hired someone for the task.

Anyone who knew Shlomie would not have asked the question. He not only gave *tzedakah,* he was a very active *baal chesed*.

Realizing that the task would be difficult for one person to accomplish, Shlomie asked a friend to come along. At the warehouse,

---
1. Pronounced "Shloimy." In some quotations in this book he is called Shloime, pronounced "Shloim'eh."

Shlomie and his friend rolled up their sleeves and began carrying 50-pound sacks of potatoes and onions, and sundry other items.

But there was no chicken; the last case had already been given away. The distribution manager offered Shlomie a coupon. "We'll get another delivery tomorrow. Show this to anyone here and you'll get your case of chicken."

"Thanks," Shlomie replied, "but I don't have the time to come back tomorrow. I'll figure something out."

The car loaded, they drove to Boro Park and stopped outside a butcher store. Shlomie took out his phone and called his wife. "Mimi," he said, "this family that I'm bringing the Pesach stuff to — what kind of chickens do you think they would want?" Shlomie's wife advised him, he made the purchase, and he was now ready to make the delivery.

When they arrived at the family's apartment building, Shlomie's friend helped him carry everything to the ground-floor elevator. When the last box had been brought in, Shlomie said, "Wait here while I bring everything upstairs. It's bad enough that *I* know how poor they are. They don't need someone else knowing about it." And he proceeded to bring everything upstairs unassisted.[2]

By the testimony of his childhood friends, Shlomie was born with a heart of gold, which he further developed as he matured. In the last two decades of his life, he was a living embodiment of the words of Rav Chaim Volozhiner, as reported by his son, Rav Yitzchak Volozhiner:

> *He always told me: Man was not created for himself; rather [he was created] to help others in whatever way his abilities allow.*[3]

In the words of Rabbi Lipa Geldwerth, a noted rav and *maggid shiur*:

> *There are some rare people who say that this is their calling — to help their brothers. It begins with a natural*

---
2. Rabbi Yitzchak Mitnick.
3. Preface to *Nefesh HaChaim*.

goodness, but then that goodness is nurtured and developed and becomes greater and greater ... Shlomie was a gaon in knowing how to cheer people up, and ensuring that they smile. When I think of him I think of the Rambam's words: "There is no greater and more glorious joy than to gladden the hearts of poor people and of orphans, widows, and converts. For whoever [does so] ... is likened to the Shechinah ..."[4]

An Israeli Rosh Yeshivah related:

A couple of years after I was first introduced to Shlomie, my wife developed complications during childbirth and her life was in danger. She delivered healthy twins, but for two weeks she remained in the ICU, connected to machines that kept her alive. The doctor told me, "There's nothing more we can do. It's in Hashem's hands."

Baruch Hashem, my wife recovered, but it was a long process. After a year, she was home and functioning as a mother to her many children, but she still lacked strength and her spirit had not fully returned.

*Around that time Shlomie was planning the wedding of his oldest child (Adina). One day I received a phone call from him. "I am sending plane tickets for you and your wife. You **must** come to the wedding — you must have a healthy wife."*

We came to New York and enjoyed the wedding. During the week of sheva berachos Shlomie took us on a horse and buggy ride through Central Park. After an enjoyable ride he said, "We have to buy presents for the children." I tried to convince him that it would be sufficient to buy one present for everyone to share, but he would not hear of it. He took us to a toy store in Manhattan and purchased a nice toy for each of my children.

That trip did wonders for my wife.

---

4. *Hilchos Megillah* 2:17.

Shlomie did all that for one reason: He truly felt another's pain. He put himself in my shoes and felt that he had to find a way to help my wife regain her former strength and spirit.

A Prince of Goodness

A FRIEND REFERRED TO SHLOMIE AS "THE PRINCE OF Jerusalem." On his frequent visits to the Holy City, he was greeted by scores of "Yerushalmis," upright men, many of them *talmidei chachamim*, whom Shlomie had assisted financially and in other ways at some point in time.

A friend related:

> *I was driving with him in Yerushalayim when we passed a famous chassidishe shul. Shlomie noticed one of his Yerushalmi friends and honked the horn to get his attention. The man hurried to the car ... and a few others followed behind him. Shlomie got out of the car and in moments was surrounded by Yerushalmis who were hugging him with genuine love.*[5]

One such Yerushalmi related:

> *Dovid HaMelech says* אַשְׁרֵי מַשְׂכִּיל אֶל דָּל *(Praiseworthy is he who contemplates the needy).*[6] *Shlomie was unusual in his ability to understand exactly what each person needed and to provide him with those needs — as I experienced firsthand.*
>
> *I was preparing to return to Eretz Yisrael after having spent two months in America with one of my children who required medical treatment. A few days before my return Shlomie said to me, "You've been away for so long, it would be proper to bring home something nice for your wife."*

---

5. Avraham Colman.
6. *Tehillim* 41:2.

> I knew that he was right, but I had no idea what to get for her. Shlomie had it all figured out. "I'm calling a women's clothing store in Flatbush. You'll go there and get a nice dress for her."
>
> The proprietor asked me, "So what kind of dress would you like to get?" I had absolutely no idea, so the person picked up the phone and called Shlomie. Shlomie said, "Pack up for him any dress that you think his wife might like — and bill me."
>
> I walked out of the store carrying a package with six or seven dresses. Judging by my wife's reaction, I can tell you that it was a wonderful idea.

Rabbi Aharon Samet, *Menahel* of Toldos Aharon in Jerusalem, said:

> I never met anyone like Shlomie Gross. He assisted the poor without a gabbai to distribute his tzedakah, without fanfare. He would come to Yerushalayim, visit the homes of broken, impoverished families, and leave behind tzedakah that helped them in a very meaningful way.
>
> To help a fellow Yid was his greatest pleasure in life.

Dancing with Rabbi Aharon Samet in Jerusalem

A Unique Individual

RABBI ELYA BER WACHTFOGEL, ROSH YESHIVAH OF YESHIvah Gedolah Zichron Moshe of South Fallsburg, New York, had a close relationship with Shlomie. In his words:

> Shlomie was a מַעְיָן דְלֹא פָּסַק, a wellspring without end, of tzedakah and chesed. He gave tzedakah without cheshbonos (calculations). There was no concept of giving maaser (one-tenth) or chomesh (one-fifth). He just gave and gave. He could not say "No" to someone in need.
>
> His heart was so great. He would have given the shirt off his back for someone else. He didn't just give tzedakah; he became involved in the person's situation as if that person were his own child — he was חַד בְּדָרָא, unique in his generation.
>
> He was wealthy, but materialism meant nothing to him. What did concern him was the chinuch of his children.

With Rabbi Elya Ber Wachtfogel

Sharing the Burden

AS HE MATURED, SHLOMIE'S GOODNESS BECAME INTERtwined with a heightened sensitivity for another's situation and an unusual level of *nosei b'ol*, sharing in someone else's pain. A friend related:

Shlomie and I often davened Maariv and then walked home together. As we walked, his cellphone would ring every couple of minutes, usually with someone calling to ask a favor. He never turned off his phone, and it was rare that he did not answer a call immediately.

Many times as we walked, he would express his anguish over a problem that someone had called him about that day. He took people's tzaros very much to heart; their pain was his pain, and it affected him in a very personal way.[7]

He did not have to know the person well to take his plight to heart, as one man testified:

My contact with Shlomie was being part of the same minyan, on occasion, at Rabbi Landau's shul in Flatbush.

One day I met him at the Diamond District on 47th Street in Manhattan. I asked him what he was doing there and he replied that his daughter was getting

---

7. Tzale Edelstein.

married the following night, and he had come to buy a piece of jewelry. He asked me what my *parnasah* (livelihood) was, and I replied that I had been laid off from work six months earlier.

When I told him my profession, he took out his cellphone and made call after call on my behalf. He succeeded in arranging a job interview for me.

Astounded, I said, "Why are you doing this? You are so busy — you're making a wedding tomorrow night!"

Shlomie did not seem to understand my question. "I should go to the *chuppah* and you shouldn't have a job?"

※ ※ ※ ※ ※ ※ ※

A tragedy occurred in Williamsburg when a young chassidishe boy was hit by a bus and killed. Shlomie called up a friend and asked, "Are you coming to the *levayah* (funeral)? I'm here; it's going on right now."

Later that day, his friend met him in Williamsburg. He accompanied Shlomie as he went to food establishments, purchasing an assortment of foods to bring to the mourners.

He did not know the family. But a Jewish child had died and a family was in pain. Shlomie had to share in their pain and help them in some small way.[8]

Chazal teach: "If someone prays on his friend's behalf and he needs that same thing, he will be answered first."[9] R' Yitzchak of Vorka interprets *"and he needs that same thing"* to mean that the person *davens* for his friend as if he himself must have his friend's need met. This was Shlomie's approach to someone else's pain.

※ ※ ※ ※ ※ ※ ※

---

8. Kalman Tabak.
9. *Bava Kamma* 92a. See *Rashi* to *Bereishis* 21:1.

Along with his natural goodness, Shlomie was born with a wild nature, and an inability to sit still for long periods of time or focus on his studies.

He was a boy who needed to overcome serious, difficult challenges.

He was the kind of child some might label destined for failure.

In the Torah's view, no one is destined for failure, though some certainly have to work much harder than others to achieve success. But as the Mishnah teaches, לְפוּם צַעֲרָא אַגְרָא, *the reward is in proportion to the effort*.[10] Sometimes, those who are especially challenged achieve the greatest success.

Such was the case with Dovid HaMelech.

Dovid vs. Esav

THE VILNA GAON WRITES THAT MAN'S PRIMARY PURPOSE on this world is *l'sakein es hamiddos*, to correct one's character flaws. But this does not mean that a person must change his inherent nature. Shlomo HaMelech says חֲנוֹךְ לַנַּעַר עַל פִּי דַרְכּוֹ, *Train the youth according to his way*.[11] The Vilna Gaon explains that a parent should not attempt to break his child's innate nature. Rather, he should channel that nature towards the good. As the Gemara states, someone who is born under the *mazal* (horoscope) of *Maadim* (Mars) is destined to shed blood. He can become a murderer, or he can channel his nature positively and become a blood-letter; or he can take it to a higher level and utilize his nature for a mitzvah by becoming a *mohel*.[12]

Dovid HaMelech, says the Gaon, is a classic example of someone who channeled his nature for the good. Dovid is described as אַדְמוֹנִי עִם יְפֵה עֵינַיִם, *red, with fair eyes*.[13] When Shmuel HaNavi

---

10. *Avos* 5:26.
11. *Mishlei* 22:6.
12. *Shabbos* 156a.
13. *Shmuel I* 16:12.

went to anoint a king from the sons of Yishai and saw that Dovid had a ruddy complexion, indicating that he had been born under the *mazal* of *Maadim*, he grew apprehensive. Shmuel said to himself, "Perhaps he is one who sheds blood like the wicked Esav!" (Esav had this same complexion; the Torah states וַיֵּצֵא הָרִאשׁוֹן אַדְמוֹנִי, *The first one emerged red.*[14]) But Hashem informed Shmuel that Dovid was יְפֵה עֵינַיִם; whatever killing he would carry out would be with the agreement of the *Sanhedrin*, who are called עֵינֵי הָעֵדָה, *the eyes of the assembly.*

The Gaon says that the secret of Dovid's success, the reason he merited to retain his monarchy despite the fact that he erred twice,[15] was that all his life he worked to overcome his nature and channel it in a positive direction. The Gaon refers to Dovid as one who was מַעֲבִיר עַל מִדּוֹתָיו, which in this context means he took his *middos*, innate tendencies, and transferred (was *maavir*) them from bad to good. For such spiritual strength the reward, measure for measure, is מַעֲבִירִין לוֹ עַל כָּל פְּשָׁעָיו, all his sins are *transferred* (i.e., removed). This is why Hashem overlooked Dovid's two sins.

Dovid's entire life was an uphill battle of spiritual struggle, a battle that he won decisively, and in that merit Jewish monarchy became his forever.

Shlomo Yehudah Gross struggled all his life. It was obvious that, as a young child, he had great difficulty functioning in a classroom setting. His dedicated, loving parents tried everything — but nothing seemed to work. He would go out the door of one yeshivah and into another, a pattern that repeated itself until the end of high school. He got a job in a summer camp and was sent home. His last official stop as a *talmid* in yeshivah was in Mirrer Yeshivah in Brooklyn. Before long he was spending most of his time patrolling the streets against anti-Semitic youths who would sometimes harass the yeshivah students.

---

14. *Bereishis* 25:25. See *Baal HaTurim*.
15. See *Yoma* 20b.

Against All Odds

A CLOSE FRIEND DESCRIBED HIS FIRST ENCOUNTER WITH him:

When I first met Shlomie, I was 19 and he was 12. It was before vacation, and a friend and I were driving to the Lower East Side to buy suits. We met Shlomie at a friend's house and he asked if he could come along.

My first impression was that this boy was not the typical 12-year-old. He was extremely wild. When we set out from Boro Park, my friend and I were in the front seat and Shlomie was in the back. But as we approached the Manhattan Bridge, we pulled over and I got out of the car and went to the back so that I could keep an eye on him and try to hold him down.

It was impossible. He was jumping around, grabbing the driver from behind, making it difficult if not impossible to drive. Finally, out of desperation, I grabbed hold of him and threatened to open the car door and leave him on the road. He calmed down somewhat after that.[16]

In the last decades of his life, Shlomie succeeded in helping a number of troubled teenagers.[17] When someone asked Shlomie

---

16. Jack Friedman.
17. See Chapter Eleven.

why he invested so much time and energy helping these boys, he replied, "I could have ended up like them."

What were the chances that someone with his "resumé" would …

> … become one of the most respected *baalei batim* in the Torah world?
>
> … become a unique *baal tzedakah* and *baal chesed* upon whom countless individuals and many *mosdos* leaned for support?
>
> … achieve a heightened appreciation of Torah and its scholars; and enjoy the love, admiration, and friendship of roshei yeshivah throughout the Torah world?
>
> … have an early-morning learning session for some 25 years with a distinguished *talmid chacham*, in which he would focus intently for an uninterrupted hour, and which he would never miss — even after his child's wedding when he was exhausted and had barely slept?

Shlomie was especially close to the Mirrer Rosh Yeshivah, Rabbi Shmuel Berenbaum

He accomplished all this without his innate nature undergoing any real change. Through sheer effort and determination, he trained himself to learn that hour each morning, rain or shine. But it did not come easy.

> *A three-hour learning seder was held one evening as a source of merit for a community member who had taken ill. Shlomie attended along with his morning chavrusa. After an hour, he closed his gemara and rose to leave. Turning to a friend who was learning behind him, he said, "It's gevaldig (tremendous) that you are able to learn for three hours straight. But I can't do more than an hour." He felt that he could not sit any longer, but he wanted those who remained to know that he admired them and wished that he, too, could do what they were doing.*[18]
>
> *One Shavuos night he walked some two miles in order to learn with his chavrusa. On that exalted night, he pushed himself beyond his normal limits and learned for 2½ consecutive hours. Shlomie's joy knew no bounds. He told his chavrusa, "I never sat so long in my life!"*[19]

Channeling His Energy

RABBI LIPA GELDWERTH REFLECTED:

> *He was so great precisely because of his inherent vildkeit (wildness). He had enormous energy, and he channeled it into great things, helping others, raising enormous funds for tzedakah, helping to build a shul, participating in others' simchos in a way that really made a difference, making others feel happy and good about themselves ....*

---

18. Rabbi Yitzchak Mitnick.
19. Rabbi Avrohom Aharon Levy.

After Shlomie's passing a stranger approached his son Aharon and related the following:

> I have a friend in Jerusalem who heads a Tomchei Shabbos type of organization that has a yearly budget of over $2 million. A few years ago when I was in Eretz Yisrael, I went to call on my friend at the organization's headquarters.
>
> A large produce shipment had just arrived. Something strange caught my eye. The fellow unloading the truck was a middle-aged American; he was sweating profusely as he unloaded 50-pound sacks of potatoes. I asked my friend why he had hired such a man for the job. He laughed heartily and informed me that this man was not his worker, he was one of America's most admired baalei tzedakah, R' Shloime Gross.
>
> I then turned to your father and asked, "What possessed you to volunteer for such work — look how sweated up you are!"
>
> He replied, "I can't understand how you can ask such a question. I love such mitzvos."
>
> After completing his work, your father wrote out a check for the organization.

Rabbi Yehoshua Leib Diskin, Rav of Brisk more than a century ago, is reported to have said, "Why did Hashem create *a krumme kop* (lit. *a crooked mind*, the ability for the mind to think in a very obtuse way)? So that we can use that ability to be *dan l'chaf zechus* (to give a person the benefit of the doubt even when it seems more likely that he is culpable.)" Every negative trait can be used in a positive way. Shlomie took his inherent wildness and channeled it toward helping others in ways that were above and beyond what would be expected of even the kindest souls.

As a friend of his youth put it: "We lived a block away from each other. He was a wild kid and the life of the party. He had a great heart, one of a kind. I saw how as the years passed, he took all the negative and turned it into positive."

Ascending the Ladder

SHLOMIE'S BASIC PERSONALITY NEVER CHANGED. HE REmained the same personable, humorous, restless fellow he had always been. A number of friends used the term "very normal guy" to describe him and explain why they always enjoyed his company.

But by the end of his life, he had changed significantly from the person he had been 25 years earlier. Shlomie worked hard to refine not only his *middos,* but all areas of his service of Hashem. He grew in Torah learning, *tefillah, shemiras einayim* (guarding one's eyes from forbidden sights), and in other ways. He would undertake a new *kabbalah* (resolution) each year before Rosh Hashanah, and keep it.

From the time of their marriage, the Grosses had a television. One day, Shlomie and his *eishes chayil* agreed to get rid of it. Their lives and the lives of their children were changed forever. Shlomie still enjoyed taking his children skiing, playing a game of tennis, and going on vacation with his wife. At the same time, he was a true *ben aliyah,* ascending the ladder of spiritual growth.

His longtime friend and business partner Yossi Friedman said:

> *His mother called me recently and said, "Thank you for being his partner all these years. I knew that with you he was in good hands." While I appreciated the compliment, I told her that in fact the opposite was true. I was the one who was in good hands. Shlomie taught us so much; he lifted us all up.*
>
> *I remember the day he came into the office carrying his television. He and his wife had decided to get rid of it and he was giving it to our worker, Carlos. Shlomie was constantly "on the move," moving higher and higher in spiritual levels. And he lifted us all up as he grew. Not*

by giving mussar; he was not that kind of person. He remained a "normal guy" to the very end. He was still one of us, and yet he surpassed us in many ways. It was impossible to watch him grow and not be affected by it.

On his voice mail Shlomie identified himself by his legal name, "Sol Gross." For most of his life, some of his closest friends would call him by this first name. One friend related:

A few years before his passing, I stopped calling him "Sol" and started calling him "Shlomie." In the last year, I called him "Reb Shloime." This was not a conscious decision; rather, it reflected the change in the way I perceived him as he went from a carefree guy who couldn't sit still to someone who was undergoing major changes before my eyes, to one who surpassed his peers in many areas of avodas Hashem.

More important, he achieved what most thought was impossible with the inborn challenges he faced. In his last year, he had become a genuine lamdan; he understood Gemara with a newfound depth and would phone a friend to clarify a point in a Ramban on Chumash. Before Chanukah, we learned and debated the Brisker Rav's Torah on the Rambam.

Three summers before he passed away, we learned a complicated piece in Ohr HaChaim on the episode of the Meraglim. The piece is long and complex, and I am certain that 20 years ago, Shlomie would have quit after a few minutes. We learned the entire piece and he was clear in about 80 percent of it. I am convinced that had we learned the piece two years later, he would have understood it perfectly.

This is how he transformed himself.

Who would have dreamed he was capable of this?[20]

---

20. Jack Friedman.

At a memorial gathering following Shlomie's sudden passing, his rav, Rabbi Avrohom Schorr, said:

> There is another Shlomie that you don't know, the Shlomie who worked against his nature to change himself, day in, day out.
>
> It was against his nature to sit in one place, yet he did this every morning for 25 years when he sat and learned.
>
> It was against his nature to solicit tzedakah from others, but he did this often because it needed to be done.

It is told that as a young child, the Netziv[21] was not interested in learning despite the fact that his parents had strained their budget to hire a private *melamed* for him. One night, young Naftali Tzvi overheard his father tell his mother in an anguished voice that he would terminate the arrangement with the *melamed* and instead enroll the boy in an apprenticeship.

That night was a turning point in Naftali Tzvi's life. He promised his parents that he would approach his studies seriously, and kept his word. Many years later, the Netziv reflected that had he not overheard that conversation, he probably would have remained an observant Jew, who *davened* three times a day and even attended a *Mishnayos shiur* — and he would have been very satisfied with himself. But Heaven would have held him accountable for not becoming the *talmid chacham* that he had the potential to be.

Shlomie Gross' life story makes this demand on all of us. In the next world, we will not be asked why we did not become another Rav Moshe Feinstein or Rav Yosef Sholom Elyashiv. But each one of us has an obligation to be the best that *he* can be. And we cannot use our inborn deficiencies as an excuse for mediocrity.

Shlomie's yeshivah years were filled with frustration and disappointment. Had he and his wife raised a family that was Orthodox but with its focus on materialism, he would have been viewed as a

---

21. Rabbi Naftali Tzvi Yehudah Berlin, Rosh Yeshivah of Yeshivas Volozhin at the end of the 19th century.

success. People would have said, "Do you know where he could have ended up?" And had he also given a respectable amount to *tzedakah* and gone to a *Mishnayos shiur* between *Minchah* and *Maariv*, he would have been viewed as a *great* success.

But Shlomie, and his family, became much more. Shlomie overcame the challenges that his natural personality presented, and as he grew, he was never satisfied with who he was. He always wanted to be better.

In a close friend's words: "How he overcame his nature was by far his greatest achievement." Another friend said, "He was able to stay the same normal guy, and at the same time, be *oleh* (ascend) in matters of *ruchniyus* (spirituality)."[22]

His story is a challenge to us all.

---

22. Eli Karman.

2

Turbulent Beginnings

SHLOMIE'S FATHER, R' AVRAHAM YAAKOV GROSS, WAS A tall, refined man who possessed a natural nobility, a sharp mind, and a good heart. In everyday life he was a true "soldier," always on time for *davening*, his daily *shiur*, and work.

R' Avraham Yaakov was born in Tissa-Oulek, Hungary; his parents were R' Shlomo Yehudah and Aidel Gross. He had one brother, Mendel Zev, and three sisters, Tzivia (Lily), Roiza, and Sheva.

R' Shlomo Yehudah and his wife were sincere *ovdei Hashem* and hard-working people. They owned a grocery store; on Shabbos guests surrounded their table. Theirs was a close-knit family, as their future generations would be.

When the Germans invaded Hungary and the deportations began, Avraham Yaakov was away in yeshivah. The rest of the family was taken to Auschwitz, where the men and women were separated. R' Shlomo Yehudah, his son Mendel Zev, and daughter Sheva were among the *kedoshim* of Auschwitz. Aidel Gross and her daughter Roiza died a month after the liberation. In Auschwitz

Aidel had told her daughter Lily, "You will survive the war and your brother Avraham Yaakov will find you."

Avraham Yaakov spent the war years in a labor camp. At war's end he searched for his sister Lily, finally locating her in a Budapest hospital where she was suffering from tuberculosis. R' Avraham Yaakov remained with her there and under his watchful eye her health was restored.[1] This sense of responsibility for others, especially family, was a legacy that R' Avraham Yaakov's son, Shlomie, inherited, nurtured, and expanded upon.

R' Avraham Yaakov Gross

In New York, R' Avraham Yaakov was the manager of a handbag factory. He was respected as hard-working and absolutely honest. He had golden hands; he renovated the basement of his Boro Park home. His family took pride in him and in his work.

At around age 50, R' Avraham Yaakov developed rheumatoid arthritis, and in 1981 he fell and never fully recovered. Over the next 17 years his condition deteriorated progressively; he was in

---

1. Eventually his sister, Mrs. Lily Perl, emigrated to America and lived first in Dayton, Ohio, and later in Los Angeles. She had one son and one daughter, and from the time her husband passed away at a young age, she and her children would spend every Pesach and Succos with her brother's family in New York. In the words of her son, Shloime Perl, "We began spending Pesach with the Grosses from the time I was seven. My cousin Shlomie and I were very close. He was so fun-loving. Whatever I would say about him would not do him justice."

R' Avraham Yaakov Gross and his sister passed away on the same date, 11 Adar, eight years apart.

both physical and emotional pain. The more his father deteriorated, the more Shlomie tried to make him feel needed and accomplished.

At the onset of his father's illness, Shlomie, who at that time was single and living at home, was enjoying his first successful ventures in the real estate market. He told his father, "Tatty, I need you to manage my warehouse where supplies for my buildings are kept." Shlomie installed some shelves and a desk at the warehouse and asked that his father sit at the desk "and make sure that nothing gets stolen." Shlomie urged his friends to visit his father at the warehouse to make him feel good. The plan had its desired effect; R' Avraham Yaakov felt that he was doing something important, and a good measure of his self-respect was restored.

Shlomie looked for every way to make his father happy. Before Pesach he would remind his dear friend, the late Luzer Brodt, to bring his father Erev Pesach matzos.[2]

Father and son

---
2. The custom, practiced today mainly by chassidim, is found in *Shulchan Aruch, Orach Chaim* 458:1.

He had caused his father much distress as he was growing up, but Shlomie more than made up for it with the love and devotion he showered upon his father in his last years. He would come every day to help his father put on *tefillin*, and to take him to doctors — even three times in one day. He would carry his father to a pool for therapy and to the *mikveh* on Erev Shabbos. And R' Avraham Yaakov derived tremendous *nachas* from seeing his son successful and respected.

A Wellspring of Faith

R' AVRAHAM YAAKOV HAD A PURE AND ROCK-FIRM *EMUNAH* (faith in Hashem), and this found expression in his devotion to mitzvos, in particular *davening*. Infirmity and icy conditions could not prevent him from attending *minyan*. When walking was impossible, he was taken by wheelchair.

Shlomie absorbed these lessons well. His lifelong appreciation for the importance of *tefillah* was learned from his father. And while Shlomie was known for his great sense of humor, anything pertaining to *Yiddishkeit* was no laughing matter.

> *Once, on his way to Eretz Yisrael, a friend seated near him reported that he had lost his cellphone. Shlomie got down on his hands and knees to search for the device. Another friend announced that telling a certain story was a segulah (auspicious omen) for finding a lost object, and he proceeded to tell a story of a childless man who entered a forest and pleaded to Hashem for mercy. The owner of the cellphone interrupted, saying that he was not interested in hearing stories. Shlomie rebuked him, "Don't make light of someone else's emunah."*[3]

---

3. Moshe Feuer.

One Shabbos morning in the Catskills, an appeal was made before Mussaf for Hatzolah. The speaker enumerated Hatzolah's impressive statistics: how many calls it answers each week, the speed of its average response time, how many lives it saves each month, and so on.

A man sitting on the other side of Shlomie's young son Nosson Tzvi said to the boy jokingly, "You believe all that stuff?"

Shlomie was clearly not happy. "Don't make jokes on my son's cheshbon (account)," he told him. Hatzolah was serious business; making light of it, especially to an impressionable child, was wrong.[4]

Mrs. Rivka Gross

SHLOMIE'S MOTHER WAS BORN IN SEILESH, HUNGARY, THE 11th child in a family of 12. Her mother died when she was 3. Her father, R' Aharon Friedman, was a Satmar chassid who was a man of modest means and modest character, endowed with every good *middah,* and loved and respected by all.

R' Aharon was a very giving individual, a trait in which his grandson, Shlomie, excelled. Though he was devoted heart and soul to his many children, he always had a candy for someone else's child.

Mrs. Gross' older sister Ruchi provided the motherly love Rivka lacked following their mother's passing. Even in Auschwitz it was Ruchi who played a crucial role in her little sister's survival. Ruchi survived the war and married Rabbi Ben Zion Halpert. The two sisters were extremely close throughout their lives.[5]

After the war Mrs. Gross was placed on a transport to Canada. When she arrived in Montreal she was welcomed into the home of the Kesslers, who considered her like family. Fortified by the

---

4. Moshe Feuer.
5. Three brothers also survived the war.

wonderful Torah home in which she now found herself, she sought a means to either find a job or continue her education. First, she enrolled in a Jewish teachers' seminary, one that was not under Orthodox auspices.

One day she received a letter that had been written upon the instruction of the saintly Satmar Rav, Rabbi Yoel Teitelbaum, bearing his signature. "Don't forget whose daughter you are," he wrote. "Such a place is not for you." That the Rav had taken such interest in her was indicative both of the Rav's love and concern for every Jew and the esteem in which he held her father.

One of her brothers who became a *chazzan* in the Boston area convinced her to move there. She was hired to teach in a local Orthodox day school. Eventually she moved to New York; in 1956, she met her partner in life, R' Avraham Yaakov Gross.

Anyone meeting Shlomie's mother must be impressed by her nobility and inner strength. And there is no doubt that it was she, together with her husband, who imparted to her son the importance of always keeping others in mind.

Shlomie and his twin sisters

On 3 Adar 5720 (March 2, 1960) Shlomie was born. He was the youngest of three, two years younger than his twin sisters, Chani and Idy. His sisters were well-behaved, diligent students, and brought their parents much *nachas*. Mrs. Gross was a Hebrew school teacher and a devoted wife and mother who ran a happy and well-organized home.

Trouble in the Classroom

THINGS CHANGED WHEN SHLOMIE GRADUATED FROM PRE-school, where a good part of the day is spent playing, and entered first grade. He quickly became a discipline problem. To make matters worse, he was a natural leader. A second-grade teacher told his mother, "When Shlomie decides to do something mischievous, he is able to get the whole class to follow."

He was bright and aimed to please, but he found it impossible to sit quietly in class and focus on the lesson for any appreciable length of time.

While Shlomie's parents recognized his inborn goodness and other redeeming qualities, they were utterly dismayed by his problems in school. Mrs. Gross had been raised to view education as the most crucial part of a person's development, and found her son's difficulties particularly troubling.

The Grosses tried everything. They hired a neighbor's teenage daughter to tutor Shlomie. After a couple of sessions she told them, "It's impossible; he can't sit still long enough to teach him anything!"

Learning Torah with his father

Turbulent Beginnings / 37

They tried therapy, but the therapist was stymied when young Shlomie responded to her questions by relating stories about himself that were quite entertaining, but had never happened. He explained to his friends that he found the whole thing boring and a waste of time, so he decided to have some fun.

A Wandering Jew

AT THE BEGINNING OF FIFTH GRADE SHLOMIE MADE A NEW start in another yeshivah. When Shlomie's parents registered him there, they did not take into account the school's proximity to the railroad tracks, which were a stone's throw away.

One day during recess the boys' ball went over the fence and landed on the tracks, which were behind a locked fence. When the boys said that they needed another ball, Shlomie asked, "Why? Why can't we get the ball on the other side of the fence?"

Some boys tried to dissuade him from doing something that no boy had ever dared to attempt, while other boys dared him to do it. Shlomie climbed the fence and retrieved the ball — and got himself expelled from the yeshivah.

That evening when his father came home from work, Shlomie told him what had happened. Mr. Gross called his brother-in-law, Rabbi Ben Zion Halpert, to ask that he intervene on Shlomie's behalf. Rabbi Halpert replied, "I can't plead for him unless I know the whole story. What did he do?"

Mr. Gross proceeded to relate the day's events. When he finished, Rabbi Halpert said, "Avrum Yaakov, I can only plead on Shlomie's behalf if there is reason to be lenient with him. But from what you're telling me, there seems to be no excuse for what he did. How can I call the yeshivah and plead for him? What can I say?"

And so Shlomie's stay at that yeshivah came to a quick end.

Apparently Rabbi Halpert, who was an outstanding *talmid chacham*, saw something special in this boy. In his address at

Shlomie's bar mitzvah, he noted that his was the last bar mitzvah of the ten male first cousins in the family. Quoting a *pasuk*, Rabbi Halpert declared, "הָעֲשִׂירִי יִהְיֶה קֹדֶשׁ *(The tenth will be holy)*![6] We will see tremendous *nachas* from this bar mitzvah!"

People looked at one another and smiled. Few, if any, believed that his prediction would come true.

At his bar mitzvah

Neighborhood Terror

IN THOSE DAYS BORO PARK WAS A MIX OF ETHNIC GROUPS. The block near 10th Avenue where the Grosses lived had only two Jewish families. The neighbors were "Jimmy," "Vinny," and friends.

Vinny was older than Shlomie but smaller. Backed by his raucous friends, Vinny taunted "the Jew boy." This was an unfortunate mistake on his part.

One day after yeshivah, before his parents had come home from work, Shlomie was sitting on the stoop when Vinny walked by. Shlomie sprang from his place and lunged forward as if he were about to attack him. Vinny was so startled that he turned and ran straight into a tree, injuring his knee. He immediately ran home to tell his parents what had happened.

Meanwhile, the three Gross children ran into the house and bolted the door shut. Vinny and his parents were banging on the door when Mr. Gross came walking down the block at his usual slow, regal pace. The would-be attackers turned to him and shouted

---

6. *Vayikra* 27:32.

Turbulent Beginnings / 39

obscenities. Mr. Gross, who quite possibly had never before heard such talk, shouted back, "You too!"

The neighborhood youths came to fear "Sol" Gross. One day, two youths were walking down the street as Shlomie and his father were coming from the other direction. One of the youths intentionally brushed against Mr. Gross as they passed. The other one was overheard saying, "Are you out of your mind? That's Sol Gross and his dad!" Shlomie was not yet bar mitzvah.

Another time, Shlomie's father was shoved in his presence. Shlomie grabbed the attacker and proceeded to teach him a lesson as his father pleaded, *"Shloime, Ich beit eich, loz em op!"* (Shloime, I beg you, let go of him!)

In a cousin's words:

> *In Europe, they would say about a wild child: "Es geit nor mit tzvei petch; oder er nemt oder er git," meaning that he would deal with a situation in one of two ways: Either he would incite someone who would respond by smacking him, or he would take the initiative and smack the other person. This was Shlomie's modus operandi in his younger years. When something exciting was happening you could be sure that Shlomie was there, either as a defender for a just cause, or on the offensive when someone needed him.*[7]

Moment of Truth

ALONG WITH HIS WILD NATURE, SHLOMIE POSSESSED A DEEP-rooted *yiras Shamayim,* an inheritance from his G-d-fearing parents and grandparents.

In moments of truth this great quality was revealed.

A friend related:

> *We were together in ninth grade; and learned together b'chavrusa (as study partners). I found his company very*

---
7. Shuli Halpert.

enjoyable, and we became friends. We both lived in Boro Park, and spent time together bein hazemanim.

One Friday morning after Succos, we decided to go fishing in Sheepshead Bay. We climbed aboard a fishing trawler heading out to sea and were looking forward to an enjoyable and relaxing few hours. After the captain had started the motor and the boat was on its way, Shlomie asked the captain, "By the way, what time are we returning to shore?"

"Four p.m.," the captain replied.

Shlomie and I looked at each other in dismay. Four o'clock! Shabbos that week began around 5:00,[8] and Sheepshead Bay was quite a distance from Boro Park. Even if the trains ran on time and we returned home before candle-lighting, there would be no time to get ready for Shabbos.

Shlomie said to the captain, "We didn't realize we would get back so late and so close to the Sabbath. We need to go back to shore."

The imposing captain did not take him seriously. "I'm going back to shore at 4 o'clock, not a minute earlier."

"If you don't turn back now," said Shlomie, "I'll jump overboard."

"Four o'clock, that's when I'm going back," the angry captain replied.

Shlomie placed his hands on his hips, stared at the captain, and said, "I'm going to jump."

The captain understood that he meant it. He turned the boat around and brought us back to shore.

Shlomie later told me that if the captain had not complied, he was going to jump overboard and swim to shore.[9]

---

8. In those days, Daylight Savings Time ended the last week in October.
9. Rabbi Meir Yehudah Lichtman.

Turbulent Beginnings / 41

Shlomie spent his high school years in three different yeshivos, seeing barely any success. But his friends have good memories of those days:

> As a 10th-grader, he was a boy with geshmak and tremendous energy. His goodness was apparent even then. Every other Friday he would use the small allowance his parents would send him to take a taxi to the only shomer Shabbos bakery in the area. He would buy a selection of pastries and put them out for everyone to enjoy on Friday afternoon.[10]

Another friend recalled:

> He was tough on the basketball court, but there was a sweetness to his toughness. He might even pat you on the cheek in a friendly way when he beat you. He was much bigger than me and could have clobbered me on the court, but he didn't — he let me play my game. And when we wrestled, I never felt defeated because I felt his friendship.[11]

He went to the Mirrer Yeshivah in Brooklyn after high school. He became the yeshivah's "protector," patrolling the streets around the yeshivah at a time when neighborhood teenagers were accosting the Mirrer *talmidim*.

He served as a vigilante in other venues as well. When a Boro Park Jew was attacked and the community staged a demonstration to demand better police protection, Shlomie led the way.

At Work and at Play

AS A TEENAGER, SHLOMIE SPENT TWO SUMMERS IN CAMP Torah Vodaath as a waiter. The first summer he was sent home after one month, in part because of his method of serving the food.

---
10. Rabbi Moshe Aharon Rosengarten.
11. Rabbi Meir Yehudah Lichtman.

Once every ten days was dubbed "hockey puck night" because the main course at supper was a piece of thick, breaded turkey roll shaped like a hockey puck. On those nights when Shlomie came to a table with his tray of food, he would toss a portion to each person as if he were flipping a frisbee. An administration member noticed this and was not happy.

However, a day after being sent home, Shlomie was told to return to camp for the second trip. Mr. Neuhaus, the camp director, was dismayed by Shlomie's antics, but at the same time, he loved him. *"Der Shloime Gross!"* he would exclaim, with a mixture of love and frustration, after Shlomie's latest shenanigan was reported to him.

During one of those summers, a Color War team came up with a plan for motivating their campers during sports activities. They formed a group which they dubbed the "*Chayos* (Wild Animals) Squad"; led by Shlomie, the group ran from activity to activity, screaming in a way that did justice to their name and banging pots and pans to encourage their team.[12]

Rabbi Lichtman

BY 1976 SHLOMIE WAS OUT OF HIGH SCHOOL AND SEEMED headed for failure. That year, Rabbi Yechezkel Lichtman opened a *yeshivah gedolah* in New Haven, Connecticut. In his long career as a Torah educator Rabbi Lichtman taught *talmidim* of all types, from borderline religious homes, *chareidi* backgrounds, Sephardim, Ashkenazim, and new Iranian immigrants. He could relate to anyone and recognize his strengths.

In his high school years Shlomie had developed a close friendship with Rabbi Lichtman's son, Meir Yehudah, who was enrolled in his father's yeshivah. Rabbi Lichtman welcomed Shlomie as a *talmid* of the new yeshivah. Interestingly, before Shlomie became his *talmid*, Rabbi Lichtman had been apprehensive about his son's

---

12. Shuli Halpert.

friendship with him because of Shlomie's reputation as a wild boy who had bounced from yeshivah to yeshivah.

The year that Shlomie spent under Rabbi Lichtman's guidance proved to be a pivotal period in his life. In those days, when special education was in its formative stages and unsuccessful students were often labeled failures, Rabbi Lichtman had the ability to see past Shlomie's restlessness and apparent disinterest in his studies. Yes, he had difficulty focusing on his learning, and he did possess a wild, uninhibited nature, but he also possessed a sharp mind and could occasionally suggest an excellent *sevara* (Talmudic reasoning). He was a *yarei Shamayim* who valued a mitzvah and felt dispirited when he sinned. And there was no denying his wonderfully kind nature.

The yeshivah eventually folded; Rabbi Lichtman became a *maggid shiur* in a yeshivah in another state. Shlomie wanted very much to join him there, but Rabbi Lichtman felt that he would not fit in with the type of *talmid* to which that yeshivah catered. And so they parted, but Rabbi Lichtman had succeeded in building Shlomie's self-esteem and his view of himself as a *ben Torah*. For this, Shlomie felt an eternal debt of gratitude.

Earning a Living

SHLOMIE WAS ALWAYS VERY AMBITIOUS. HIS PARENTS OFFERED him a weekly allowance, but when he could he declined it, preferring instead to earn his own money. At age 15 he worked for a camp luggage firm, carrying heavy trunks and duffel bags from morning to night for days on end.

When he received his driver's license, Shlomie drove a truck delivering camp luggage. Once, he drove the loaded truck onto the front lawn of a camp, and to the director's dismay the truck tore out some of the grass and created a ditch. Years later, Shlomie's daughter Adina became engaged to the director's grandson. As the *chasan's* grandmother walked into the "*l'chaim,*" Shlomie

In the *aravos* business with his friend Yitzchak Mitnick

said to his family, "I sure hope she doesn't remember what I did to her lawn." In fact, she did remember the story, but could laugh about it at that point. She and her family were proud to become *mechutanim* with Shlomie Gross.

During those teenage years he drove a truck for Kedem wines during the Pesach season. The company owners loved him, despite his antics, for they recognized his inherent goodness and integrity. He did not always follow instructions, choosing to do things his way, but he always got the job done, and with a smile.

Once, when he unloaded an order in a store's warehouse, the manager told him gruffly, "You put them in the wrong place. Move them over there!" — and he pointed to another spot. Had he spoken nicely Shlomie probably would have complied, but because of the way he said it, there was no chance; Shlomie was not moving those boxes.

"Move them or I'll shoot you," the manager threatened.

"Shoot me right here," replied Shlomie, pointing to his stomach. The man did not shoot and Shlomie did not move the boxes.[13]

---

13. Rabbi Meir Yehudah Lichtman.

Turbulent Beginnings / 45

Kedem had another wholesale customer, a husband and wife who were both physically disabled. They were friends of Shlomie's future in-laws, the Cypersteins, and told them at the time of his engagement: "Shlomie has a heart of gold. We've had many delivery boys come to us over the years. He was the only one who on his own always carried the boxes inside and put them exactly where we needed them."[14]

He was popular not just because he was fun to be around, but because he was a friend in the truest sense. Below are the words of two friends:

> *We were friends from our youth. Shlomie taught me early on the meaning of friendship. I was not very popular, and Shlomie befriended me. He instilled confidence in me and we developed a trust in one another.*

▰▰▰▰▰▰▰

> *In 1981, when I graduated medical school, I had an offer to buy the medical practice of a Dr. Fishbain, a Williamsburg doctor who was retiring. One night at around 1 a.m. I got a call from Shlomie. "Let's go check the place out," he suggested. They were asking a hefty sum for the purchase of that practice, and Shlomie wanted to help me decide whether or not it was worth it.*
>
> *We drove to Williamsburg, pulled up in front of the doctor's office, and emerged from the car. As we looked the building over, some chassidim walked by. Shlomie asked them whether they thought that the practice was successful. We did not get a clear answer until someone said, "In Williamsburg, if you want some good schmaltz herring, go to Flaum's. If you want a good pastrami*

---

14. Aron Cyperstein.

> *sandwich, go to Gottlieb's. And if you have an ingrown toenail, go to Fishbain."*
>
> *That clinched it. I bought the practice and have never regretted it.*
>
> *Recently I met Shlomie at a wedding. Turning to another friend, I said, "Did you ever meet Shlomie Gross?"*
>
> *My friend replied, "Yes, many years ago when you and I were about 18. We were coming home from a restaurant in Manhattan when our car broke down. It was one o'clock in the morning. You called Shlomie and he came down right away to drive us home."*[15]

When he was a successful, popular "name" in the community, Shlomie was still the man to call when a friend or relative was experiencing car trouble. He would never say, "Why don't you call AAA?" or something similar.

A friend related an incident from recent years:

> *I was once driving up to the country on Route 17 with Shlomie when we realized that we had passed a Yid whose car had a flat tire. My feeling was that we should just keep on going, but Shlomie insisted that we get off at the next exit and return to that spot. Shlomie changed the tire.*

Shlomie was always ready and eager to help, and no task was beneath his dignity.

---

15. Dr. David Kreiser.

3

Marriage

IN 1985 SHLOMIE MARRIED HIS LIFE PARTNER, MIRIAM (MIMI) Cyperstein. His *kallah's* family background was very different from his own. The fact that he had such a close relationship with his father-in-law and extended family says much for the warm, accepting, and non-judgmental nature of both the Grosses and the Cypersteins.

As mentioned, Shlomie's parents were born and raised in Hungary, in chassidic communities that were light years away from the Lithuanian enclave into which Shlomie's father-in-law, R' Nosson Tzvi Cyperstein, was born.

Shlomie and his parents at his wedding

R' Nosson Tzvi's father, Rabbi Avigdor Cyperstein, succeeded his father-in-law, Rabbi Aharon Rabinowitz, as Rav of Lida, a town in Lithuania. The Chofetz Chaim visited Lida during Rav Aharon's tenure and stayed in his home.

Rav Avigdor, who descended from a distinguished family, was orphaned at a young age. When he learned in Slabodka, the Alter of Slabodka, Rabbi Nosson Tzvi Finkel, drew him close and profoundly influenced him. It is not surprising that Rav Avigdor named his son after the Alter.[1]

The Second World War

DURING THE WAR RAV AVIGDOR AND HIS FAMILY JOURNEYED to Kobe, Japan, and later Shanghai, via the port of Vladivostok, Russia. They did not travel with the Mirrer Yeshivah; Rav Avigdor had his own rabbinic visa. In Japan they joined the yeshivah, where Rav Avigdor became a *chavrusa* of the legendary Rosh Yeshivah, Rabbi Chaim Shmulevitz. In later years a Cyperstein visit to Eretz Yisrael inevitably included a visit to the Shmulevitz family.

Rabbi Avigdor Cyperstein (right) with Rabbi Chaim Shmulevitz

---

1. The great Rav of Vilna, Rabbi Chaim Ozer Grodzensky, was the child's *sandak*.

One of Shlomie's close friends, Dr. David Kreiser, is a nephew of the late Ponovezher Rosh Yeshivah, Rabbi Dovid Povarsky. As a bachur, Dr. Kreiser learned in Ponovezh and lived in his uncle's home.

After Shlomie's marriage he began his custom of spending Yom Kippur and Succos in Eretz Yisrael. When his oldest child, Adina, was still an infant, he called his friend David the day after Yom Kippur and asked that he arrange an appointment for his family with the Ponovezher Rosh Yeshivah Rabbi Elazar Menachem Shach. Shlomie, his wife, and child were accompanied by R' Nosson Tzvi Cyperstein and his wife.

After visiting Rav Shach the men went to daven Minchah in the yeshivah. After Minchah, the family was standing on the pavement outside the yeshivah when Rav Dovid Povarsky emerged from the building surrounded by talmidim who were "speaking in learning" with him.

With Rabbi Elazar Menachem Shach

> *David approached his uncle and said that his friend from America would like to greet him. Rav Dovid shook hands with the men; upon hearing the name Cyperstein, he asked Shlomie's father-in-law, "Are you related to Rav Avigdor?"*
>
> *"Yes, he was my father," came the reply.*
>
> *Rav Dovid lifted up his hands and said with excitement, "What a great man he was!"*

Shlomie's father-in-law R' Nosson Tzvi became a bar mitzvah in Shanghai. The young boys in the Mir-Shanghai community were paired with *bachurim* who studied Torah with them for some two hours a day. Nosson Tzvi's mentor was Rabbi Nachum Partzovitz, who became the son-in-law of Rav Chaim Shmulevitz and a leading Rosh Yeshivah in Yeshivas Mir Yerushalayim. After the war the Cypersteins settled in America.

R' Nosson Tzvi was a lawyer by profession, but Torah was his life's passion. Three nights a week he delivered a *shiur* in his study to a group of friends, some of whom were from the Mir. The *rischa d'Oraisa* (heated Torah debate) that went on in the Cyperstein home on those evenings still rings in the children's ears.

R' Nosson Tzvi married Sarah Bakst, whose father, R' Yaakov, hailed from Volozhin where he had studied before moving on to Telshe. R' Yaakov's wife Yenta had been living in America since 1925 when her family had emigrated from Pinsk. When Yenta reached marriageable age her brother, who was a student in Volozhin, wrote to her that if she wanted to marry a *ben Torah* — not easy to find in America at that time — she should return to Lithuania and meet his friend, Yaakov Bakst.

They married and moved to America, where R' Yaakov became a *shochet* and *mashgiach*. Their home was one of Torah and *chesed*. Guests were always welcome and many would come to receive R' Yaakov's sage advice.[2]

---

2. Mrs. Bakst was related to the family of Malka Greenberg, who later became the rebbetzin of Rabbi David Feinstein, Rosh Yeshivah of Mesiftha Tifereth

Welcome to the Family

SHLOMIE CAME FROM A HOME WHOSE HALLMARK WAS *emunah peshutah*, sincere, unquestioning faith in Hashem. The home of his bride-to-be was of Lithuanian, intellectual bent. It did not seem like an ideal *shidduch*.

As the courtship progressed, Shlomie's future brother-in-law Aron Cyperstein made inquiries about Shlomie. The person he spoke to was a serious, orderly fellow, a very different personality than the one he was being asked to describe. "Shlomie," the man said, "is a *vilde* (wild type) — but what a sweet *neshamah!*" The *shadchanim*, Mr. and Mrs. Bernie Nagelberg, also stressed Shlomie's unusual good-heartedness.

When the engagement seemed imminent, R' Nosson Tzvi asked his daughter, "What do you see in him? That he's big and tall? Reb Aharon (Kotler) wasn't tall, Reb Moshe (Feinstein) wasn't tall — many *gedolim* weren't tall!" Mr. Cyperstein himself was not tall.

As the years passed, R' Nosson Tzvi came to love Shlomie. He once told his daughter jokingly, "Even if you were to leave him, I would still be his friend!"

The Shiur

R' NOSSON TZVI CYPERSTEIN, AN ASTUTE, LEVEL-HEADED individual, was undeterred by the reports he heard about Shlomie's wild nature. However, he did have a talk with Shlomie at the time of the engagement. He asked him how he planned to support his daughter; he also told him that *limud haTorah* was paramount in his family, and he expected his future son-in-law to devote time to learning on a regular basis.

Though Shlomie's father attended a daily *shiur* and inculcated in him an appreciation for Torah, at the time of his marriage

---

Jerusalem. When Malka's father died suddenly as a young man, R' Yaakov Bakst borrowed money so that the widow could make an investment that would provide her family with a means of support.

Shlomie was not learning very much. He did not attend a *shiur* or have a *chavrusa*. His future father-in-law made it clear to him that he expected him to attend his *shiur* at least once a week. Shlomie heeded this request; immediately following his marriage he would drive from Brooklyn to the Cyperstein home in Queens on Monday nights. On a week when he did not come, he would receive a phone call from his father-in-law asking why he had been absent.

Shlomie was an active participant in the *shiur* and was not afraid to argue with the others, each of whom was old enough to be his father. He thoroughly enjoyed the give and take, and forged a deep, loving relationship with his father-in-law.

Once a year the members of the *shiur* would go on vacation to Florida or another resort city. They always chose a *sugya* (Talmudic topic) in advance that would be the focus of their learning during the vacation. Shlomie often went along and, being a young, energetic, fun-loving fellow, made sure that the trip was interesting and "*geshmak.*"

Members of the *shiur* while on vacation together. Standing (left to right): Binyamin Shore, R' Nosson Tzvi Cyperstein, Rabbi Shalom Katz (in background), Rabbi Moshe Shmidman and Shlomie. Seated (left to right): Heshy Schechter, Henry Grossbard, Dr. Bertram Neuman and Izzy Schertz

On Well-Prepared Soil

AT THE CYPERSTEIN SHABBOS AND YOM TOV TABLE, R' NOSSON Tzvi enjoyed raising a *hashkafah*-related question that ignited a lively discussion. Shlomie was always a very vocal participant; his opinion often revealed the pure, uncompromising faith and passion for truth that his parents had ingrained in him.

In retrospect, it seems that the merging of the Gross and Cyperstein families' *chinuch* was ideal for Shlomie. He came into his marriage knowing what was truly important in life. His father-in-law's prodding placed upon him a responsibility to learn at the very least on a weekly basis. This set the stage for further spiritual development.

For many years the change in Shlomie was gradual, but unmistakable. As is common, a person's parental upbringing has taken root and begins to grow most dramatically when adolescence ends, and especially when a young man marries and begins to establish a family. So it was with Shlomie. His parents had prepared the soil well; with Shlomie's marriage to Mimi Cyperstein, he began a new stage in life. Slowly at first, he developed a more mature appreciation for the importance of becoming a more serious *ben Torah*. His growth surged in the final decade of his life when he became a *ben aliyah* (one who strives spiritually) to a degree that left his peers in awe.

Like a Son

IN R' NOSSON TZVI'S FINAL YEARS WHEN HE WAS ILL AND HAD to make frequent doctor visits, Shlomie would carry him in his arms from the house to the car, from the car to the doctor's office, and then reverse the process to go back home. When R' Nosson Tzvi was hospitalized, Shlomie was there every day.

Shlomie's mother-in-law, Mrs. Sarah Cyperstein, spoke about her son-in-law and their special relationship:

Mrs. Sarah Cyperstein with Shlomie, his wife and their children at Aharon's bar mitzvah

When the shidduch between Shlomie and our daughter was developing, we were apprehensive. We were Litvish, and Shlomie came from a Hungarian background. And we had heard about the different aspects of his personality. But we decided to let the shidduch proceed, and of course, it was the right decision. Shlomie and our daughter Mimi had a wonderful marriage.

Shlomie and my husband were chavrusos and friends. They were very different, yet their relationship grew and grew.

Little did we know what Shlomie would develop into, what kochos (strengths) he had, how much he would accomplish for Klal Yisrael and for the countless individuals whom he helped privately.

Whenever something was needed, Shlomie was there. When something needed to get done, Shlomie took care of it almost before you said anything. "Don't worry," he would say, and before we knew it, it was done. It was something magical. It was not only for us that he was so helpful; he was this way with everyone.

He once drove us to a wedding, and on the way he was on the phone raising $5,000 to give one of the mechutanim towards the expenses. After securing the pledges, he handed the mechutan $5,000 at the wedding.

My husband was a talmid chacham and an attorney, but when he came to know and understand who Shlomie was, he would sometimes call him for advice. The love they felt for each other was something special. I do not recall either me or my husband ever having an argument with him. Everything was with a smile.

With his father-in-law

> *My husband took sick at age 62. Shlomie cared for him during that period with love and devotion. During the shivah, a doctor looked around the room and asked why Shlomie was not seated among the mourners. We told him that he was a son-in-law. The doctor was amazed; he had assumed that he was a son.*
>
> *When my husband passed away, Shlomie took over as head of our family. He was there for me, for my children and grandchildren. He gave us the strength to go on. And he gave us the strength we need to go on now that he is no longer with us.*

After R' Nosson Tzvi's passing Shlomie and his friend Yosef Tabak had a *sefer Torah* written in memory of his father-in-law that was donated to Yeshivas Mir Yerushalayim, where they had spent many a Yom Kippur together. Whenever Shlomie was at the yeshivah on Simchas Torah he was honored with a *hakafah;* he would always ask to hold this *sefer Torah*.

At the *hachnasas sefer Torah* in Mir Yerushalayim. Rabbi Nosson Tzvi Finkel is speaking. At far right is Shlomie's brother-in-law, Eli Cyperstein.

Marriage / 57

A Place for the Shechinah

SHLOMIE AND HIS WIFE ESTABLISHED A HEALTHY, HAPPY HOME. Shlomie was a model husband, never allowing his assistance to others to come at the expense of his wife's needs. He answered phone calls from her (and his children) no matter what he was in the midst of doing. Every Sunday morning, before he got busy with his *tzedakah* and *klal* work, he would first go with his wife for a walk in a park.

On the last Purim day of his life, as he was accompanying a rosh yeshivah to raise funds, he told him, "We have to stop soon — my wife is waiting for me to go to the Purim *seudah* in Lakewood." Minutes later, he merited *siyata diShmaya* as the last person they visited handed them a very generous donation.

His partner in life was a true *eizer k'negdo*; together they built a home whose focus became ever more spiritual as the years passed. For example, they agreed to celebrate the bar mitzvah of their older son, Aharon, in a modest catering hall, though they could have afforded a more lavish affair.

They allowed their home to be influenced by the outlook of the *talmidei chachamam* from whose wellsprings Shlomie drank. Together they raised their sons and daughters to revere *talmidei chachamim* and to understand that Torah study is the greatest of mitzvos and the foundation upon which the world stands. That their daughters sought husbands who were budding *talmidei chachamim*, and that their sons would devote their lives to Torah, was the realization of their deepest *tefillos* and yearnings.

Chazal teach that good *middos* are the foundation of Torah. The following anecdotes speak volumes about the *middos* of this special family.

Choosing a Name

THERE IS A 12-YEAR GAP BETWEEN SHLOMIE'S YOUNGEST CHILD, Nosson Tzvi, and his sister, Tzipora. He was born in the summer around a year after the passing of Shlomie's father. No one had been named after R' Avraham Yaakov at that time.

Shlomie's father-in-law, R' Nosson Tzvi Cyperstein, had passed away a number of years earlier, and there were already grandchildren who bore his name.

Shlomie's wife, Mimi, had suffered three miscarriages during those 12 years, and she very much wanted to name the baby after her father, but Shlomie felt that the baby should carry *his* father's name. They decided to seek *daas Torah* and consulted Rabbi Avraham Yaakov Pam. Rav Pam advised that a *goral* (lottery) be cast, and that Mrs. Gross be the one to pick the lot. The paper she chose had her father-in-law's name.

The baby had been born on Shabbos. On Friday night, the night before the *bris,* neither of the baby's parents slept very much; both were troubled by the issue of the name. In the morning Shlomie told his wife, "I want to name the baby after your father." While his wife was grateful, she had one reservation. "We have to ask your mother how she feels about it." When Shlomie's mother came to

With Nosson Tzvi

her children's bungalow and was told about their discussion, she replied, "What's the question? Mimi has been waiting 12 years for this child — of course she should choose the name."

When Rav Pam heard what had happened, he asked to speak to Shlomie's mother, to express his admiration for what she had done and to say what a great *zechus* it was for her and her deceased husband.

In the Blink of an Eye

THE FOLLOWING WAS RELATED BY RABBI YOSEF GELMAN, *Menahel* of Masores Bais Yaakov.

> This story happened a number of years ago, when Shlomie's daughters were students at our school.

Being honored at an annual dinner of Masores Bais Yaakov. (Left to right): Rabbi Yosef Gelman, Shlomie with his daughter Adina, Jeffrey Mehl, Dr. Michael Schwartz

One Friday morning at around 4 a.m. we received a phone call from the maintenance crew at Masores that there was a flood in the basement. A pipe had frozen and cracked. We could not have school that day unless the pipe could be repaired quickly. At around 7 a.m. we called Shlomie and asked if he could recommend a plumber who would come immediately. He responded, "You'll have someone there within 15 minutes."

Shlomie was a man of his word. A short while later a plumber appeared and fixed the pipe. School opened that morning as usual.

Only much later did we learn the whole story.

A pipe in Shlomie's house had frozen. When Shlomie received our phone call, there was a plumber working in his house trying to fix the problem. When we reached Shlomie, he was not at home. After receiving our call, he called his wife and asked if she could pack up the kids so that they could go away for Shabbos; they would fix the pipe after Shabbos. His wife, being the eishes chayil that she is, readily agreed. That is how he was able to send the plumber to Masores.

Shlomie and his wife built a home whose foundation is *chesed*.

4

Reaching Higher

As a young married man, Shlomie enjoyed life. His real estate business was doing well, he and his wife were blessed with children, and he made time for vacations and recreation. He and his friends enjoyed one another's company. And he would distribute generous sums to *tzedakah*, though nothing near the amounts he would give in later years.

A turning point in Shlomie's life happened some 25 years before his passing, when he was a young, successful entrepreneur. On a visit to Eretz Yisrael he stopped in at Kollel Tiferes Tzvi to speak with his friend Kalman Tabak. In his friend's words:

> *Shlomie walked in looking like he did in those days: wavy hair, no hat or jacket, fitted shirt and slacks — not exactly like a yeshivah bachur. The kollel was in the midst of learning, so I was not comfortable speaking with him there. We walked outside and I asked him if there was something he needed.*
>
> *His answer took me by surprise. He wanted me to introduce him to my Rosh Yeshivah, Rav Avraham Yehoshua*

Soloveitchik of Brisk, where I had learned before joining the kollel.

I studied Shlomie's appearance and tried to talk him out of it. I didn't think the Rosh Yeshivah would appreciate the visit, and Shlomie would not benefit from it. But Shlomie insisted that he wanted to go. I told him that it would have to wait until bein hasedarim (lunch break) and that if he still wanted to go then, he should meet me at my apartment, wearing a hat and jacket. I also told him that it would be proper to give a donation for Brisk. Truthfully, I was hoping that by bein hasedarim he would change his mind.

A couple of hours later his car pulled up in front of my apartment. He was wearing a jacket, and a hat he had borrowed from someone. I got in the car and we went to the Rosh Yeshivah's house. He led us to his table, we sat down, and Shlomie was uncharacteristically silent.

I introduced Shlomie as "an old friend who has come to be mechazek (i.e. lend support for) the yeshivah."

The Rosh Yeshivah turned to Shlomie and asked him his name and his father-in-law's name. After Shlomie responded,[1] *the Rosh Yeshivah asked him, "Vos lerntz du?" (What do you learn?)*

Shlomie did not respond. The Rosh Yeshivah persisted, "Do you have some sort of seder (learning session)?" Shlomie was not comfortable answering. He said that he learned with his father-in-law once a week and a bit more before the Yamim Tovim.

The Rosh Yeshivah asked, "Did you learn in a yeshivah?"

Shlomie replied, "Yes, I learned in the Mir."

---

1. The Rosh Yeshivah recognized the name Cyperstein. At the outbreak of World War II when thousands of *bnei Torah* and their *rebbeim* streamed into Vilna, R' Nosson Tzvi Cyperstein and his parents stayed in the same house as Rebbetzin Ettel, Rav Avrohom Yehoshua's mother.

The Rosh Yeshivah seemed upset. "Someone who learned in a yeshivah does not understand that a day cannot go by without limud haTorah? How long should you learn each day? ... I don't know ... let it be half an hour. But how can a day go by without learning?"

I was shocked. This was not like the Rosh Yeshivah; he is not one to give mussar, certainly not to a stranger, a well-to-do fellow who was introduced as someone who came to give a donation for the yeshivah.

*The Rosh Yeshivah had one more thing to say. "You think that by coming home from work and taking your wife out to a restaurant you will have shalom bayis (domestic harmony)? If you make for yourself a learning seder, **then** it will be good for you."*

Shlomie did not say a word. He handed the Rosh Yeshivah a check for $500 that he had prepared, shook his hand, and got up and left.

Outside the Rosh Yeshivah's home, Shlomie took out his phone, handed it to me, and said, "Get me a chavrusa."

I called the pay phone at Yeshivah Bais HaTalmud in Brooklyn and asked for my friend, Rabbi Avrohom Aharon Levy, who was in the yeshivah's kollel at the time. I explained what had just happened and asked if he could become Shlomie's chavrusa. He said that he needed a few days to think about it.

Shlomie flew home a couple of days later, and as soon as he entered the terminal at Kennedy Airport, he called me and asked, "What's doing with the chavrusa?" I immediately called Rabbi Levy, and he agreed to learn with him.

The next morning, their learning seder began. And it continued until Shlomie's last day.

I was amazed at Shlomie's determination to make this happen. It was obvious that he had an inner desire to change his life in a major way. And this chavrusashaft (partnership in learning) did change his life, and the lives of his wife and children as well.

In the first years, when he and Rabbi Levy would complete a masechta, Shlomie would call me and say, "Tell Rav Avrohom Yehoshua about our siyum."

Learning to Learn

THEY LEARNED GEMARA WITH *RASHI* AND *TOSAFOS*, AND Rabbi Levy would always present the primary approaches to the *sugya* as found in the major commentaries.

It was not easy for Shlomie. He had always found it very hard to sit in one place and focus. He was also not used to being in a beis midrash every morning at 6 o'clock. During the first couple of years of their *chavrusashaft,* Shlomie would sometimes oversleep. There was no way for Rabbi Levy to awaken him other than to call the house phone. Shlomie's wife told Rabbi Levy that it was all right for him to call at that early hour, despite the fact that the ringing awakened her as well. She understood how important this learning session was, and considered this a small sacrifice.

As time went on it became easier for Shlomie to sit and learn, and he enjoyed it. He was not content with just "putting in his hour." He wanted to master whatever he learned, to understand it well. He was bright, and as time went on his questions became sharper, his *sevaros* (reasonings) often reflecting a commentator's opinion. And though sitting and focusing for long periods of time was always a challenge for him, it did get easier as his passion for learning grew.

Dancing with Rabbi Avrohom Aharon Levy

The Learning Imperative

HE WOULD NEVER MISS THESE MORNING SESSIONS, NOT ON Erev Yom Kippur and not on the morning after his child's wedding.

If he went out of town within the same time zone, they would learn by phone as usual at 6 a.m. When Shlomie and his wife went to the West Coast on vacation, creating a three-hour time difference, they would learn at 10 p.m. New York time. They learned every day during July and August, when Shlomie was in the mountains and Rabbi Levy was in the city. In the last summer of Shlomie's life Rabbi Levy spent a month with his *talmidim* in the mountains. When Shlomie came up to the mountains for weekends, he drove to Rabbi Levy's bungalow on Friday and Sunday mornings.

Two years before Shlomie's passing Rabbi Levy accompanied him on a visit to Rav Avrohom Yehoshua Soloveitchik in Jerusalem. Reflecting on what Shlomie had achieved in the past 23 years, the Rosh Yeshivah saw it as a powerful lesson of what a few well-placed words of reproof can accomplish. His reproof made such an impact because Shlomie was very open to criticism and willing to change.

Even when on vacation, Shlomie always maintained his morning learning *seder*.

Ten Minutes

FROM THE TIME THAT THEIR *CHAVRUSASHAFT* BEGAN, THEY would spend 10 minutes every Friday learning *mussar*, beginning with Rabbeinu Yonah's *Shaarei Teshuvah*. These 10-minute sessions were life-changing moments for Shlomie, because he internalized whatever he learned.

His heart was in the right place, but at that point in time he did not yet view himself as a *ben Torah*. This was reflected in the language he would sometimes use in business, as well as in other ways.

The first Rosh Hashanah after he and his *chavrusa* began learning together Shlomie accepted upon himself to avoid all forms of improper language.

Carlos, his trusted worker, would often serve as his driver. Carlos enjoyed reading *The New York Post*, which he usually left in his car. Shlomie enjoyed reading Carlos' paper, especially the sports section. On the second Rosh Hashanah of his *chavrusashaft*, Shlomie accepted upon himself to avoid reading the *Post*.

Learning with his *rebbi*, Rabbi Shmuel Berenbaum

He began to ask his *chavrusa*, as well as other *talmidei chachamim*, about the Torah *hashkafah* on various topics. Once he understood what was correct, he accepted it and was ready to defend it fearlessly. He had become a *mevakesh*, one who seeks pure, undiluted truth.

He put every halachah he learned into practice. When a *talmid chacham* mentioned a certain *chumra* (stringency) that his family observed regarding *bedikas chametz*, Shlomie announced this to his family, in the rabbi's name, on the night of *bedikas chametz*. He taught his children, through words and by example, to serve Hashem with joy, to love every mitzvah, and to seek to do mitzvos the optimum way.

The last 25 years of his life saw him climb the spiritual ladder, rung by rung. By the end of his life, some of his closest friends referred to him as a *"tzaddik."*

But this did not happen overnight. As mentioned earlier, the change was gradual, gaining momentum in the last decade of his life.

Minchas Chinuch

IN THE LAST YEARS OF HIS LIFE SHLOMIE EXPERIENCED accelerated growth in his learning. As his friend Jack Friedman recalled:

> We spent our summers together. Around five years ago my chavrusa Yitzchak Brown and I began learning Sefer Minchas Chinuch together Friday nights on my porch. About a year after we began, Shlomie started coming by to join us. At first he would leave after about seven minutes. Minchas Chinuch is quite analytical, and he did not have patience to listen for long. Slowly, he developed a taste for it.
>
> Three years later, Shlomie was sitting calmly for an hour and a half, thoroughly enjoying the Minchas Chinuch's insights and participating in the discussion. No

matter how tired he was, he would not miss this Friday night learning session.

If for some reason we would become distracted, it was Shlomie who would steer us back to the Minchas Chinuch. If we succeeded in learning uninterruptedly for an hour and a half or two, he would be excited beyond words.

He liked to play chess, but he usually lost, because he could not maintain for long the full concentration needed to win. He never developed patience for this or similar mundane activities. Only with regard to learning Torah did he transform himself, going from someone who could not focus for more than a few minutes to someone who could concentrate intently on a difficult Tosafos for an hour or more.

For His Offspring

SHLOMIE'S EFFORTS IN *LIMUD HATORAH* WERE NOT FOR himself alone. A friend related:

At Aharon's bar mitzvah

I recall the tremendous effort he put into learning with his son Aharon. This was years ago when he was first beginning to learn every day, and it was very hard for him to sit and focus. I would observe him in the evening in a local shul with his son, learning on a regular basis. I knew that it was not easy for him, but he did it anyway.

Tefillah

THOSE WHO KNEW SHLOMIE 25 YEARS AGO RELATE THAT already then he had an appreciation for *tefillah*, a spiritual inheritance from his father. "If a business trip forced him to pull over to the side of the road and *daven Minchah* there," recalled a friend, "his *Shemoneh Esrei* was not rushed and you could see that he understood what it means to be *omed lifnei haMelech* (standing before the King)."[2]

As Shlomie's appreciation for learning grew, so did his appreciation for *tefillah* and *kvod hatefillah*. For many years he had been comfortable running in to *Minchah* directly from the tennis court. In his last years, he always came to shul wearing a hat and jacket, and he would sit at a table where no one engaged in conversation. If others conversed he would motion to them to stop or put his arm around the person in a friendly way. It was not his way to deliver sharp rebuke, certainly not in public.[3]

Shlomie's vacations were always planned around the need to *daven* with a *minyan*. When he took his sons on an overnight skiing trip, they often spent the night near Monroe where there were regular *minyanim*. They would arrive early enough for *Minchah* and arise in the morning in time for an early *Shacharis* before heading out to the slopes.

A friend related:

> *Every weekday morning Shlomie learned with his chavrusa in Rav (Ben Zion) Halberstam's shul. We have a Vasikin minyan downstairs; some mornings, Shlomie would join us for Shacharis. Everyone will agree that when he davened with us it was a different davening. He would daven aloud and walk around as he did. His feeling for the davening was real, and it energized our minyan.*[4]

---

2. Yosef Tabak.
3. Jack Friedman.
4. Yechezkel Paneth.

He once spent Yom Kippur in Manhattan's Sloan Kettering Hospital with a relative who was ill. This meant walking up and down 19 flights in order to *daven* with the *minyan* on the ground floor. Shlomie later said that he drew inspiration from a patient, a boy, who struggled up and down one flight to join the *minyan*. He also said that the *davening* on that Yom Kippur was the most moving of his life.

Khal Tiferes Yaakov

IN THE YEAR 2000 SOME *BAALEI BATIM* IN FLATBUSH ASKED Rabbi Avrohom Schorr to begin leading a weekly *shalosh seudos* in their neighborhood. After a few weeks Shlomie's friend Willy Beer invited him to join. Rav Schorr's words captivated Shlomie. His *divrei Torah* were inspiring, and what especially resonated with Shlomie was the Rav's call to shun a life of materialism and focus on *avodas Hashem*. Rav Schorr wanted to lift up his *kehillah*-in-formation, and Shlomie was someone who had already made positive changes in his lifestyle and aspired for more.

With friends Willy Beer (right) and Jay Tepper

After a few years of meeting only on Shabbosos, the *kehillah* moved to its present location and became a year-round *beis midrash*. Shlomie recognized the impact that Rav Schorr and the *kehillah* had on him and his family. He dedicated the shul in his father's memory, and was one of its most active members. He would encourage his friends and acquaintances to "try *shalosh seudos* just once"; often they too were inspired to join the *kehillah*.

He took great pride in the *kehillah* and its accomplishments. When *talmidei chachamim* from Eretz Yisrael were in Flatbush, Shlomie would sometimes arrange for them to come to the shul during learning or *davening* hours, or to address the *kehillah* at *shalosh seudos* if Rav Schorr was not there on a particular Shabbos.

At a *hachnasas sefer Torah* at Khal Tiferes Yaakov.
Rabbi Avrohom Schorr is to the right of Shlomie.

Seeking Daas Torah

SHLOMIE WOULD SEEK ADVICE OF *TALMIDEI CHACHAMIM* IN every important endeavor. Before he and his wife agreed to a prospective *shidduch* for their child a *talmid chacham's* approval was needed.

One summer, after some of his children were married, he wanted to fly everyone to St. Moritz for a family vacation during *bein hazemanim*. He would not do so, however, without first seeking *daas Torah*. Was it correct, he wanted to know, to take *kollel* couples on this sort of luxury trip? Was it perhaps contrary to the kind of life they were living? The fact that he could afford it was irrelevant. Uppermost in his mind was his children's spiritual welfare and whether he might be doing something that was contrary to proper *hashkafah*.

One day he walked into his office with his television and presented it to his worker Carlos as a gift. Turning to his cousin Shuli Halpert he said with a laugh, "I got rid of the television. I don't know how I'm going to know the scores in the morning, but I did it."

He had been an avid sports fan, but from the time he gave up television, he ceased following professional sports. The hours he used to spend watching ball games were now used for *chesed* and *limud haTorah*.[5]

His *chavrusa*, Rabbi Levy, put it this way: "He was constantly mindful of the concept of *daas Torah*, always asking himself, 'What would a *talmid chacham* say about this?' If he was not sure, he would ask."

Inconspicuous

AS THE YEARS PASSED AND SHLOMIE GREW IN HIS UNDERstanding of Torah and attachment to it, materialism became increasingly less important in his eyes.

---
5. Shuli Halpert.

For most of his life, he liked dressing well and wore expensive suits and ties purchased in famous stores like Barney's and Saks Fifth Avenue. In the last years of his life, as he made great strides spiritually, clothing became much less important.

He was ever attuned to Yaakov Avinu's words to his sons: לָמָּה תִּתְרָאוּ, *Why should you make yourselves conspicuous?*[6] He did not want his wealth to arouse envy in others.

For many years his family lived in a simple home. A renowned rosh yeshivah and his executive director paid a fundraising visit to Shlomie in that house. Such visits for this rosh yeshivah are usually brief, but this time he sat conversing with Shlomie for a while. Later, his executive director commented about the length of their visit.

"When I go to a luxurious house," the rosh yeshivah explained, "I feel uncomfortable and I am eager to leave. However, in this house I felt at home because they live simply."

When this comment was repeated to Shlomie, he replied, "It's to my wife's credit."[7]

That house had some glaring deficiencies; it lacked proper insulation and was very cold in winter. On cold mornings Mrs. Gross would turn on the oven and electric heaters to warm the kitchen as the children ate breakfast. Once, an old friend told him, "Shlomie, I really think you can do better than this."

Shlomie was happy in that house, but he agreed that an upgrade would improve his family's life.

They were close with the neighbors on the block, and therefore their first choice would have been to renovate their house according to their needs. A respected contractor told them that the renovations would be so expensive, it paid to tear down the house and build a new one in its place. Shlomie would not hear of it. "Tear down a house that's livable? That's [a transgression of] *bal tashchis*."[8]

---

6. *Bereishis* 42:1.
7. Related by the executive director.
8. The prohibition against destroying anything of value. See *Devarim* 20:19.

He could have afforded to build one on an empty lot to his family's specifications, but Shlomie was adamant that they had to buy an existing house that was in almost move-in condition. He felt that to build from scratch would be making a statement that materialism was a major factor in his life, which was not the case. He also did not want his time to be taken up with the details of major construction. "I should build a house and be busy with it day and night?" was how he put it.[9]

He was also concerned that this might arouse jealousy. "I don't want the whole world walking by and seeing that Shlomie Gross is building himself a house." The house they bought is surrounded by a high fence, which pleased him, for this way the house does not attract attention. It came with many outdoor lights along the front and sides to illuminate the property at night. Shlomie never allowed these lights to be turned on, in order not to draw attention to the house.

Outside their old home on East Eighteenth Street

---

9. Rabbi Berel Karniol.

Reaching Higher / 75

Before making a final decision on the house, Shlomie brought a *talmid chacham* to see it and assure him that it was not showy.

To the Grosses, "low-key" was the approach in any public venue. When Shlomie made a parlor meeting, his wife served salads, chocolates, cakes, and candies. Even if the organization wanted a lavish affair, Shlomie and his wife would not allow an elaborate menu of hot dishes to be served. It was simply not their style.

Shlomie was upset when a *mosad* he supported delivered a very expensive bottle of wine to his door on Purim. He felt that offering extravagant *gashmiyus* was not the way to raise money for *ruchniyus*.[10]

His Means of Travel

SHLOMIE, WITH HIS 6'4", 240-POUND FRAME, APPRECIATED AND enjoyed driving a luxury car. In his early years as a man of wealth he drove a Volvo, then an Infinity, but as he grew spiritually, he worked on himself to control this passion.

He confided in a *talmid chacham,* "I have a *yetzer hara* to buy an Infinity 35," but the scholar, who was very close to Shlomie and recognized his spiritual striving, discouraged him. "It's not for someone like you," was his simple response. Shlomie responded that to buy a very plain car might appear arrogant, as if to say, "I'm rich but I don't need anything fancy." He settled on a Honda Pilot, which was somewhere in between plain and luxurious. His last car was a Honda Accord, quite a small car for a fellow of his size and means.

He confided to a close friend, "You know that I have a *yetzer hara* for fancy cars, but I have to control myself." He would sometimes borrow a luxury car from a friend for a few days, to enjoy such a car without owning one.

When he flew overseas with his children he would fly economy and purchase an extra seat to give himself more room. Business

---
10. Eli Cyperstein.

class was far more comfortable, and though he could have afforded it, indulging in such "luxuries" was, to his mind, not proper *chinuch* for his children. By the time an 11-hour flight to Eretz Yisrael landed, Shlomie ached all over from having to squeeze into a tight seat with little leg room. When he and his wife flew alone, they sometimes flew business class.

It bothered him when others demonstrated a warped sense of values.

When his neighbor's daughter was of *shidduch* age, Shlomie received a phone call inquiring about the family. The caller was asking foolish questions such as "Do they use Rosenthal china? Do you know if they ever use paper plates for Shabbos or Yom Tov?" As Shlomie later put it, "My blood pressure was going through the roof." He had no patience for such shallowness.

Spend Wisely

AS BOTH FAMILY AND FRIENDS REPORT, SHLOMIE WAS VERY free with his money. A couple of friends would sometimes join him for dinner at a Williamsburg restaurant. There was never any discussion about who would pick up the tab; Shlomie would never allow the others to pay for their meal.

When a close friend would celebrate a child's engagement, Shlomie would often show up with an expensive bottle of liquor.

When he felt that one of his children could use an incentive to do well in school, he made sure to offer a reward that would make the effort worthwhile.

But he absolutely would not waste money for naught. He visited Eretz Yisrael often. A friend who owned an Israeli cellphone would lend it to him, whenever possible, for his trips there. Why spend money on a phone when one was readily available at no cost?[11]

---

11. When that friend would visit Eretz Yisrael soon after Shlomie's last visit, the phone would ring constantly, as Shlomie's many Yerushalmi friends (see Chapter Seven) were trying to reach him.

At his office, before discarding a stack of financial reports he removed all the paper clips, to be reused. Manila envelopes that arrived in the mail were recycled.

Intense and Relaxed

HE WAS INTENSE ABOUT HIS SPIRITUAL GROWTH AND FAILURES, and relaxed about mundane mistakes. Once, his brother-in-law Eli Cyperstein asked that he accompany him to a business meeting in Florida. Shlomie offered to make the travel arrangements. On the way to the airport he commented, "We'll be able to *daven Minchah* in the kollel."

Eli was dumbfounded. "There's no kollel in Tampa …"

"Tampa?" Shlomie replied. "I thought the meeting was in Miami!"

He calmly called his travel agent, cancelled the tickets — at a loss — and ordered new tickets for the next flight to Tampa, totally ignoring what had happened. There was no discussion of who was at fault; it was not important. Later, Shlomie would relate this episode as an amusing story.

Regret and Resolve

IN THE LAST YEARS OF HIS LIFE HE HAD CONVERSATIONS WITH those closest to him that revealed a heightened spiritual striving. He told an old friend, "We're going to get such *petch* (smacks) [in the Next World] for things we did when we were young." As an example, he reminded his friend of the time they were traveling together and suddenly realized that they would never make it to a shul in time for *Minchah*. They parked the car near a pair of pay phones, and each took a receiver in his hand and *davened* quickly, appearing as if he were talking into the phone.[12]

---

12. This was commonly done 30 years ago when one needed to pray in a public place but was embarrassed to do so.

"What kind of *davening* was that?" Shlomie thundered. "*Davening* into a phone for a minute and a half?"

His friend had a different viewpoint. After all, what they did was preferable to not *davening* at all. "And besides," his friend continued, "why do you say we'll 'get *petch*'? Isn't there something called *teshuvah*? You wouldn't *daven* into a pay phone again, would you?"

"Never!" he replied emphatically. "*B'li neder*, I will never *daven* like that again."

A Blending of Mitzvos

SHLOMIE PAID CAREFUL ATTENTION TO HALACHAH, AND HIS great heart made sure that others were able to as well. A young man related:

> For my first Seder at my in-laws', I brought a bottle of white Moscato d'Asti. We did not have a corkscrew, so I went to their neighbors, the Grosses. Shlomie saw the bottle and asked, "White wine at the Seder?"[13] I replied that this white wine was preferable because I found its taste superior.[14] Shlomie responded that the same type of wine was available in red — and he sent his son to get a bottle of Malvasia. The bottle was opened and given to me to take back home. Ten years later I still use that wine at the Seder — and I never forgot the lesson Shlomie taught me to be sure that a mitzvah is done in the optimum way.[15]

Love for Our Land

SHLOMIE HAD AN INCREDIBLE LOVE FOR ERETZ YISRAEL. HE traveled there often, even more frequently after his children married and lived there. For him, a trip to Eretz Yisrael was an

---

13. "It is a mitzvah to seek to use red wine (for the Four Cups)" (*Shulchan Aruch, Orach Chaim* 472:11).
14. See *Rema* ad loc.
15. Rabbi Yehudah Deutsch.

Visiting Rabbi Yaakov Meir Shechter in Jerusalem. Rabbi Chaim Yosef Gefner is standing.

opportunity to recharge his spiritual batteries. He loved walking the streets of Jerusalem, visiting *gedolim*, learning with his children and visiting their *kollelim,* and spending time with his many Yerushalmi friends, some of whom he would bring to his hotel to join him for a meal.

As exhausted as he was on these trips, he would not allow himself the luxury of a nap; he just kept on going until his day ended or sleep overtook him.

In the Judean Desert with his son Nosson Tzvi

One year he and his brother-in-law Avi Szenberg were in Meron for Lag BaOmer. They were walking together when suddenly Shlomie disappeared! Avi's repeated calls to Shlomie's cellphone were not answered.

An hour later, Shlomie appeared. He had sat down to rest for a moment and immediately lapsed into a deep slumber.

In Meron with his son Aharon

Spiritual Sensitivity

THOSE WHOSE EMPLOYMENT TAKES THEM OUTSIDE THE sheltered confines of the beis midrash are faced with the often difficult daily test of *shemiras einayim,* guarding one's eyes from viewing improper sights. Shlomie's dealings brought him into the company of all kinds of people, including women who were not properly attired. He worked hard on training himself to avoid looking where the Torah does not permit one to look.

A rav to whom he was very close marveled at the strides he made in *shemiras einayim.* No one else could have known, because Shlomie was not one to brag. But to this rav in whom he often confided, he said one day, "I had such a *nisayon* the other day in *shemiras einayim* — and I was *matzliach* (successful in looking elsewhere)!"[16]

---

16. Shuli Halpert.

He would not walk into the women's section at a wedding even to greet his mother, and he would take his friends to task if he saw them entering the women's side. He didn't "give *mussar*." It was a frank, straight-from-the-heart "What are you doing there? You don't belong there."

Once, he was driving a friend when he noticed that his friend was looking out the window at an improper sight. Shlomie slapped him lightly on the cheek and said, "Stop it." And his friend did. It was a tribute to their friendship and to his friend's acknowledgment that Shlomie himself put much effort into guarding his eyes.

As detailed in a later chapter, there were troubled teenagers whom Shlomie befriended and upon whom he had tremendous influence. Once, he took a boy along with him to a *simchah*. As soon as he entered the ballroom, he blanched. There was no *mechitzah* (partition), and some women were not dressed properly. He quickly led the boy outside, apologized for bringing him there, and gave him money to buy supper in a restaurant.

From the time he heard a rav criticize the practice of referring to a friend's wife by her first name, he would not do so.

During Shlomie's first years of marriage, he was comfortable walking from his bungalow to the pool in his bathing suit. In his later years, this was unthinkable.

As he changed for the better in many ways, Shlomie's essential personality remained unchanged. He never conveyed an impression that "I'm working to grow and therefore I am superior." He was the same humorous, lovable, spirited Shlomie Gross.

His true inner yearnings were once expressed in the recovery room after he underwent minor surgery. Rabbi Avrohom Aharon Levy paid a visit when Shlomie was first waking up and was not fully coherent. Shlomie muttered, "I want to do *retzon haBorei* (the will of the Creator)."

He certainly did.

5

The 'Great Connector'

SHLOMIE WAS CHARISMATIC. HE WAS BRIGHT, WARM, passionate, and humorous. All these qualities contributed to his great success in the business world.

In a friend's words: "Shlomie was the 'Great Connector.' There was something about his handshake that made you feel an instant connection to him."

His most important quality in business was his *ehrlichkeit* (integrity). He earned a reputation for impeccable honesty. He possessed a pure, powerful *emunah*, which manifested itself in how he viewed life and in particular how he approached business.

The *yiras Shamayim* his parents instilled in him was apparent even in his early years in real estate, before he was studying Torah daily or striving spiritually in other areas. A friend related:

> *My father and I had our own real estate business. We sold a certain property to an Orthodox Jew. We were also in the mortgage business, and we arranged a mortgage for the buyer on this property. Later, Shlomie, who was then*

a young entrepreneur, bought the property from that buyer, which meant that he would assume the mortgage. One day he called us up. "Did you write a heter iska for this mortgage?"[1] In those days, many observant businessmen, myself included, were unfamiliar with heter iska. I told Shlomie that we had not made use of it.

Shlomie therefore took out another mortgage from a bank at a higher interest rate and paid up our mortgage in full so that he would not have to pay us any interest, which would involve a Torah transgression.

Partners Like Brothers

ONE OF SHLOMIE'S CLOSEST FRIENDS WAS YOSSI FRIEDMAN, his long-time partner in the real estate business they founded. Mr. Friedman talked about their years together in business:

He was a very honest guy. I never looked over his shoulder to see how much of our money he was giving to tzedakah, or even how he was distributing monies from our investments.

In our 28 years as partners, we had our disagreements in hashkafah and other non-business matters — but it was never about trust. We never fought over a business decision, we never argued over money, and we never had to keep an eye on each other.

The same trust applied to investing our company's money. If one of us would say that he was taking a sum of money to invest in a property, the other one would never check to make sure that he had actually taken that specific amount and invested it. Our trust in each other's word was absolute.

---

1. The Torah forbids a Jew to charge another Jew *ribis* (interest). A *heter iska* is a halachic permit whereby a potential loan is transformed into a joint business venture. See *Shulchan Aruch, Yoreh Deah* ch. 177.

With Yossi Friedman (right) and Emil Friedman

Sometimes I would make a mistake in a deal, and sometimes Shlomie made a mistake. We never got upset at each other for this.

The uniqueness of our partnership was not a recent thing. In our early years a very serious matter arose that required litigation. When a lawyer suggested a certain course of action, I told him firmly that this was in the category of mesirah (informing on a Jew), and I would not do it. The lawyer, who was not an Orthodox Jew, did not understand me. He turned to Shlomie and asked, "You're going to let this guy bring you down?" Shlomie replied without hesitation, "Whatever my partner says, that's what we'll do."

The Man Who Made Things Happen

When we needed big money to close a deal, Shlomie would make the phone calls. His honesty was beyond reproach and he was very likable; these qualities were important reasons why others invested with us.

The 'Great Connector' / 85

He had a scintillating personality, and when we would go together to work out a deal, he would loosen everyone up with his conversation and humor. Sometimes I would tell him before such a meeting to concentrate on the details, but he didn't always listen to me. He would get busy schmoozing with someone on the other side of the table. But this worked to our advantage, because he made the atmosphere light and congenial.

The last such meeting we had before his sudden passing was at a bank to obtain financing. A bank official was listing off conditions, and I caught one that was incorrect. I turned to Shlomie and asked, "Did you hear what she just said?" He hadn't heard a thing; he was in the midst of an animated conversation with the bank vice president. I took care of the nitty-gritty while he put everyone into a good mood.

After Shlomie's passing many of the non-Jews we dealt with expressed genuine sadness over the loss. They told me, "He was a great guy ... wonderful to do business with," and similar sentiments. They recognized that he was a special person and truly enjoyed his company. And now they miss him.

Beyond the Letter of the Law

YOSSI FRIEDMAN CONTINUED:

In business Shlomie would go beyond the letter of the law when other people's money was concerned. His policy was "Treat others as you would want others to treat you." Shlomie would say that if someone was looking for "heteirim" (legal loopholes within the confines of Halachah), he could get away with a lot. He never looked for heteirim; he wanted to do what was right.

In one instance, I felt that Shlomie was going too far, that he was being unnecessarily generous to others who had invested with us. He was adamant that his approach was not generosity but yashrus, the straight and correct way to go. I disagreed.

I called a respected beis din, and they agreed with me. We asked a noted talmid chacham, and he agreed with me. Shlomie took the case to our rebbi, Rav Shmuel Berenbaum, and he agreed with me. But despite his respect for all these people, Shlomie's feeling for what he felt was "ehrlich" (honest), combined with his goodness of heart, did not allow him to give in. So I gave in, and our investors did very well. I gave in because when it came to such matters, to anything relating to וְעָשִׂיתָ הַיָּשָׁר וְהַטּוֹב[2]*, you could not budge him. (Truth be told, an incident that occurred 15 years later made me realize that although halachically I was correct, there was merit to Shlomie's insistence on going beyond the letter of the law in this case.)*

His bitachon (trust in Hashem) guided him in business. He truly believed that no one can deprive you of what Hashem has decreed is yours. Therefore, he would never touch a deal that he felt rightfully belonged to someone else.

We had a firm policy never to become involved in a deal that might hurt another Jew — for example, in a case of foreclosure, where the bank might offer the owner a good deal if others did not show interest in the property. There are enough deals available out there without our having to make things hard for our own people.

---

2. Lit. *You shall do what is fair and good* (Devarim 6:18), the Torah's command that we go beyond the letter of the law when dealing with others. See *Bava Metzia* 35a.

Above and Beyond

A FRIEND RELATED:

> When my son left kollel and decided to enter the real estate field, I asked a number of friends and acquaintances to advise him in any way that they could. No one did for him what Shlomie did.
>
> Shlomie went through his list of important contacts and introduced my son to everyone he thought my son could benefit from. If my son came to him with an idea he had for a deal, Shlomie would lead him by the hand, putting him in touch with the people who could make the deal happen. In fact, he even tried to arrange deals for my son to negotiate.
>
> I never saw anything like it. Generally, people are willing to help others in their field up to the point where their own success might be compromised. Shlomie was not like that at all. He was ready and eager to help my son in any way, and was very happy to see my son close a deal that otherwise might have been his own.

The mother of one of Shlomie's closest friends, a wise and perceptive woman, gave Shlomie some of her savings to invest. Every year he would bring a check to her for that year's profits. Her grandson once asked, "Bubby, do you ask Mr. Gross for a statement of the investment earnings? Does he give you anything other than a check?"

She replied, "I trust him implicitly. There is no need for any proof."

Shlomie would accomplish what others considered impossible, whether this meant doing a difficult business favor or saving someone in dire financial straits. This required not only supreme goodness, but also the infallible trust that others had in him. Everyone knew that with Shlomie Gross, "a word was a word."

Integrity and charisma are key components for success in the investment world. Shlomie also had many other sterling qualities that endeared him to everyone whose path he crossed.

No Grudge

THERE WERE TIMES WHEN HE HAD OPPORTUNITIES TO EARN large sums of money, but opted to allow someone else to invest so that that person could establish a successful livelihood for himself. Later, Shlomie might try to contact that person to help with some project, and the person would not return his phone call. Shlomie did not bear a grudge.

He bore no grudge against someone who declined to participate in a *tzedakah* campaign he was spearheading. If that person later called him for a favor, he would do his very best to help him and would not mention how the person had disappointed him.

He looked away when he spent money and did not receive its value in return. One Chol Hamoed in Eretz Yisrael, he rented a bus to take his family, extended family, and friends to a certain destination. He paid for a coach bus but was sent one that was old and dilapidated. He paid the full price without a word about not getting his money's worth.

Similarly, when someone who drove him from Jerusalem to Bnei Brak in an old jalopy charged him the full price of a taxi, Shlomie paid without a word.[3]

In the early years of his marriage Shlomie, his wife, and in-laws spent Succos in Eretz Yisrael, where they were hosted by relatives. During Chol HaMoed the family took a one-day trip and stayed overnight in a hotel. Shlomie's father-in-law was planning to pay for everyone. However, when he was given the bill he was shocked; it was far more than he had expected. He felt that the management was being dishonest.

---
3. Aron Cyperstein.

With his father-in-law in the Old City

Shlomie went into the office to speak to the management. Unbeknownst to his father-in-law, Shlomie gave the manager $200 towards the bill. He emerged from the office smiling. "I worked things out," he said.

In the early years of his marriage, before he was well-to-do, his sister-in-law drove his car to the Catskills and was involved in a crash. Thankfully no one was hurt, but the car needed major repairs. Of course Shlomie would pay for it, and his sister-in-law felt terrible. She recalls, "I really felt bad, but it was obvious that the whole thing did not bother him one bit. Money had no value in his eyes except for doing mitzvos."

In Confidence

HE WAS INVOLVED WITH COUNTLESS FAMILIES WHO CONFIDED in him their financial, familial, or emotional worries. A close friend related, "I knew that he knew what was going on in the lives of many people, and truthfully, at times I thought that because of our closeness he would share some of this information with me. But he never did. He was a *shomer sod* (guarded people's secrets)."

Deep Emotion

SHLOMIE WAS A PERSON OF DEEP EMOTION. HE CRIED UPON reading a *tzedakah* letter detailing a family's tragic situation.

His sensitive *neshamah* had a deep feeling for *neginah,* as his long-time friend Abish Brodt recalled:

> *For many years we had a lively mesibah in my home on the first night of Purim. Around 20 years ago R' Shmuel Brazil composed "V'yaazor," and we sang it Purim night for some two hours. My children were very young at the time. For over an hour Shlomie danced around the room with a Brodt boy on each of his shoulders.*
>
> *In recent years we had a kumzitz on the second night of Purim in the home of my brother Luzer, z"l. For much of the evening the mood is one of dveikus; it becomes freilich (joyous) towards the end.*[4] *Shlomie would not miss it for anything. Even when he traveled to Lakewood for the Purim seudah, he would be back in time to participate in our mesibah.*
>
> *I received the news of Shlomie's passing while in Cracow. I had to be at that levayah. I flew from Cracow to Germany to Tel Aviv, arriving in time for the levayah, and returned to the States that same night. I cried like a child.*

Rejoicing at the Purim *mesibah*

---

4. One year Shlomie, in a heightened state of joy, danced on the table.

The 'Great Connector' / 91

Abish once invited Shlomie to a *siyum haShas* made by a man who was a quadriplegic. After the actual *siyum*, Rabbi Mattisyahu Salomon spoke, and then Abish led a *kumzitz*. Shlomie cried the entire time.

Fearless

A FRIEND RELATED:

> *Years ago, before cellphones were common, the employees at my security company would communicate via two-way radios. One day, a worker on the job put his radio down and it was stolen. Later, we got a call from that radio. The person claimed that he had "found" it and said, "If you want it, you have to pay for it." He asked for $200 and gave his address in a run-down Brooklyn neighborhood.*
>
> *The radio was worth $1,500. I wanted it back but was afraid to go alone. So I called up Shlomie; of course, he agreed to go with me.*
>
> *When we met the fellow he was holding the radio. Shlomie took the radio and told him, "You stole it; we're not paying you." The man looked at Shlomie open-mouthed and did not say a word. It was obvious that he was the thief, and he did not put up a fight. We got back in the car and drove off. I never heard from the fellow again.*[5]

One morning, a thief broke into a house around the corner from Shlomie's and made off with some silver. Providence arranged that his escape route took him through Shlomie's driveway. At that early hour Shlomie was sitting in the front room of his house and heard noise in the driveway. He looked out the window and saw the thief. Shlomie ran outside and let out a yell that woke up much of the block and frightened the thief, causing him to drop all his loot and run.[6]

---

5. Dovid Langer.
6. Jack Warshavchik.

One night, a neighbor across the street awoke in the middle of the night and heard an intruder outside his bedroom. He grabbed a baseball bat that he kept next to his bed, called the neighbor closest to his house, and then the police. He and his family were unharmed, but when Shlomie heard what happened, he was upset. "The first person you should have called was me," he said.

Early one morning Shlomie looked out his window and saw a man enter the enclosed porch of his neighbor across the street. Still clad in his robe, he ran out of the house and dashed across the street to accost the apparent intruder. It turned out that the fellow was delivering the morning paper. Shlomie apologized, but remained alert to any strange happenings on his neighbors' property.

He was visiting Eretz Yisrael when Gilad Shalit was released from captivity. On the day of his release the Israeli Army and police were in a heightened state of alert and were stopping cars randomly. When Shlomie was stopped he showed his driver's license, but he did not have his passport. He explained truthfully that from Israel he was heading to Russia and Poland, and he had left his passport at one of the embassies.

"Then you're coming to the police station," the officer said.

"No problem," replied Shlomie. "Let's go right now."

With Nosson Tzvi and a member of Israeli Hatzalah

The 'Great Connector' / 93

His confidence made the officer realize that he was telling the truth, and he let him go.

Once, a young non-Jewish driver cut him off on the highway, then blocked his car and jumped out, ready for a fight — not realizing how big Shlomie was. Before getting out of the car, Shlomie told his companion, "This guy is gonna get it."

When the fellow saw Shlomie's frame he looked frightened, but he need not have worried. Shlomie could not hit another man, even when provoked. He made do with a good tongue-lashing, then drove off.

When he found out that a girl from an Orthodox home was on the verge of becoming engaged to a non-Jewish boy, he went to a dangerous neighborhood to convince the boy to break up with her. He succeeded; the girl eventually returned to her family's way of life and married an observant Jew.

Man of Principle

HE WAS A MAN OF PRINCIPLE. THIS, COMBINED WITH HIS fearlessness, caused him to take action in ways that others would never consider.

Once, he and a business acquaintance were on a plane together. The other fellow switched on his screen and began to view an inappropriate film. Shlomie ordered him to switch channels. He did, but the second film was not much better than the first. Only after the man's third try was Shlomie satisfied.

Shlomie would go to great lengths for *pidyon shevuyim*, to help free Jewish prisoners. When a friend told him of an Israeli who had just been arrested and had no one to advocate for him, Shlomie quickly arranged a meeting of *askanim* to determine what could be done to help this man.

At one point, the prisoner let a friend know that he was having a difficult time procuring kosher food. The friend called the prison chaplain but was told that the chaplain was busy and could

To Sanctify His Name

AT A *SHELOSHIM* GATHERING FOR SHLOMIE, RABBI YITZCHAK Scheiner, Rosh Yeshivah of Yeshivas Kamenitz in Jerusalem, stated: "One who truly loves Hashem prays that His Name should be sanctified in this world. There was no one I knew who lived for this idea like R' Shloime Gross. Everything he did was *l'kadesh Shem Shamayim*."

A business acquaintance recalled:

> *Shlomie and I invested in a property in Knoxville, Tennessee. Shlomie decided to go out there to check on the property. We arranged for him to be shown around by the property manager. Upon his return to New York, Shlomie sent the manager a box of New York doughnuts (a novelty in Knoxville). When I spoke with Shlomie about his trip, he mentioned the doughnuts and said, "I sent them out of hakaras hatov, and to make a kiddush Hashem."*

With Rabbi Yitzchak Scheiner

The 'Great Connector'

> *This made a deep impression on me. While Shlomie was such a normal guy, good middos, serving Hashem, and kiddush Hashem were always in the forefront of his mind.*

A friend related:

> *Building commissioners and other officials in the New York City government still speak of Shlomie with the highest praise. They recall his integrity, how pleasant it was to deal with him, and how he treated everyone with respect.*
>
> *Recently, I was at a meeting and an assistant commissioner told me, "You should know that at meetings, this man's [i.e. Shlomie's] name comes up often. He is so missed."*
>
> *A short time ago a city official was speaking with me and mentioned Shlomie's name. I asked him, "Do people still remember him?" He replied, "Of course they remember him. Just last week, we were discussing the problem of people who do not honor their commitments. Someone said, 'We could use a Sol Gross.'"*[8]

Shlomie often played tennis at the Prospect Park Tennis Center. After his passing the Center's director sent a condolence letter to the family:

> *Sol was known at the Prospect Park Tennis Center for his kind and generous personality and for his keen sense of humor. He will be sorely missed by all here. We wish to express our heartfelt sympathy for your loss.*

Eight staff members signed under the director's signature. One wrote, "I will miss his sense of humor. He was a wonderful person."

---

8. Kalman Tabak.

One worker at the tennis center sent his own note:

> I will always remember Sol for his generosity. After finding out in a conversation that I had always wanted to attend a championship tennis match but had never done so, Sol got me a ticket to the match. His diligent effort to get the ticket for me is something that I will never forget. He will be missed.

His Humor

SHLOMIE HAD A GREAT SENSE OF HUMOR.

On a trip to Russia for Vaad L'Hatzolas Nidchei Yisroel, someone took a picture of Abish Brodt standing near a cow. When Shlomie was shown the picture he said, "Abish, we'll use this for the cover of your next Regesh album and call it 'Abish and Friends.'"

With Abish Brodt

Shlomie's uncle, Rabbi Ben Zion Halpert, was ill during his final years and for a time was a patient at a rehabilitation facility. On a visit one Erev Shabbos, Shlomie and a friend noticed that R' Ben Zion was given only one challah roll for his Friday night meal. He told them, "Usually *lechem mishneh* is not a problem because my roommate and I lend each other our rolls. But my roommate is not here this Shabbos, so I need another roll." R' Ben Zion then smiled and said, "Well, if I put the roll opposite the mirror, I'll have two."

He and Shlomie remarked simultaneously, "But when it comes to eating it, I want the real one!"

To celebrate a brother-in-law's birthday, Shlomie hosted a restaurant dinner which his parents-in-law, their children, and spouses attended. Most of those attending had to leave early. At the end of the meal, the only ones remaining were the guest of honor and his wife, and Shlomie and his wife. Shlomie turned to the other couple and said, "Now if we leave, you pay the bill!"

When he heard a good story, he sought to share it with others.

The last morning of Shlomie's life, someone told him that he had met Shlomie's old friend, Dr. David Kreiser. Shlomie responded, "I must tell you a story David once told me — it's one of my favorites."

> *When David was attending college, he earned money as a salesman in a shoe store. The store was owned and run by non-Jews, and though David wore a yarmulka, he blended in with his surroundings in his T-shirt and jeans.*
>
> *One day, a man dressed in rabbinic attire came in to buy a pair of shoes. David suggested a pair, which the man tried on. "They feel good," he said, "but I can't take them because people in my community don't wear such shoes."*
>
> *"What do you mean?" David retorted. "Rav Dovid Povarsky and his sons wear them!"*

The rav could not believe his ears. "Rav Dovid ... how do you know him?"

"I'm Rav Dovid's nephew," David replied.

Not long after Shlomie heard this story for the first time, Rabbi Sholom Povarsky[9] visited the States and was in Flatbush for Shabbos. On Friday night he was scheduled to visit a friend of Shlomie's, who invited his neighborhood friends to come to meet his distinguished guest. It was a bitter cold evening and few ventured outside. When Shlomie arrived, his friend said, "You came to speak in learning with the Rosh Yeshivah?" Shlomie replied, "Actually, I came to see his shoes."[10]

Another of Shlomie's favorite stories was the time David was learning in Ponovezh and found himself alone one afternoon in Rav Dovid Povarsky's apartment. He opened the trunk containing his belongings, took out his basketball, and began to dribble it

On a trip to Lithuania in 2011. Dr. David Kreiser is at top left.
Rabbi Binyomin Povarsky is at bottom right.

---

9. A son of Rav Dovid and a Rosh Yeshivah at Yeshivah Kol Torah in Jerusalem.
10. Rabbi Yaakov Beinenfeld.

around the apartment. A few minutes later a *bachur* knocked on the door and said, "I'm learning downstairs with Rav Shach. He asked that the carpenter stop banging."

A Good Time for All

HIS WILD NATURE NEVER LEFT HIM, THOUGH HE BECAME QUITE adept at harnessing it and using it for the good. At his summer vacation home he would have fun hosing people as they came out of the pool. He enjoyed it and he hoped that his targets enjoyed it as well. But the moment someone told him that a certain individual was not happy about it, his face underwent a transformation. The last thing he wanted to do was to hurt someone. He would apologize and stop.[11]

Because he was so fun-loving, people often assumed that when he approached them at the pool or anywhere on the colony grounds, it was to engage in some sort of fun.

One day, a man was taking out the garbage when he noticed Shlomie approaching him. Wanting to initiate some fun, the man flung the bag at him, forgetting that inside was a large, glass juice bottle — which hit Shlomie squarely on the head, with great force. Shlomie mumbled a quick "Have a good day," and hurried inside. He was in pain and had a huge welt, but never made mention of it.[12]

Shlomie worked in the city from Monday through Thursday and would drive to the mountains for weekends. Aside from his learning session by phone with his *chavrusa* and an hour or two of tennis, Shlomie spent the rest of his Friday and Sunday entertaining not only his young son Nosson Tzvi, but also a whole troop of children. He was the unofficial "counselor" who took these children swimming, horseback riding, hiking, or gave them rides on his private golf cart.

---
11. Jack Friedman.
12. Eli Cyperstein.

On Shabbos afternoon in the mountains Shlomie and his wife would go for a walk; often, they were accompanied by a throng of White House Estates children who wanted to see the cows up the hill.[13]

He was "Uncle Shlomie" to every child at White House Estates. He had a smile, a *knip*, or a kind word for every little boy and girl. When he would stop at a friend's house in the city it was not uncommon for a child to get out his or her camera to snap a shot of Shlomie with the family.

Summers at White House Estates will never be the same.

Every child's "Uncle Shlomie"

---

13. One Shabbos, five-year-old Nosson Tzvi was standing next to his mother when a bullet ricocheted off a tree and grazed Mrs. Gross's arm, opening a gash that bled profusely. The bullet came from the rifle of a retired police officer who was hunting in the woods. The family held a *seudas hodaah* for the fact that Mrs. Gross was only lightly injured (she required seven stitches) and Nosson Tzvi was unharmed.

The 'Great Connector'

6

His Great Heart

At the wedding of Shlomie's oldest child someone said to me,

"You think you're one of Shlomie's best friends?"

"Absolutely," I replied.

"Well," said the fellow, "everyone else here feels the same way."

(related by Bernie Nagelberg)

RABBI YOSEF MAYER, A NOTED *MAGGID SHIUR* AND *gabbai tzedakah,* had a close relationship with Shlomie. He said, "Shlomie's heart was as huge as his frame."

A friend who would often spend recreation time with Shlomie related: "When he would turn his phone on after it had been off for an hour, I would try to guess how many calls he had missed. Often, it was between 20 and 30 calls. He had so many 'friends' for whom he was the first address for help, not just for money but also as a shoulder to lean on."[1]

---
1. Eli Karman.

His father had a cousin, Gedaliah Greenzweig, a Holocaust survivor who lived in Toronto. He would often come to New York to be with family for Yom Tov. He always chose to stay at Shlomie's house, saying, "I like being with him."[2]

Many acts of kindness that others considered unusual, Shlomie viewed as ordinary. Once, he was informed that a businessman had gotten into trouble with people who had underworld connections. His very life was in danger; he needed to leave the country fast.

With his father's cousin, Gedaliah Greenzweig

Shlomie drove him to Toronto, drove back to New York, and then sat with the man's young wife in a passport office until she filled out the necessary papers and her application was accepted.

When he was told that a *bachur* — not his relative — needed a car for a date, he readily handed over his car keys. He lent his car often, and would remark, "So I lend out my car — what's the big deal?"

Once, someone was coming to New York with his sick child and needed a car but could not afford to rent one. A friend of Shlomie's knew that Shlomie was leaving for Eretz Yisrael. He called to ask if the person could borrow his car.

"Is he responsible and trustworthy?"

"Yes."

---

2. Mrs. Chana Sosowsky.

"Tell him the car is in front of my house. The keys will be on top of the visor."

A friend related:
> I was working in Connecticut and I mentioned to Shlomie that I found the drive from Brooklyn difficult. The next day I received a call from him. "I spoke to someone near your place of work and he gave me the phone number of a fellow who might be interested in driving you to and from work every day."
>
> This was typical. As soon as Shlomie heard that someone needed something, he went into action.[3]

There were times when Shlomie gave generously to a cause though he believed that it was less important than many others. He did so because the solicitor was sincere and was having a difficult time raising funds. Shlomie felt that a generous check would lift the man's spirits, and he would do anything to make another person feel good.

He was always thinking of others. A man who had invested with him passed away. When one of the children was soon to be married, Shlomie showed up at the widow's door with an envelope. "Your dividends are due in a few months, but we figured that you could use the money now."

Thinking About Others 24/7

RABBI BINYOMIN POVARSKY, A *MAGGID SHIUR* IN JERUSALEM[4] with whom Shlomie enjoyed a close relationship that spanned decades, had this to say:
> The stories of Shlomie's kindness are endless. It is correct to say that he was thinking about others 24/7. His greatest joy in life was getting others to smile. He would do anything to make that happen.

---
3. Dr. Yitzchak Brown.
4. He is a son of the Ponovezher Rosh Yeshivah, Rabbi Berel Povarsky.

I recall the time someone lost his entire business. Shlomie supplied the funds to help the man start anew. The money might have been his own, or he might have raised it; it makes no difference. The point is that he was determined to get that man back on his feet financially, and he succeeded in doing it.

One summer my parents were flown to America so that my father could deliver shiurim during bein hazemanim in various bungalow colonies. Shlomie informed me that he was sending me a plane ticket so that I could relax in the Catskills and also spend time with my parents.

He arranged for me to spend Shabbos as his guest in White House Estates. My parents were staying at a colony down the road. Shlomie set up an eruv techumin so that I could visit my parents on Shabbos.

Friday morning, while my father was delivering a shiur, Shlomie brought my mother to his summer home so that we could visit with her, as he and his wife served us a sampling of the Shabbos foods.

Left to right: Aharon Gross, Rabbi Binyomin Povarsky, Shlomie, Rabbi Yosef Gutfarb

The last time I saw him was on his last visit to Eretz Yisrael, some four weeks before his passing. He was preparing to return to the States and was sitting on the porch of his daughter's apartment. I brought him a cellphone for a friend of mine, a rosh kollel, who was fundraising in America and whose cellphone had broken. I told Shlomie that my friend would be in touch with him so that he could come to the Gross home to pick up his new phone.

Shlomie would not hear of it. "Why does he have to come to me? Give me his contact number and address; I will bring the phone to him."

And what was he talking about on that Motza'ei Shabbos, as he spent his last hours in Eretz Yisrael with his children? Finding an apartment in New York for someone from Eretz Yisrael who was coming to the States for a few months.

That was Shlomie, thinking about others 24/7.

With Rabbi Berel Povarsky in the Catskills

Getting to Know Him

IT WAS EASY TO DEVELOP A RELATIONSHIP WITH HIM, AS ONE man recalled:

> *I first met Shlomie when a friend of mine was in deep financial trouble. I called Shlomie in his office and in five minutes I felt that he was my friend, though I was some ten years younger. I felt drawn to him; he was someone with whom I wanted to have a relationship.*
>
> *We spoke only briefly over the next couple of years. Then, when this same friend of mine began to marry off his children, I called Shlomie and he invited me to come to his home.*
>
> *We spoke for an hour and a half about all kinds of things. He made me feel very good, and very happy to be strengthening our relationship. He helped my friend that night and continued to inquire about him over the years.*
>
> *Once, he asked me about my friend and I replied that, as a matter of fact, my friend had been unable to reach him by phone. Shlomie was distraught. "He called me and I didn't pick up? I would never ignore someone's phone call." He immediately asked for the man's phone number, called him up, and apologized for not being reachable.*
>
> *A lot of times when you need someone's help, you're uncomfortable making the call. It's just hard asking others for help. With Shlomie, it was easy picking up the phone because he made you feel like a million dollars. When you left his house with a check, he thanked you.*
>
> *He was real through and through. He had no agendas, no ulterior motives. He just wanted to make you feel good and help you in any way that he could, without expecting anything in return.*

Here to Help

A FRIEND RECALLED:

> When I was once talking with Shlomie he mentioned with dismay how so many people were struggling to make ends meet. He remarked that recently a friend had married off a child, and he knew that the friend would have to go into debt to make the wedding. Shlomie called him up and asked, "So how much do you need?" The friend was uncomfortable accepting money and did not want to answer. But Shlomie was persistent. Finally, his friend said, "I need a couple of thousand dollars."
>
> Shlomie told me, "If he finally admitted to a 'couple of thousand,' he probably needs much more. So I sent him much more."
>
> Then I mentioned to Shlomie that my wife had just opened a business. We struggled to make ends meet and were hopeful that the business would "take off." Shlomie became very excited. "Whatever you need for the business — a building to expand — whatever it is, be sure to call me."
>
> I miss him in so many ways.

He was always attuned to the needs of friends and family. When he happened to hear that a fine *bachur* of his acquaintance was not being accepted as a staff member to a camp that he had attended as a camper, he immediately starting making phone calls. The boy's parents were shocked when Shlomie called, instructing them to call someone who might be able to help.

Someone close to him was buying a house. He had the down payment to obtain the mortgage, but not much more. Renovations would have to wait — or so he thought.

One day Shlomie approached him. "That house is going to need some fixing. This should help." The check he handed him covered all renovations.

In the recipient's words: "It was just hard to believe it when he did that. Like a mother or father, he had figured out how much money we would need to get the house in shape, and he provided it."

But it was not only with money that he zeroed in on another's needs. His sister-in-law, Mrs. Malki Cyperstein, recalled:

> We lived in Eretz Yisrael for the first few years after our marriage. When we returned to the States I began working for the first time, and my husband, Aron, entered law school. It was a difficult adjustment in many ways. Shlomie perceived that and called us soon after our return: "Call me when you need something." He would call us often to see how we were doing and to help wherever he could.
>
> But it was not just family or close friends whom he touched. After he passed away, people from our shul who had met him only once told us how impressed they were by his warmth, his smile. He was a pure neshamah and loved everyone.
>
> Ahavas Yisrael is often compromised because we zero in on those aspects of a personality that we don't particularly like. Shlomie was above that. He saw beyond the externals. When he looked at someone he saw his neshamah, and all he felt for him was pure, unadulterated love.

With Boruch Friedman

His Great Heart

Multi-Tasking

HE WOULD OFTEN DEAL WITH MANY DIFFERENT ISSUES simultaneously. On a given day he could assist more than a dozen individuals with their personal issues, placing phone calls to the right people for each particular situation. He could be helping one person to close a real estate deal, another to avoid foreclosure on his home, another to gain admittance to the right doctor or hospital, and another to raise the funds needed for a wedding or medical procedure — all at the same time.

Friends from his youth would marvel at how Shlomie, who had such difficulty staying focused, could maintain in his mind the many details of each case so that he could deal with them as if the problem were his very own. This was how he lived his life, day after day.

In many instances the person who approached him had no previous relationship with him. He came because his problem was not easily solved and he was told, "Shlomie Gross can help you."

He was so thought-out in the way that he helped a person, so efficient in addressing *every* aspect of the person's situation, that each person felt that *he* was Shlomie's primary object of focus, the one with whom his mind was preoccupied. If he came to someone's aid and overlooked a detail that could have brought the person some additional joy, he was upset with himself.

He took a person's pain to heart and did not forget about it. A week after he extended himself to help someone, he would make inquiries about how everyone was, and if there had been any improvement in the situation.

Instant Chizuk

RABBI YOSEF GUTFARB WAS ONE OF SHLOMIE'S CLOSEST Yerushalmi friends. He related:

> *I first met Shlomie some 13 years ago. One of my children was not well, and we were advised to seek medical*

help in Seattle. I had never left Eretz Yisrael before. It was decided that I would spend two weeks in Brooklyn's frum community before heading out to Seattle with my child.

Heaven arranged that I should spend some time learning in a Flatbush shul where one of Shlomie's friends, Yosef Tabak, was learning. We "spoke in learning" and were soon friends. Shlomie was observing shivah for his father, and R' Yosef took me along to the shivah. When he introduced me to Shlomie, R' Yosef told him why I had come to the States. Shlomie looked up at me and said, "I'm coming with you to Seattle."

I cannot express what those few words meant to me. America was a new world to me, and while people were very nice, I still found it very difficult. I knew that as hard as Brooklyn was for me, Seattle would be much more difficult. And here was a man whom I had just met telling me that he would accompany me to Seattle.

When Rabbi Yosef Gutfarb married off his oldest child, Shlomie could not attend because the wedding coincided with the engagement of his son Aharon. Shlomie therefore hosted a combination *vort* in honor of the engagement and *sheva berachos* for Rabbi Gutfarb's *simchah*, in Jerusalem. In this photo, taken at that celebration, Rabbi Gutfarb is dancing with Aharon. To Shlomie's left is his friend Rabbi Yitzchak Porush.

His Great Heart / 113

> *In the end, circumstances did not allow Shlomie to accompany me. But he kept in touch with me and the friendship between us would only get stronger as the years passed. He always stood ready to help me in any way possible.*

"You'll Be Home for Chol HaMoed"

A CHILD FROM JERUSALEM WHO HAD TO UNDERGO SURGERY in Baltimore arrived in Brooklyn with his father on Erev Yom Kippur. Someone had arranged for them to stay at the home of a certain *askan*, but due to a misunderstanding the guest rooms were already taken. The *askan* arranged for them to stay somewhere else. Their new host was very nice, but he was not an *askan*. He could offer them room and board, but not the financial help or emotional support that they desperately needed.

Someone suggested that the father call Shlomie. When he did, he mentioned the name of one of Shlomie's Yerushalmi friends. Shlomie called his friend and, after confirming that the story was true, called the young man. "Please join my family for an Erev Yom Kippur *seudah*."

At the *seudah*, Shlomie told him, "I will take care of everything you need in Baltimore, and with Hashem's help, you and your child will be back home by Chol HaMoed."

And that is exactly what happened. From then on, Shlomie would stop in to visit this young man and his family when he was in Jerusalem.[5]

"Tell Me a Joke"

YONASAN SCHWARTZ, A RENOWNED *BADCHAN*, RELATED:
> *I arrived in the States from Eretz Yisrael some 24 years ago feeling very lost. I had been orphaned at age 10, could not speak English, and had no means of support.*

---

5. Rabbi Yosef Gutfarb.

I knew that I had the talent to be a badchan, but who would want to hire a newcomer, a young fellow with an Israeli accent, to be mesame'ach (inspire joy) at their simchah? Who would help me?

I could not pay my rent. I was so desperate that I took to collecting for myself each morning in the local shuls. One morning I had the good fortune to come to Khal Bais Avraham in Flatbush, where R' Shloime Gross davened. Another meshulach was kind enough to tell me, "You see that yungerman over there? He is a great baal chesed. Go ask him for a donation."

After davening I went over to R' Shloime, explained my situation, and concluded, "Please help me. I don't want to be a beggar. I want something from you that is bigger than money. I need help to become a badchan. I have the talent but I can't get anyone to hire me."

R' Shloime asked me to tell him one of my "badchan jokes."[6] *I did, but I was terribly shy. I could see the pain in his eyes, how he was feeling my pain. He wanted very much to help me.*

He told me, "Tomorrow night I am making a sheva berachos for a close friend. Come there and perform, and I will take care of you."

I prepared non-stop the rest of that day and all of the next day, for what was to be my first badchan performance. I was nervous and had little self-confidence.

As soon as I walked into the hall R' Shloime greeted me and did his best to make me feel comfortable and calm. And when the moment came, he stood up and

---

6. The term *badchan*, which literally means "jester," does not do justice to the *badchan's* role at chassidic weddings. While many *badchanim* do lighten the atmosphere with jokes, much of their repertoire includes *divrei hisorerus* about the awesome responsibility of building a Jewish home, and about the lineage of both the *chasan* and *kallah*, all sung in rhyme. It is for this reason that the *badchan* plays an important role at weddings in the courts of chassidic rebbes.

announced, *"AND NOW WE WILL HEAR FROM THE PERFORMER OF THE CENTURY — YONASON SCHWARTZ!"*

His introduction boosted my confidence, and my performance went very well. After that, R' Shloime became my "agent." Whenever someone he knew was planning a wedding, he would call up and say, "If you're thinking of hiring a badchan, make sure to take Yonasan Schwartz." He made all these phone calls for my sake.

It did not take long before I was a success. Over the years, R' Shloime and I met many times at weddings where I performed. I know that he derived great pleasure from watching the badchan in whom he instilled the confidence to succeed.

I will never forget the man who helped me to "stand on my own two feet," by giving me a livelihood to support my family, and putting an end to my loneliness and helplessness. He helped me for one reason — because I am a Jew. He never asked for anything in return.

First-Hand Look

A FRIEND RECALLED:

> There was no one who was nosei b'ol (shared his fellow's burden of troubles) like Shlomie. It made no difference what the problem was. I recall that when someone was having difficulties with an inheritance in the Midwest, Shlomie flew there to see the property firsthand so that he could offer the best possible advice.

Rav Yisrael Salanter said that a person's face is a *reshus harabbim* — it is viewed by the public. It is important that one greet others cheerfully even when he has reason to be worried or depressed. One's personal problems cannot interfere with his obligations to his fellow man.

Shlomie's life was not always smooth sailing. There were times when business was not going well, or other situations of difficulty arose, as they do in the course of life. He worked on himself to be in control of his emotions so that regardless of his situation, he could make others feel good with his warm smile, sense of humor, and genuine concern.

Guaranteed Investment

HE WAS ONCE PREPARING TO INVEST IN A VENTURE THAT seemed guaranteed to earn significant returns. He contacted someone close to him who earned a good living but was far from wealthy, and urged him to invest as well. However, this person was not interested. It troubled Shlomie. He knew that this man had children to marry off, and this seemed like a "sure-fire" venture.

"Listen," Shlomie told him, "invest the money and I will guarantee it. If the whole thing flops, I will refund your investment." The man refused the offer, but he remains amazed at Shlomie's selflessness. Shlomie wanted so badly to see his friend earn the expected profit that he was willing to use his money as insurance and possibly suffer a major loss.

There were other reasons why he sometimes encouraged business ventures, as one employee recalled:

> *I was once in Shlomie's car when he was on the phone talking business with some fellow — I had no idea who it was. He was telling him, "Listen, I want you to meet these people, you'll make a deal with them, you'll pay me back, and the rest of the profits will be yours."* Shlomie saw I was very curious, so when he hung up he explained:
>
> "This man owes me money for a long time and was not doing anything to pay me back. So I found him a deal that will generate enough profit for him to pay me back and leave a nice amount remaining for himself."

One Mitzvah Leads to Another

MORE THAN A DECADE AGO, SHLOMIE'S COUSIN YOSEF PERL was diagnosed with a serious illness that required him to spend a year in the States for medical treatment. The first person he called after receiving the diagnosis was Shlomie, who shortly thereafter met him at Kennedy Airport. Their first order of business was to find an apartment for Yosef and his family. After a few phone calls and some apartment-hunting, they signed a lease on an empty Flatbush apartment.

"Now," said Shlomie, "we need to get you some furniture."

No sooner had he said those words than his cellphone rang. A friend was calling to ask for a favor. He owned a house in upstate New York and needed to remove all its furniture. Could Shlomie provide him with his company driver and truck for this task? Shlomie readily agreed.

Then came the next question. "Shlomie, any ideas as to where I can put all the furniture?"

"Yes," Shlomie responded, "I know exactly where to put it."

During the year that followed, Shlomie visited his cousin *every day* until his health was restored and he was able to return home. Sometimes Shlomie brought along roshei yeshivah who would offer *chizuk*; other times, he brought with him a doctor whose assessment might prove useful.

Dancing with his cousin Yosef Perl at his daughter's wedding

In Times of Grief

ON A VISIT TO ERETZ YISRAEL HE HEARD THAT A YOUNG father, whom he did not know, had passed away. He went to the *shivah* house and told the widow, "I am paying for after-school *chavrusos* for all your sons for as long as you feel it will benefit them." This greatly relieved the woman; now she knew that there would be money for whatever help her sons would need to develop their potential as *talmidei chachamim*.

Hope for the Despondent

AT A WEDDING IN JERUSALEM SHLOMIE NOTICED AN OLDER *bachur* who seemed somewhat different. He inquired and was told that the *bachur* was a good person, capable of marrying and building a home, but that the behavior Shlomie had noticed, which was not something that could change, made it very difficult for the *bachur* to find a *shidduch*.

Shlomie approached the boy's father and told him, "If you offer to buy certain things for the new couple that will make their life more comfortable, it will be easier for you to find a *shidduch* for your son. You find the *shidduch* and I will pay for these expenses."

A *shidduch* was found, and Shlomie kept his part of the deal. However, after a short time, the marriage ended in divorce.

When Shlomie found out, he called the father and said, "Find him another *shidduch* and we'll have the same deal as before."

A *shidduch* was found, and now, years later, the couple is happily married and merited wonderful children.[7]

A Sleepless Night

AN ISRAELI ROSH YESHIVAH RELATED:

> My wife accompanied me on one of my trips to America. We made plans to have someone drive us from

---
7. Rabbi Yosef Gutfarb.

New York to Toronto on Motza'ei Shabbos. Shlomie was not happy about this. He felt that the long trip would leave me exhausted. He offered to pay for plane tickets, but I refused.

We traveled through the night. Shlomie called me a number of times during the night to make sure that we were all right. I felt bad that he was up worrying about me. He claimed that his sleeplessness had nothing to do with me. But I believe that he stayed up because of his concern for our well-being.

For a Special Child

R' SHOLOM STERN, AN ELDERLY *TALMID CHACHAM*, OFTEN comes to visit his children in White House Estates. R' Sholom enjoys imparting to others the Gemara *shiurim* he heard from his *rebbeim*. Whenever R' Sholom visited, Shlomie would come to his lodgings on Shabbos afternoon and enjoy hearing a two-hour *shiur* from him.

During the winter R' Sholom sometimes spends Shabbos with his children in Flatbush. On those Shabbosos, Shlomie would come over in the afternoon. On one visit he found another visitor there. A boy with special needs who lives in the neighborhood was on the floor playing with a toy doctor's kit. Shlomie lay down on the floor and with a big smile said, "Give me a check-up."

Silent Chesed

A FRIEND RELATED:

It happened around 10 years ago. I had lost my only son and was doing my best to cope. But one Shabbos morning was particularly tough.

As davening began I realized that I was going to be the only person sitting at my table that morning. Usually my brother-in-law sat there, as well as some friends. We didn't talk during davening, but knowing that I was sitting with family and friends was comforting.

But that Shabbos morning everyone at my table had gone away for Shabbos. I was sitting all alone and felt overcome by a feeling of sadness — but not for long. I looked up from my siddur, and there was Shlomie sitting at my table directly opposite me. He had noticed that I was sitting alone and had come from the other side of the beis midrash to sit with me. He remained there for the duration of the davening. He did not say a word to me other than "Good Shabbos" when davening was over.

Words cannot adequately describe what his presence meant to me. It was a true nechamah, without his having uttered a word.

Surprise Package

HE WOULD OFTEN SEND SUITCASES AND PACKAGES TO HIS children in Eretz Yisrael containing a variety of useful items. The *gabba'ei tzedakah* were happy and eager to have an opportunity to do him a favor and take the package. He would always call ahead to his children so that they could pick up the package right away.

There was one time when he did not call ahead. When his son-in-law received the package he was surprised to find that it contained nothing but a few snack items. He called his father-in-law and asked why he had sent it.

Shlomie replied, "I really had nothing to send you, but this Yid wanted so badly to do me a favor and take something for me. I didn't want to disappoint him so when he came to my office, I quickly put together some nosh and tied it up tightly so that he should not know what I sent you."

His Great Heart

Special Delivery

A FAMOUS CHASSIDISHE REBBE IN ERETZ YISRAEL WAS IN need of a very expensive medication that was available only in America. The medication had to be mixed at the time of purchase and delivered within 36 hours. Shlomie, who did not know the Rebbe, was asked to undertake this mitzvah. Every two months he would send his worker to New Jersey to pick up the medication, which he paid for, and then he would find someone to bring it to Eretz Yisrael. His family knew nothing about this.

Once, his son-in-law picked him up at the airport in Tel Aviv and Shlomie told him, "I must go to the ____ Rebbe immediately."

"Why?" his son-in-law asked.

"I have a meeting with him," he replied.

His family feels that he kept such information from them not because he wanted to do these mitzvos *b'hatzne'a leches* (anonymously), but because he did not consider such deeds extraordinary, and therefore there was no reason to discuss them. Who wouldn't help a Jew in need?

Flowers for Yom Tov

WHEN HE SPENT SHAVUOS IN JERUSALEM, ORGANIZATIONS that he supported would send him beautiful bouquets of flowers in honor of the Yom Tov. Shlomie would contact a Yerushalmi friend and pay for him to hire a taxi and deliver the flowers to people who were ill or had other life challenges. "Just don't say it's from me," he would caution.[8]

Hands-On Chesed

ON ONE VISIT TO ERETZ YISRAEL SHLOMIE TOLD HIS BROTHER-in-law Eli Cyperstein, "I'm going to pick you up at 2 in the morning. You're going to see something you never saw in your life."

---
8. Rabbi Yosef Gutfarb.

At that hour, with the streets of Jerusalem quiet and almost all its citizens asleep, these two American businessmen delivered food packages to the doors of poor families in Meah Shearim and other neighborhoods. Shlomie excitedly told Eli, "This is an unbelievable way of doing *chesed*. The families are asleep; they have no idea who is delivering all this food. They'll wake up in a few hours and find it at their door."

To one family they delivered not only food, but also a refrigerator. The organization for whom they were delivering had learned that this particular family was desperately in need of this appliance.

Trans-Atlantic Thoughtfulness

A *TALMID CHACHAM* RELATED:

> Once, I attended a funeral in Eretz Yisrael of a man from the States. Shlomie knew the man only casually, but he attended the funeral. I noticed that he had his cellphone on both in the funeral home and at the cemetery so that

With the *Gaavad* of Jerusalem's Eidah Chareidis, Rabbi Yitzchak Tuvia Weiss *someone in the States could listen to the hespeidim. I asked him, "Are you the shamash here?" He replied, "What's the big deal? The niftar has a sister who wasn't able to make the trip. This way she can be part of it."*

Eviction Notice

A WOMAN ONCE CAME TO SHLOMIE'S OFFICE WITH AN elaborate food platter as a token of appreciation. She was a widow, and a significant part of her income was the rent of an apartment she owned. Squatters had taken over the apartment and she was unable to evict them. When Shlomie was informed of the problem he sent his non-Jewish workers to first remove all the furniture from the apartment and then convince the squatters that *they* had a lease for the apartment and did not take kindly to its

Shlomie with (left to right): Shlomo Singer, Chaim Friedman (background), and Yossi Friedman

occupation by others. The squatters left, and the woman could not thank Shlomie enough.

When Shlomie once went to check on one of his buildings in the Bronx, an elderly woman walked by. The building manager, Shlomo Singer, mentioned that she was the only white tenant. Shlomie struck up a conversation with her and she mentioned that she was Jewish. Shlomie asked her, "Do you have anyone helping you?" "No," she replied, and she added that it had been many, many years since she had last tasted challah. Shlomie instructed the manager to deliver fresh challos to her door every Friday. And when this woman took ill, Shlomie's wife visited her.

"You're Too Late"

ON A SUMMER SUNDAY A PARLOR MEETING WAS HELD IN Monsey. The choice of location was ideal for those traveling to and from the Catskills. Shlomie was heading toward the city when he arrived there. A *gabbai tzedakah* who knew him asked if he could arrange a ride for him from the meeting to the Catskills. Shlomie went from person to person, but no one was going to the town where the *gabbai* was heading, and apparently no one felt that he could afford the extra time to take him there.

With no alternative, Shlomie told the man, "No problem. I'll take you where you need to go."

Someone who overheard this said, "Shlomie, that's ridiculous. You're heading to the city; why should you turn around and go back to the mountains? I'll take him where he needs to go!"

"You're too late," Shlomie replied. "I got the *zechus*, and now that it's mine, I'm not giving it up."[9]

Rabbi Berel Karniol[10] related:

> I once called up Shlomie and said, "I'm coming from Monsey to Boro Park to pick up my son from kollel and

---
9. Eli Cyperstein.
10. Executive Director of Machon L'Hora'ah.

then take him to Kennedy Airport. What's the best way to get to the airport from Boro Park?"

Shlomie asked me, "Where is your son's kollel located?" I told him. Then I heard him calling, "Carlos, please go to this address; someone there has to go to the airport."

Out-of-Town Simchah

RABBI TZVI KAHAN[11] RECALLED:

My first grandchild was born seven years ago. I always travel to America during bein hazemanim (intersession) so that my fundraising does not interfere with the zman (semester). Therefore, I had no choice but to miss my first grandchild's shalom zachar. I actually went straight from the hospital where I saw the baby to the airport at Lod.

I landed at Kennedy Airport and went to Flatbush. Shlomie met me in the street. He knew about the simchah and immediately took hold of me and began to dance.

I spent Shabbos with my steady host in the States, a good friend of our yeshivah. This friend and Shlomie surprised me by arranging for a shalom zachar. Shlomie brought a number of people whom I know and we had a lively "farbreng" together. Apparently they thought that I felt bad about missing the shalom zachar in Jerusalem. I certainly appreciated what they did for me.

Genuine Comfort

A ROSH YESHIVAH IN JERUSALEM RELATED:

A number of years ago Shlomie asked that I accept a certain bachur into our beis midrash. I was reluctant, because this bachur was somewhat different than the talmidim of our beis midrash. That day I attended the funeral in

---
11. Rosh Yeshivah of Yeshivah Imrei Noam in Jerusalem.

Jerusalem of Rabbi Uri Shraga Hellman, longtime Menahel of Bais Yaakov High School of Boro Park. One of the maspidim mentioned that Rabbi Hellman would accept girls to the school who did not exactly "fit in" if he felt he could work with them. I called Shlomie, told him what I had just heard, and said that we would accept this boy and work with him.

That very evening Shlomie went to the aveilim, whom he did not know, told them what had happened, and said, "You see, Rabbi Hellman is still helping Yiddishe kinder in this world."

Gifts From Gedolim

WHEN OTHERS ACCOMPANIED HIM ON VISITS TO GEDOLIM, Shlomie would always ask for a *berachah* for his companions, even before asking for himself. On one trip to Eretz Yisrael he was accompanied by a friend who had been unsuccessful in finding a *chavrusa* back home. Shlomie asked each *gadol* for a *berachah* that his friend should find a *chavrusa*.

A close relative wanted very much to own items of clothing worn by *tzaddikim*. Shlomie brought him a *gartel* worn by one *gadol* and a *yarmulka* worn by another.

And his children follow in his ways. His younger son, Nosson Tzvi, returned from Eretz Yisrael following Succos 5773 (2012) with a gift for his uncle — an *aravah* that had been used by the Toldos Aharon Rebbe.

After Shlomie passed away, his wife entered a store that she knew he frequented. When she introduced herself as "Shlomie Gross' wife" the proprietor told her:

My son works behind the counter alongside me. One day Shlomie came in and at some point became aware that my son has a penchant for nice watches. He left the store and returned around 20 minutes later with a watch for my son. [Shlomie had a friend who sells good watches at discount prices.] Then he left and returned again with a watch for me. Apparently he was concerned that I might feel bad that he had gotten a gift for my son and not for me.

Helping From Afar

A FRIEND RECALLED:

Eighteen years ago I was appointed menahel of a new day school in an out-of-town community. The school was built by a very wealthy family; essentially, this family was my employer.

I was apprehensive, and not just because I was a first-time menahel in a new school. I had gone through some tough times before accepting this appointment and moving my family to this faraway community. I was anxious that things should work out.

Visiting Rabbi Aharon Leib Steinman with his son Aharon

One day I looked out my office window and saw a limousine pull up in front of the school. Out stepped the head of the family that had founded the school, and moments later he entered my office. I was nervous; what was this unannounced visit all about?

He proceeded to place a few thousand dollars in front of me and said, "Rabbi, you've been doing a fine job, and we want to show you some appreciation. Take this money and use it to take your wife and kids on a well-earned vacation.

I was stunned. "This is so generous of you ... why are you doing this?"

The man replied, "To be truthful, I wouldn't have thought of it on my own. You see, recently I went to see a famous chassidishe rebbe. In the waiting room I met a fellow named Shlomie Gross. As soon as he heard where I was from, he got all excited, saying that he knows you

With the Toldos Aharon Rebbe

for many years. He could not stop raving about you, and at the end of our conversation he told me, 'He's a very good man; make sure that you take good care of him. He deserves it.'

"So I decided to follow his advice."

From Santo Domingo

A FRIEND RECALLED:

One evening I was coming home to my apartment in Brooklyn when I was accosted by a pair of muggers. They stabbed me nine times, took my briefcase and wallet, and warned me not to move until they were out of sight.

I staggered to the closest house and rang the bell. The man took one look at me, gave me a chair to sit on, and called Hatzolah. They arrived in minutes and began administering first aid.

A local rav walked by and when he heard what had happened, he immediately contacted my cousins in Bnei Brak to daven for me. My cousins knew how close I was to Shlomie. One of them called Shlomie's house and was told that Shlomie was in Santo Domingo at that time. My cousin was given Shlomie's cellphone number.

A half-hour after I was attacked, I was wheeled by Hatzolah into a local emergency room. As soon as I got there a nurse said to me, "You have a phone call from Santo Domingo. It's one of your friends, but we can't let you talk to him." Shlomie sent a friend to the emergency room to make sure I was given proper care and attention.

I was released from the hospital a week later. Around the same time my office was totally destroyed in a fire. I was really depressed.

One day I received a call from Shlomie. "We're going to Eretz Yisrael for a week." He made all the arrangements for a week-long stay. I had been with Shlomie in Eretz Yisrael, but only during Yom Tov. This was a regular week, and it was an incredible experience. It was like walking with the prince of the city. Wherever we went, people greeted him: "Reb Shloime, Reb Shloime!"

His phone was constantly ringing. It was as if all of Yerushalayim wanted to speak with him. This created a problem. Shlomie had rented three rooms in the Plaza Hotel; one for me, one for himself, and one for his cousin who had joined us for the trip. All three rooms were registered in his name.

One morning at breakfast his cousin complained to Shlomie, "A few times during the night, my phone rang. People were calling you, probably for money."

"And what did you tell them?" Shlomie wanted to know.

"I told them, 'Loz mich shlofen!' ('Let me sleep!')."

Shlomie laughed.

During that trip, Shlomie took me to chassidishe rebbes and roshei yeshivah, to yeshivos and organizations in which he was involved. We visited a soup kitchen in Yerushalayim, and a facility in Tel Aviv to help childless couples.

One of the gabba'ei tzedakah with whom he was close is well connected with government officials. He took us to the Knesset, where we attended a session, and also brought us into a cafeteria reserved for Knesset members so that we could meet some of the politicians. All doors were opened for Shlomie.

He really went all out to make that trip enjoyable, to take my mind off my worries.

Not a day goes by that I don't think about Shlomie.

Health Crisis

A FRIEND RELATED:

> *Six years ago I had a meeting scheduled with Shlomie in his office at 10:00 a.m. It was in the summer, and my family was up in the mountains. At 10:30 Shlomie called me to find out why I had not shown up. I did not respond coherently and he grew concerned. He called my neighbor, who came over and took me to the hospital for a CT scan.*
>
> *While I was waiting in the emergency room, Shlomie arrived. He had left his office and driven 30 miles to be with me. The scan was negative, and the doctors had no idea what was wrong with me. Shlomie called his friend Rabbi Shuky Berman of Refuah Resources, who arranged for me to be seen immediately by a Manhattan specialist. Shlomie took me there. Thank G-d, it turned out to be nothing serious, but I never forgot what Shlomie did for me that day.*

Another friend related:

> *I was the victim of a hold-up; needless to say, it was a frightening experience. The first person to call me afterwards was Shlomie. "You must go on vacation. I'll pay for it." I told him that I did not need a vacation and I was not in the habit of taking vacations, but he would not accept that. He spoke to friends of mine, asking them to convince me to accept his offer. That is how he was. He always wanted to help, and he could not rest if he was not successful in providing help.*

A Friend's Dilemma

A FRIEND'S BUSINESS COLLAPSED. SHLOMIE WOULD SPEAK with him often, encouraging him that matters would turn around. But as Pesach approached nothing had changed.

Shlomie met his friend and asked him if he had come up with a plan for providing his family with their Pesach needs. The friend tried to avoid a direct answer; it was obvious that he had no plan. Shlomie would not let him leave until he gave him his checking account number. The next day this man discovered that a substantial sum had been placed into his account.

When a friend lost his job, Shlomie sent some money. Then he called his friend's wife and asked how her husband was coping.

"Not so great," was the reply.

"Is it the money, or is it the void?" Shlomie wanted to know.

"Both," was the reply.

"I'm sending more money," Shlomie said. "Now let's work on the void." And he proceeded to make phone calls to try to find his friend a job.

He found other ways to help his friends. A *shidduch* was suggested for a friend's daughter. Shlomie knew the boy and his family, and thought it was a wonderful idea. He wanted to help move matters along by speaking to the boy's parents, but was concerned that he did not know the girl. His enthusiasm was based on his friendship with her father and her father's assessment of her.

Shlomie came to their house on an Erev Shabbos and sat watching the family interact as they prepared for Shabbos. Now he could tell the boy's parents his firsthand impression of the girl and her entire family.

The Thousand-Dollar Tie

SHLOMIE WORE NICE TIES AND SOMETIMES RECEIVED COMPLIments for his good taste. Often, upon receiving such a compliment, he would remove the tie and present it to the person as a gift.

Once, he presented someone with a most unusual tie.

A friend was making a wedding out of town and Shlomie knew that money was tight. He called him before the wedding and asked, "Is the wedding covered?"

"Yes, just about."

"Well," Shlomie said, "there's still something I want to give you — a tie."

The man laughed. "A tie? What for? Anyway, I'm leaving for the airport soon and there won't be time for me to pick it up."

Shlomie took down the flight information. After hanging up, he prepared a package and hired someone to take it to the airport, find a Jew who would be on that flight, and ask him to give the package to his friend. The plan worked; the *baal simchah* laughed again when he open the package and withdrew a used tie. His laughter gave way to shock when he discovered $1,000 stuffed inside the tie.

After Shlomie passed away, a friend related: "I was preparing for my child's wedding while struggling just to make ends meet. Someone asked me, 'How do you plan to pay for the wedding?' I responded, 'I can always count on S.G.'"

Many felt this way. As someone close to him put it, "Shlomie was 'the last line of defense.' If all else failed, you could always count on him to bail you out of a financial crisis."

A friend recalled:

> When I made a wedding, Shlomie knew that I needed money. On the day of the wedding he handed me an envelope and said, "It's a loan, but don't worry about paying it back. Whenever you have the money is fine."
>
> I had hired the musician until 11 o'clock. But Shlomie went over to the musician and told him that he would pay for an hour of overtime.

A Friend's Simchah

SOMEONE ONCE SAID, "UNFORTUNATELY, WHEN A *SHIVAH* IS being observed, people go out of their way to attend. It's not always that way with a *simchah*."

To Shlomie, a friend's *simchah* was something not be missed.

> *We were neighbors with the Grosses in our first years of marriage. After we moved to the West Coast, we stayed in touch and remained close friends.*
>
> *When our oldest son became engaged in Toronto, we were shocked when Shlomie walked in the door to join us for the l'chaim. To this day, I don't know how he found out where it was being held. I certainly did not tell him. When I asked him why he had made such an effort, he replied simply, "A friend's simchah — what's the question?"*[12]

Rabbi Meir Yehudah Lichtman, a lifelong friend, related:

> *Our daughter got married in the Midwest three weeks before Shlomie passed away. He told me that he had a business trip to California scheduled for that week and did not think that he would make it to the wedding. But I asked my wife to make a seating card for him, because I knew that if it was at all possible, he would come. And he did! On a snowy day, he surprised us. He did not say a word about the difficulties involved in getting there, or that he would have to get up at 5 to make the plane the next morning.*
>
> *During the wedding, which was on a Thursday night, people were watching the snow coming down hard. Someone said to Shlomie, "Why did you come?"*
>
> *Shlomie didn't understand the question. "What do you mean? For a friend ...?" He added, "And I **will** be back with my family for Shabbos." He was.*

He used his natural liveliness and magnetic personality to draw others into the dancing at a wedding and increase the joy for the *baalei simchah*.

---

12. Avraham Colman.

One friend put it this way:

> *What sometimes appeared as wildness was actually a manifestation of Shlomie's desire to get others to smile. I attended a wedding of two older singles at which Shlomie was "the life of the party." He carried on for two hours straight. This was not uncontrolled wildness; it was an effort to make the greatest, most memorable wedding for a couple that had waited a long time for it to happen.*

A rosh yeshivah recalled watching Shlomie dance at the wedding of an orphan. "He danced with the energy of a *bachur*."

A neighbor recalled: "When a friend made a *simchah*, he was as happy as if he himself was making the *simchah*. When my first daughter became engaged, he showed up at the *l'chaim* with an expensive bottle of liquor. When I protested that it was not necessary, he replied with a smile, 'For the first daughter? You need it.'

"The funny thing is, he did the same thing when my next daughter got engaged."

Dancing at the wedding of his son Aharon

Saved by the Simchah

ON ONE OCCASION, HIS EFFORTS TO ATTEND A FRIEND'S *simchah* led to a business-related salvation:

> Shlomie flew to Los Angeles to attend our son's *aufruf*. In the car on Erev Shabbos he told me about a deal in which he and his associates were about to invest heavily. Being in business myself, I was familiar with similar deals, and told him emphatically that it was a fraud. We discussed it, and I convinced him. He leaned over to me, gave me a kiss, and said emotionally, "Thank you so much for saving me."
>
> Monday morning we heard the news that those who had invested in this venture had unfortunately lost all their money.

Uninvited Guest

THERE WERE TIMES WHEN HE WOULD CONTRIBUTE GENEROUSLY to help marry off a child of a New York family whom he did not know. Often he was not content to merely give the money. He wanted to feel the parents' joy when they led their child to the *chuppah* with their financial burden eased. Quietly, he would make inquiries to discover the location of the wedding and go there to watch and *shep nachas*.

Perhaps most instructive were the weddings he attended of *baalei simchah* with whom he was acquainted but not close enough to be invited. Often he would attend such *simchos* simply because he was very happy for them and he knew that his appearance would bring them joy.

When he heard that his cousin's cousin was engaged, he called up the parents to wish *"Mazel tov"* and to say that he knew the *mechutanim* and that they were wonderful people. He was not invited to the wedding; he did not know either party that well. But he went to the wedding anyway, to wish them *"Mazel tov"* again.

His Great Heart / 137

He had another reason for coming. He was a *tov ayin*; he rejoiced in another's success, in another's *simchah*.

Thankfully, today's *frum* community is blessed with many *simchos*. Often, when one is not invited to a wedding or bar mitzvah, the reaction is a sigh of relief: "*Baruch Hashem*, I can stay home that night." Shlomie's attitude was altogether different. Though he was an extremely busy person, he always had time to bring joy to someone else, even if he was not invited.

A *simchah* of a relative or close friend was, understandably, especially important to him. One Erev Shabbos when he was in Eretz Yisrael, his friend Shimon Bertram called with the news that his son was engaged; the *vort* would be held on Motza'ei Shabbos. Shlomie's return flight was on Motza'ei Shabbos. "What?" he exclaimed. "You're making the *vort* without me?"

A few hours after the *vort* had ended, the *baalei simchah* heard knocking on their front door. Shlomie had taken the first flight out after Shabbos and had made it from the airport to Brooklyn in record time. Rather than be upset at having been awakened, his friend was ecstatic. "I can't believe it," he repeated as they hugged. Shlomie responded, "For a friend I had to do it."

Luzer Brodt, z"l

ONE OF SHLOMIE'S CLOSEST FRIENDS WAS ELAZAR (LUZER) Brodt, who passed away in 5759 (1998), leaving behind a wife and children, some of whom were very young at the time.

In the words of one of Luzer's sons:

> It's really not possible to describe their relationship in words. I see before my eyes Shlomie z"l twirling my father z"l around on the dance floor at family simchos. They shared so many good times together; and they shared chesed projects, some of which are known and some which will never be known.

Luzer's brother, יבל"ח, Abish Brodt, recalled: "I was at an Agudas Yisrael convention when I received word that my brother Luzer, *z"l*, had been diagnosed with a serious illness. I left immediately for the hospital. By the time I got there, Shlomie was already there."

A friend recalled, "I never saw a person cry at a *choleh's* bed like I saw Shlomie cry at the bed of his dear friend, Luzer Brodt. Torrents of tears flowed as he recited *Tehillim* for him."

From the time that his friend passed away, Shlomie would come by often to spend time with the Brodt children. This was especially true on Erev Shabbos in the summer when he patronized a *mikveh* near the Brodts' summer residence. As the oldest of the children recalls, "Shloimy was so full of life and fun. We waited for his car to pull up and were really disappointed when, for whatever reason, he could not come."

When Moshe Nochum, the youngest of the Brodt children, was becoming a bar mitzvah, Shlomie asked him what he would like for a gift. "A camera," the boy replied. Shlomie was not satisfied to take the boy to a local camera store. One day after Moshe Nochum finished yeshivah, Shlomie was there, along with his son Nosson Tzvi, to pick him up for a trip to a well-known camera store in Manhattan.

In the store, Nosson Tzvi whispered to his father that he too would like a camera. "Today is Moshe Nochum's day," he told his son. "We can come back another time to get you a camera."

Following is an excerpt from a letter sent by one of the Brodt children to Shlomie's family after his passing:

> *I remember the days when our father, z"l, was in a coma and people came by non-stop to visit. When Shlomie, z"l, came there was a breath of fresh air, a smile, a good word, a change in everyone's mood.*
>
> *But it didn't end there.*
>
> *[In the years that followed], Shlomie would stop by — in his words "just because." Sometimes he said he was coming for a piece of potato kugel, sometimes he said he "owed" something to one of the kids. He would sit down and get everyone to join him at the table. He was*

all smiles and noticed each one of us with a comment, a good word. It might have been a comment about a new bike one of us was riding, or the many apples someone was peeling. He always had a good word to say.

I can fill a book with stories of Shlomie's maasim tovim (good deeds).

Shimmy Biegeleisen, Hy"d

AMONG SHLOMIE'S CLOSEST FRIENDS WAS SHIMMY BIEGELEISEN, who was killed in the Twin Towers attack on September 11, 2001. Shimmy's wife recalled:

Shlomie was always there for us. Our two youngest sons were ages 8 and 11 at that time. Shlomie would appear at our door at random, usually twice a week, always bringing along little Nosson Tzvi. We feel such hakaras hatov for all that he did.

Shlomie took the two young boys down to their basement and taught them how to say *Kaddish*.

With Shimmy Biegeleisen

Dancing with Mo Biegeleisen on his shoulders.
Mordechai Biegeleisen is behind Shlomie on right.

When a Biegeleisen child celebrated a birthday, Shlomie was there with a cake.

When the youngest son, Mo, approached Shlomie to sponsor his swimming in a Chai Lifeline swim-a-thon, Shlomie said, "If you swim 500 laps, I'll give you $1,000." The boy kept his part of the deal and Shlomie got another sponsor to donate $200 so that Mo could get the top prize — a scooter — for raising $1,200.

As a two-year-old, a Biegeleisen grandson was afraid of Shlomie. Shlomie decided to buy the child a toy in the hope that this would calm his fears. He called the boy's mother to ask what toy he should buy, and settled on a motorized car.

Shimmy Biegeleisen was a beloved member of the White House Estates summer community, where he was Shlomie's next-door neighbor. Shimmy was a Belzer chassid and he loved "Kadeshihi," a lively Belzer *niggun*. After his passing, at every wedding of their summer friends, Shlomie would have the band play "Kadeshihi" and would announce, "This is for Shimmy!" The men would place their arms around each other's shoulders and dance like brothers.

A Powerhouse of Giving

FOLLOWING IS AN EXCERPT FROM A LETTER WRITTEN TO the family by a close friend of Shlomie's, Volvi Elbogen:

> Shlomie was a powerhouse of giving. It was not only because he gave huge sums to a multitude of causes; he lent an ear and gave sympathy, empathy, and love from a heart so big he simply didn't know when or how to stop giving.
>
> In the summer of 2004 our middle child, Tehila, then 13 years old, was diagnosed with cancer. Witnessing our daze, Shlomie called Rabbi Shuky Berman of Refuah Resources and within hours Shlomie put us on a plane to Boston, to one of the best surgeons in the country.
>
> Two and a half years later, Shlomie made arrangements for Tehila's kevurah. Unbeknownst to us for the first two

With Volvi Elbogen

> years of its existence, Shlomie founded an afternoon kollel in Tehila's name in a moshav right near the cemetery where she is buried; the kollel is named "Mesivta Tehilas Hashem."
>
> Sunday, 17 Adar (less than a week before Shlomie's passing), was Tehila's fifth yahrtzeit. My son-in-law, Shimmy, was going to make a siyum Mishnayos and I asked Shlomie to join. Apologizing that he couldn't make it because he was going on a business trip (as a favor to

someone else), he came over on Motza'ei Shabbos (the night of the yahrtzeit) and said, "Let's learn Mishnayos l'ilui nishmas Tehila."

He called his wife that Tuesday asking her to tell my wife that many people on the moshav have become baalei teshuvah as a result of the shiurim delivered at Mesivta Tehilas Hashem.

On the plane he told his companion, "Let's learn Mishnayos for Tehila Malka."

Shlomie was warm, considerate, funny, loved to laugh, and so, so sensitive. He didn't hesitate to express his love for all of us. An only son, he would occasionally introduce me as his "brother." And I loved him more than a brother. It was from him that I learned what it means to be a friend and what it means to give, even though I know that I will always fall woefully short of his example.

My feeling, my lament, aside from my sorrow, is one that is shared by his many friends and the many who benefited from his incredible generosity: A person like Shlomie comes along once in a generation. There is no one like him.

In *Pirkei Avos*, Rabban Yochanan ben Zakkai asked his *talmidim* to discern which one quality a person should strive to perfect, so that this will be the catalyst to refine his entire personality. R' Yehoshua responded: *chaver tov*, a good friend.[13] *Rabbeinu Yonah* explains that this does not mean to find a good friend. Rather, it means to develop within oneself the *middah* of being a good friend, even to one person. By being a true friend to one individual, one can come to love all of mankind.

Shlomie Gross personified the *middah* of *chaver tov*, and he came to love all Jews, of all backgrounds, with genuine, unconditional love.

---

13. *Avos* 2:9.

7

The Ultimate Baal Tzedakah

SHLOMIE ONCE TOLD A *TZEDAKAH* COLLECTOR, "YOU and I are partners in the same business. My job is to give, and your job is to receive." He lived by Rabbi Samson Raphael Hirsch's understanding of the word צְדָקָה as relating to צֶדֶק, *justice*. In Rabbi Hirsch's words:

Why should G-d give you more than you need unless He intended to make you the administrator of this blessing for the benefit of others?

A noted rav said, "Sometimes philanthropists have agendas: They like to support a particular kind of cause and channel virtually all their *tzedakah* in that direction. Shlomie had no agenda other than to fulfill the will of Hashem. If a cause was worthy, he was ready to contribute and to encourage others to contribute as well."

He once gave an acquaintance a large check to help with someone's wedding expenses. The acquaintance told someone close

With his *mechutan* Moshe Feuer (center) and Rabbi Yehudah Svei

to Shlomie, "I'm not comfortable taking so much money from him. He's so generous — what if he's giving me more than he can really afford?"

The man responded, "The money is not staying in his account. Shlomie views it as money that was given to him to give to others. If you don't get it, someone else will."

The Rosh Yeshivah of Yeshivah Gedolah of Philadelphia, Rabbi Shmuel Kamenetsky, told one of Shlomie's *mechutanim*, Moshe Feuer, "You should know that if your *mechutan* Shlomie had only one dollar left in his wallet and I asked him for it, he would give it to me without any hesitation."

A noted *gabbai tzedakah* related:

> Shlomie would give me money each year for a variety of worthy causes. I hesitated to ever ask him for more because I knew that his goodness made it hard for him to say "No" even when it was hard for him to give.
>
> Once, I found myself in the midst of a major crisis. I needed a lot of money, and quickly. Hashgachah (Divine Providence) arranged that Shlomie and I traveled somewhere together, and I told him of the crisis. He wrote out 25 postdated checks, one per month. The crisis was over.

The Ultimate Baal Tzedakah / 145

During a recent tax season his accountant warned him, "No one gives such a large share of his earnings to charity. You're liable to be audited."

Shlomie responded by handing over boxes of *tzedakah* receipts, proof that his deductions were accurate.

Sometimes after making a huge profit in a deal, he would tell a friend, "I'm no better than people who don't make this kind of money. Why should I have it and not them?"

As a young entrepreneur, his standard donation to anyone who came to his office or rang his doorbell was $100.

Twenty-five years before his passing, when he was first becoming successful in the real estate business, he borrowed $25,000 privately for the sole purpose of distributing it to *tzedakah*.

Unusual Outlook

A FRIEND RELATED:

> In the early 1990s Shlomie and I would exchange business information and developed a close relationship. At one point Shlomie called me to say that he needed to talk — he had just suffered a major stock market loss. He said, "What a shame, what a waste! I invested this money and it went down the drain. Do you know how many yeshivos could have benefited from the money I invested?"
>
> I was thunderstruck. The average person would have been focused on how the loss of money affected him personally. With that attitude, someone experiencing such financial loss would quite possibly fall into a depression. But Shlomie, at that young age, had an entirely different focus. His sole concern was that he could have used that money for tzedakah, specifically the support of yeshivos, and now it was gone.

He sought the guidance of rabbanim for his *tzedakah*-giving, how to prioritize, and what to do when he was running low on funds. He was well thought out in how much, and how often, he gave to each solicitor. He confided to a *talmid chacham* that when the recession affected his earnings, he drew strength from the Gemara that teaches regarding spending for Shabbos foods, "*Hakadosh Baruch Hu* says to the Jewish people, 'Borrow on My account and I will repay you.'"[1]

Prior to the wedding of one of his children, when the real estate market was depressed, Shlomie borrowed a substantial sum to distribute to *tzedakah* causes in honor of the *simchah*. Soon after, he made back the money in a successful deal.

For the Sake of Yeshivos

AS SOMEONE WHO HAD A HEIGHTENED APPRECIATION OF THE importance of Torah study, Shlomie was a supporter of many yeshivos and kollelim, both in America and in Eretz Yisrael.

The head of one yeshivah recalled:

> *Shlomie would give our yeshivah a $5,000 donation a couple of times a year. I developed a very close relationship with him; he was a dear friend.*
>
> *Once, I called him for his usual donation. He said, "I can tell from your voice that you're under stress."*
>
> *I could not deny it. The financial situation of our yeshivah at that time was stressful.*
>
> *"I'll tell you what," Shlomie said. "I'll give you $5,000 and loan you $25,000."*
>
> *I thanked him but declined the offer; I do not borrow what I cannot pay back and I did not see how, at that time, I could repay such a loan.*

---

1. *Beitzah* 15b.

> *Shlomie invited me to come to his house to pick up the check. When I arrived he said, "What's the problem? I want to lend you the money. Why can't you take it?"*
>
> *"Because I don't want to lose a good friend," I replied. "I don't see how I'll be able to repay such a loan."*
>
> *Shlomie thought for a moment. "In that case," he said, "I'm going to give a donation of $25,000."*
>
> *He wrote a check, handed it to me, and said, "You can still call me this year if you need more."*
>
> *Nine months later, I called him and he gave another $5,000.*
>
> *The following year I came to him for his usual donation. Shlomie asked me, "How much did I give you last year?" I replied that last year was a special situation. "It makes no difference if it was 'special,'" he responded. "I want to know how much I gave."*
>
> *I told him that his donations totalled $30,000. He promptly wrote 12 post-dated checks, each for $2,500.*

An Israeli rosh yeshivah recalled:

> *Our yeshivah was in a serious financial crisis and I did not know where to turn. I was under enormous pressure to come up with a large sum. On Erev Shabbos I took my entire family to Kever Rochel and we davened that Hashem save our yeshivah.*
>
> *On Sunday morning my good friend Shlomie called. After a brief exchange, he said, "You sound under the weather. What's wrong?"*
>
> *I told him my problem. He responded immediately that he was sending me the full amount I needed. I told him that I was not sure if and when I would pay it back. "Don't worry," he responded, "you'll pay it back. And if not, it's also okay."*
>
> *Baruch Hashem, I did pay it back, but I never forgot how he perceived my worry and came to my rescue.*

A rosh yeshivah recalled:

> *He would tell me, "Pressure me to give more. What I decide in the end is my business, but you should pressure me." One time I did pressure him. He said, "I understand you and you are right, but right now it is hard for me. Keep bothering me; I will try to do what you ask."*

Honoring His Word

RABBI TZVI KAHAN, ROSH YESHIVAH OF YESHIVAH IMREI NOAM in Jerusalem, related:

> *Once, I received a phone call from Shlomie at around 2 a.m. his time. "What happened in the end?" he asked me. "Did I give you the donation I promised or not?"*
>
> *I was upset with him. "You couldn't wait until morning to call me with this question? Why did you have to call me when for you it's the middle of the night?"*
>
> *"It was disturbing my sleep," he replied.*
>
> *I told him that he had not yet made good on his pledge. "But don't worry," I assured him. "You can mail it out."*
>
> *Eight o'clock that morning, he personally delivered the check to our New York office.*

Whether Big or Small

THOUGH HE DISTRIBUTED *TZEDAKAH* ON A GRAND SCALE, he appreciated when someone offered a small donation that represented a true sacrifice.

> *The gaon Rabbi Shmuel Auerbach requested that Shlomie spearhead a fundraising campaign for the family of a man who had died suddenly, leaving behind a wife and many young children. A mailing was sent out with Shlomie's name and office address. Among the checks was one for $6 with a note:*

"Every Rosh Chodesh, we buy our children ice cream as a special Rosh Chodesh treat. This month [with the children's agreement], instead of buying ice cream, we are sending the enclosed check to help these unfortunate children."

Shlomie was so touched by this that he kept a copy of the check in his pocket to show to others. Eventually, he taped the copy to a wall of his office, where it remains to this day.

The first Pesach after that fundraising campaign, Shlomie sat at the head of his *Seder* table and with tears in his eyes said, "To whom are they going to ask the Mah Nishtanah in that home tonight?"

With Dignity

THE PONOVEZHER RAV, RABBI YOSEF SHLOMO KAHANEMAN, was a great builder of Torah, and as such, he spent much of his

With Rabbi Shmuel Auerbach at a *hachnasas sefer Torah* celebration in Jerusalem

time fundraising. He is reported to have said that the shame he sometimes experienced from being received with less than proper respect was actually a blessing. Every bit of shame he endured was an atonement and would make it easier for him in the next world.

He would have experienced no such "blessing" had he knocked on Shlomie's door.

At home, Shlomie would receive those who came for *tzedakah* in his study downstairs. A side entrance was the shortest way to this study, and for a while after he moved into his home, this was the entrance *gabba'ei tzedakah* would use. But something troubled Shlomie. These were honorable people, and some were outstanding *talmidei chachamim*. He felt that asking them to enter his home through a side entrance did not accord them proper respect; instead he welcomed them at the main entrance and invited them into his living room.

"I'm Jealous"

A NOTED *ASKAN* RECALLED:

> *When I was a bachur in my teens, I volunteered to spend an evening helping a Yid from Yerushalayim make the rounds of Flatbush collecting. One of the main addresses on our list was that of Shlomie Gross. I knew he was well-to-do and that he had a heart of gold.*
>
> *Somewhat nervously I knocked on the door, hoping that the maid would let me speak to him. I was quite surprised when a smiling Shlomie opened the door himself, and brought us into the kitchen where he was having a snack. He invited us to join him. I was amazed at how comfortable he made us feel, as if we were his relatives or good friends.*
>
> *My companion told Shlomie his tale of woe and mentioned that we did not know each other but that I had offered to accompany him. Shlomie handed him a*

generous check and then, turning to me, he said, "I'm jealous of you. I envy your mitzvah. I'm sitting here in my comfortable house writing a check, while you're trudging from door to door, collecting money for someone you barely know, having doors slammed in your face. You're doing the real thing. How I envy your reward!"

His words warmed my heart and encouraged me to continue helping this Yid. Later, I brought other meshulachim to his door, and I received the same warm reception.

Another noted *askan* expressed a similar sentiment:

I take meshulachim around from house to house helping them to raise funds. It's not easy. Sometimes people don't let you cross the threshold, other times they let you in but make you feel uncomfortable.

Shlomie was always one of my first stops. He was very warm and welcoming. He was quick with his checkbook and gave very generously. And one time when he saw that I was a bit frustrated he told me, "Don't stop what you're doing! Helping these Yidden is an incredible mitzvah. I envy your zechus."

His words were a great source of chizuk to me.

A neighbor, Jack Warshavchik, recalled:

I lived directly across from the Grosses. I could not believe the number of meshulachim that would ring their doorbell and be welcomed in. On Purim, there were times when he was not home.[2] The meshulachim would ring my bell and ask, "Are you Gross?" or "Where is Gross?"

I came to the conclusion that Shlomie was really a malach (angel) and I was just a person.

---

2. As mentioned elsewhere in this book, Shlomie would spend part of Purim taking his son collecting. Some years, he would also accompany a rosh yeshivah or *gabbai tzedakah* on their *tzedakah* collections. He never spent the entire Purim away from home.

Fundraisers' Headquarters

TO AN OUTSIDER, THE OFFICE OF SHLOMIE AND YOSSI FRIEDMAN, his partner of 28 years, seemed like an American headquarters for overseas *tzedakah* fundraisers. These gentlemen would sit comfortably around a table in the office, drinking coffee and conducting their business on their cellphones. But Shlomie was not satisfied with that. He would share various tidbits about his business and other happenings with these men, making them feel that they were not *"shnorrers"* (beggars) — a term he despised as degrading — but rather, his friends, which they were.

He would become upset if someone referred to a solicitor as a *shnorrer* or even as a *meshulach* (collector).[3] To him, every Jew who arrived from overseas to raise funds, whether for himself or for an organization, was a *"gabbai tzedakah"* (charity treasurer) or a *"sheliach mitzvah"* (mitzvah emissary). Shlomie would say that he too was a *gabbai tzedakah*. "I just give out what Hashem gave me to distribute." And he would ratify this statement with a comment of the *Ohr HaChaim*.[4]

A *bachur* whom Shlomie hired to work in his office for a few weeks told his parents, "Mr. Gross doesn't really work; he hires people to do that. He sits and writes checks all day." Of course, this was not an accurate statement, but it does reflect how much time Shlomie devoted to dispensing *tzedakah* on a daily basis.

A secretary, Mrs. Chana Fonfeder, recalled:

> *His office message books are something to behold. People from all walks of life would call and come to see him: Litvishe, chassidishe, Sefardim, young and old, men and*

---

3. In Shloimy's vocabulary, a *tzedakah* collector was a *"gabbai tzedakah"* and an employee was "someone whom I work together with." In this book, we sometimes use the term *"meshulach"* to distinguish between poor people who solicit *tzedakah* for themselves and *gabba'ei tzedakah*, who collect on behalf of others.
4. *Shemos* 22:24. "One should not act haughtily towards the poor man [with the attitude] that he is giving to him [and is therefore deserving of his adulation], for he is merely giving him what is [rightfully] his."

women. Sometimes when he would receive a phone call, he would tell me, "I can't talk now; please take a message." But most of the time he would buzz me moments later, "Put the call through." He was so kindhearted, he found it impossible to ignore people's requests.

Once, a woman from Eretz Yisrael came seeking support for her program for autistic children. She brought with her a device to help these children communicate by typing their thoughts with the help of a shadow. She wanted to demonstrate how it worked. I knew that Mr. Gross had no time for this (and probably would have given her the same donation regardless), but he saw that the demonstration was important to her. So he asked me to come over and serve as her "student" so that she could show him how it worked.

Everyone's Welcome

YOSSI FRIEDMAN RECALLED:

As time went on, our office resembled Jerusalem's Central Bus Station. It was something that I never dreamed would happen in my office, and I don't believe Shlomie thought it would either. The meshulachim often knew each other and would sit around the conference table conversing, talking on their phones and on our phones ... It got to a point where even Shlomie realized that the situation was difficult. So we installed a lock, a buzzer, and a camera for the outside door.

But these innovations did not really change the situation, because Shlomie found it almost impossible to disappoint someone and send him away empty-handed. If a meshulach rang the bell, he was let in. At most, he would be asked to return at a less busy time. But he was never rejected.

Of course, all this meant that Shlomie spent a good part of his workday listening to these people and writing checks for them. That was fine, because we were more like brothers than partners. There was never any discussion over who was spending more time on business-related matters. We were both busy, though in different ways, and we were both fine with that.

Often, meshulachim would come in to thank me for a check that Shlomie had written from the company account. I had no idea who these people were or how much Shlomie had given them. I left it up to him.

I have to be honest. At first, I tried to hold him back, both regarding the amounts he was giving and the number of people he was giving to. But I saw how badly he wanted to do it. And I said to myself, "Who knows where the berachah comes from?"

What never ceased to amaze me was how he could sit patiently for half an hour or more listening to a meshulach pour out his heart and his tzaros (troubles). All his life, Shlomie found it hard to sit still and stay focused. Yet, for these needy individuals, many of them broken souls, he could sit, listen, empathize, and advise.

And there was something else that was highly unusual about our office. One minute a distinguished rosh yeshivah was sitting with Shlomie, and a few minutes later a "kid at risk" was sitting pouring out his troubles to him. Shlomie was beloved by and comfortable with both.

The Best Advice

A YOUNG MAN WHO WAS ENTERING THE REAL ESTATE FIELD asked if Shlomie could meet with him to provide some tips for success. An appointment was made.

Shlomie greeted the fellow, asked that he be seated, and to the young man's surprise, withdrew his own checkbook. He proceeded to date 12 checks, one per month, for the next 12 months. He said, "If you want to be successful, write 12 head checks, one for each month of the year. Choose a worthy *tzedakah* and fill in an amount that will be a generous portion of your profits. That's the best advice that I can give you." He then proceeded to explain the ins and outs of real estate dealings.

Jerusalem's Jewels

A CLOSE FRIEND SAID, "SHLOMIE WAS THE ADVOCATE OF THE Yerushalmi Yidden (Jews of Jerusalem)."

He had an appreciation for the loftiness of the typical "Yerushalmi." He knew from visiting their homes that they and their families happily do without many of the comforts that Americans take for granted. He recognized the *dveikus baShem* of these noble Jews, that they are great in Torah knowledge and awe of Hashem.

His *neshamah* perceived the greatness of their *neshamos* and he loved being in their company. To the Yerushalmi *gabba'ei tzedakah* the respect, love, and concern that Shlomie showered upon them was a bright spot in the difficult *"galus"* they are forced to endure when spending weeks and sometimes months in America collecting for their respective causes.

A friend recalled:

> *I was invited to the sheva berachos of one of Shlomie's children, hosted by some of his friends. It was held in a small catering hall. There was no head table; the first table in the front was set aside for Shlomie and his family. When I entered the hall I was shocked to see that sitting around the table with Shlomie were a number of his Yerushalmi friends. They were his "family," and he felt honored to have them sitting with him.*

Rabbi Avraham Ausband, Rosh Yeshivah of Yeshivah Telshe Alumni (Riverdale), reflected:

Shlomie was a unique individual.

The Gemara says that one who gives tzedakah to a poor man merits six berachos, but one who comforts him, who gives tzedakah with a smile, merits 11 berachos.[5] *Shlomie took the mitzvah of giving tzedakah to a higher level. He not only put himself in the solicitor's situation, he made the person feel that he was his good, trustworthy friend, that he was enjoying the person's company and was genuinely happy to have a relationship with him.*

His children's weddings were something special. In addition to the hundreds of American friends and relatives, it seemed as if every rosh kollel, rosh yeshivah, and gabbai tzedakah from Eretz Yisrael was there. But that was not all. Shlomie took each one of them into the middle of the circle and danced with him alone, making him

Making a point to Rabbi Avraham Ausband (center) and Rabbi Yaakov Horowitz

5. *Bava Basra* 9b.

The Ultimate Baal Tzedakah / 157

feel special. He felt a true yedidus (friendship) toward every one of them, and he also felt that they deserved recognition for their role as עוֹסְקִים בְּצָרְכֵי צִבּוּר *(those who busy themselves with the community's needs). He made them feel that* **they** *were doing* **him** *a favor by involving him in their sacred work.*

His brother-in-law Aron Cyperstein recalled:

The wedding of Adina, their oldest child, was a real eye-opener for us. There were all these meshulachim, honored guests at the chasunah! And the whole night, Shlomie was very concerned that they each had a seat, that they were happy and being properly served.

The common attitude is that it's very nice to allow a meshulach into your home and give him some money.

At the wedding of Meir and Adina Kaplowitz (left to right): Rabbi Avrohom Schorr, Rabbi Osher Porush (in background), the *chasan*, Aharon Gross, R' Abish Brodt, Rabbi Tzvi Kahan, Rabbi Chaim Yosef Gefner, Rabbi Aharon Samet

The relationship ends until he rings your doorbell a year later. Shlomie introduced us to an entirely different attitude towards these Jews.

At the wedding of one of his children, the *maitre d'* asked Shlomie if he would like the staff to keep all *meshulachim* out of the hall, as their collecting might interfere with everyone's enjoyment. "Absolutely not," he replied emphatically. "Their presence is what makes the celebration complete. And they're not *meshulachim*, they're *sheluchei mitzvah*."

At each of his children's weddings, he came well prepared to distribute *tzedakah* to the scores of collectors who came. At his son Aharon's wedding, his pockets were empty when the wedding was far from over! Shlomie approached a friend and borrowed $2,000 which he proceeded to distribute.

Perceiving Their Purity

SHIMON ECKSTEIN RELATED WHAT TO HIS MIND WAS THE SECRET of Shlomie's special relationship with Yerushalmi Yidden:

I knew Shlomie since our days as bachurim in Mirrer Yeshivah.

Shlomie loved pure, humble, sincere people. He was their friend, their advocate.

I saw the love he felt for roshei yeshivah, for kollel yungeleit. When he perceived someone's tzidkus, he went all out for that person. I think this is why he loved the pure Yerushalmi Yidden. He loved them as people.

Eventually, we became neighbors on East Eighteenth Street and I was able to see firsthand how he dealt with these meshulachim. Usually when a poor person comes to the door, you hand him a check and that's all. With Shlomie, you could see him becoming emotionally involved with the person and his plight. He loved their spirit, their humility, their innocence. He enjoyed their company.

"That's Who He Was"

AFTER SHLOMIE'S PASSING, THE FAMILY RECEIVED A LETTER from a Yerushalmi who wrote:

> ... I was moved by something amazing. For many days after we heard the news, everywhere I went, I heard people talking about the personal relationship that they had with R' Shloime. Each person had his own incredible story to tell. And whenever the person would finish his story the others would respond, "That's not a chiddush (something newsworthy) — that's who he was!"

For a Brother

SHLOMIE ONCE TOLD A YERUSHALMI FRIEND, "I DON'T THINK I'm going to get [Divine] reward for the *tzedakah* that I give. When I give, I feel like a brother to the person — and who wouldn't help his own brother?"

A young *talmid chacham* in Jerusalem fell ill and was advised to fly to Arizona for surgery. A large sum had to be raised quickly. Someone told the young man's father to call Shlomie Gross. The father made the phone call and explained the situation. Shlomie responded, "עָלַי וְעַל צַוָּארִי (*Upon me and on my neck;* i.e. I take responsibility)."[6] The father's relief was indescribable.

In relating this story someone commented, "Only someone who felt like a brother to the recipient could make such a commitment."

When he helped someone, he became totally involved in the person's situation and thought of every possible way to ease it. Once, he realized that a *meshulach* had not eaten supper. He took him to a store and bought over $100 worth of food so that the two of them could enjoy an expensive meal together. He was not one to spend such money for a regular weekday meal, but in this instance he thought that an elaborate spread would make the *meshulach* feel good and lift his spirits.

---
6. From *Pesachim* 8b.

For his oldest child's wedding, a number of Israeli *gabba'ei tzedakah* and heads of *mosdos,* along with their wives, were in attendance. For some, it was their first time in America. At 9:30 a.m. on the morning after the wedding, Shlomie attended a breakfast for some of these guests hosted by a friend. At 11 a.m. he took some of these guests on a trip to Manhattan, to show them some tourist attractions and to help them choose gifts to bring back to their families, all of which he paid for.

Without Being Asked

A FRIEND WHO TRAVELED WITH HIM TO ERETZ YISRAEL TOLD HIM, "Shlomie, I can't go with you to the Kosel — it's *sakanas nefashos* (dangerous)!" He was referring to the crowds of *meshulachim* who would surround Shlomie almost as soon as he was noticed.

At the Kosel with his son Nosson Tzvi

He enjoyed *davening Vasikin* (at sunrise) at the Kosel. However, when *meshulachim* would learn of his presence there, they often went to meet him, which made it difficult for him to *daven.*

On what was to be his last trip to Eretz Yisrael, Shlomie decided one morning to *daven* in a quiet shul where no one would know him. During the *davening* he noticed a Yerushalmi crying profusely as he poured out his heart to his Creator. As soon as *davening* ended, Shlomie sent someone to the man with a few hundred dollars, asking that it be given anonymously.

The Ultimate Baal Tzedakah / 161

Perceiving Their Needs

A FORMER EMPLOYEE RELATED:

> *Once, I was supposed to drive Shlomie to Manhattan for an important meeting. We left the office very late and hurried out to the car. As Shlomie got into the passenger seat, a meshulach — not someone with whom Shlomie was close — ran up to the car and asked Shlomie for a few minutes of his time. "I'm sorry, but I'm late for a meeting," he replied. "But please come back again and we'll talk."*
>
> *The man would not take "No" for an answer. He held onto the car, insisting that he needed to speak to Shlomie **now**. I was shocked at the man's chutzpah. Shlomie, however, had a different attitude. I guess he interpreted the man's behavior as an act of desperation. He handed the man a few hundred dollars and said kindly, "I really want to give you more. Come back to me."*

He was once asked to provide funds for a New York wedding in which both *mechutanim* struggled to make ends meet. Along with his check towards wedding expenses, he added $250 as a gift for the *chasan* and *kallah*.

A friend related:

> *One year he approached me before Pesach and said, "One of our chaveirim (friends) doesn't have money to make Pesach. Give this to him, but don't tell him who it's from." He handed me $5,000.*
>
> *I delivered the money. The man started to cry. "My wife and I just said we need to go shopping for Yom Tov. I didn't know where to turn."*

Once, a couple from out of town who were marrying off a son in New York stayed at a friend of Shlomie's. One day, Shlomie spoke to the friend. "These people don't have money for the wedding and I want to help them — but I don't want them to known that the money is coming from me. Can you help me?"

The friend arranged for a third party to give the couple an anonymous $3,600 gift. The grateful father said, "I honestly did not know how we were going to pay for our share of the wedding."

Some years ago, a family in New York suffered the sudden loss of a child. When someone mentioned to Shlomie that he knew the family, Shlomie replied, "I have heard that the family does not have much money. Do you know if they were able to pay for the *kevurah* (burial)?" The man looked into the matter and reported that it had been paid for with borrowed money. Shlomie then gave a sizable sum.

Making Their Problem His Own

WHEN A PERSON'S SITUATION TOUCHED SHLOMIE'S HEART — and it was not very difficult to accomplish this — Shlomie was not satisfied with giving a generous check. He became involved with every detail.

A couple living in Eretz Yisrael had a newborn with a medical issue that required care in America. This meant that the entire family had to temporarily relocate to America and needed a place to stay. The young man's *rosh kollel* phoned Shlomie and requested his help.

The lease on Shlomie's car was expiring, so he renewed it and gave them the car. He set them up in an apartment, and his wife pitched in by driving the parents and their baby to the doctor in Washington Heights.

When the baby's situation stabilized, doctors allowed them to return home. On the appointed day, Shlomie and his worker, Carlos, arrived at the family's apartment to take them to the airport. Shlomie personally loaded the many suitcases into one car which his worker drove, while Shlomie drove the family in the other car. As the young man put it, "I felt like he was my brother."

One day he met a young man in Flatbush who had come to America seeking medical treatment for a sick child. An appointment had been made with a specialist in Boston; he was on his way to Boro Park from where he would go with his wife and child via car service to Newark Airport.

"What for?" Shlomie asked. "I'm going to the airport today. I'll be happy to take you." In fact, he had just decided that he was going to the airport so that this young man could be driven by his new friend, Shlomie Gross, and not by a stranger.

That trip was the beginning of a close relationship. Some time later, when the family was again preparing to travel from Brooklyn to Boston, Shlomie rented a chauffeur-driven limousine and told the driver, "I will pay for you to stay in Boston for as long as necessary until they are ready to return to New York."

A Gabbai's Testimony

RABBI CHAIM YITZCHAK COHEN IS A RENOWNED *GABBAI tzedakah* in Jerusalem. He related:

> *I have met many wealthy people in my lifetime, but Shlomie was unique. He was very sharp and was very good at sizing up a person, so that when people came to him for the first time, he was able to determine how far to go in helping them. As tall and broad as he was, that is how great his heart was.*
>
> *I would sit and watch as he gave a solicitor a donation and then made phone calls for an hour or two on the person's behalf. This chesed was much more than the money. The needy individual's spirits were lifted when he saw that Shlomie felt for his plight to the point that he wanted to get others to help as well.*
>
> *I know of cases where Shlomie asked the person, "How much do you need to raise?" The person would name a sum, Shlomie would raise the full amount, then summon*

his driver to take the person to the airport for his trip back home.

Rabbi Cohen continued:

When I arrived in America for the wedding of one of Shlomie's children, I was not in good spirits. I had just been informed that my daughter was seriously ill. Shlomie knew about this, and at the wedding, he tried to lift my spirits, pulling me into the circle and dancing with me.

The morning after the wedding, he called me up and asked that I meet him at his office at 11 a.m. I protested that he must be exhausted after the wedding, but he insisted that I come. When I arrived, he told his secretary that he was taking me somewhere and that she should not forward any phone calls to him while we were out.

Right to left with hands joined:
Rabbi Chaim Yitzchak Cohen, Shlomie, Willy Beer, and Rabbi Chaim Yosef Gefner

> We went to Manhattan, where he hired a horse and buggy to take us on a tour of the city. After half an hour, he noticed that I did not look happy. "R' Chaim Yitzchak, you're not enjoying it?" I told him the truth, that I was cold, and therefore found it hard to enjoy myself.
>
> Shlomie had the driver stop at the nearest clothing store, which was known for its expensive merchandise. He bought me a pair of gloves and a scarf. When I protested, "I can buy 20 scarves for that price!" he insisted that I take it.
>
> We then continued our ride, and I did enjoy myself. He succeeded in lifting my spirits.
>
> But he was not finished. He called his secretary and instructed her to prepare 10 checks for my tzedakah fund.
>
> Shlomie is an example for everyone to learn from. He obligates the wealthy to use their money wisely; he obligates everyone to set aside fixed time each day for learning; he obligates us all to put our whole heart into feeling the plight of others.

He perceived the needs of fundraisers in other ways as well. A former employee related:

> Once, Shlomie spent a few days assisting a rosh yeshivah to raise funds. He said to me, "This man is my ticket to Olam Haba." He did not merely help him obtain money. He made sure that the man ate a good supper every night. One evening, Shlomie himself brought him supper. Another night, he sent an employee to a take-out store to buy food for him. He was totally involved with taking care of this man.

An Israeli rosh yeshivah recalled:

> My wife accompanied me on one of my fundraising trips to America. Our phone rang at 8 in the morning. It was Shlomie, saying that he had spoken to the owner of a

clothing store who was happy to offer us a "very good price" on any item in his entire stock.

With that understanding, we enjoyed a mini shopping spree at the store. When it was time to pay, the owner informed us that Mr. Gross was paying the bill.

A *gabbai tzedakah* once came to the office wearing a shirt with French cuffs, but no cufflinks. When Shlomie asked him about this, the man replied that he had lost one cufflink in the snow. Shlomie immediately removed the cufflinks from his own shirt and insisted that the man put them on.

Always Prepared

HE KEPT A WAD OF BILLS IN HIS POCKET JUST IN CASE HE would meet someone who needed a large sum of money.

At a wedding, Shlomie was entertaining some guests with a story when a friend approached him. "A rosh yeshivah just told me that there's a fellow here at this wedding who desperately needs $1,000 by morning."

Shlomie continued with his story as he withdrew a wad of bills from his pocket and counted out the money. It was nothing major as far as he was concerned; that's what his money was for.

A distinguished *talmid chacham* met Shlomie and asked if he could contribute $500 towards a worthy cause. Shlomie withdrew his checkbook and wrote a check ... for $1,000. The *talmid chacham* responded with a hug and a kiss.

Always Available

WHEN HE WAS AT HOME, HE WOULD SHUT OFF HIS CELLPHONE at night, but while he was away, it was never turned off. Sometimes, business took him to the West Coast, which is three hours behind New York. *Gabba'ei tzedakah*, unaware that he was not at home, would awaken him at 5 a.m. Pacific time. He would answer the phone as if it was the middle of the day, never hinting that he had been awakened.

Sometimes he would come home from work subdued because of the sad stories he had heard from *gabba'ei tzedakah* that day.

When his children in Eretz Yisrael would call and say that they were on the way to the Kosel, he would sometimes tell them, "*Daven* that I should have money to give to *tzedakah*."

Without Delay

ONE SIMCHAS TORAH IN ERETZ YISRAEL, HE WANTED TO BUY the *Kol HaNe'arim aliyah* for his son-in-law — but he fell asleep during the bidding. When he awoke, he approached the man who had won the bid and asked that he sell it to him. This man, who was involved with a renowned *tzedakah* organization, told Shlomie, "For a $15,000 donation to help tutor children from impoverished families, I'll give you the *aliyah*." The deal was made.

On Motza'ei Yom Tov the man called the organization's director to proudly inform him of the donation he had arranged. "We know," the director replied. "Mr. Gross dropped off the check a short while ago."

He was quick with *tzedakah* in other ways as well. He was once in Eretz Yisrael to attend the wedding of a friend's child. In the car on the way to the wedding, someone asked Shlomie if he could assist a Yerushalmi family that was marrying off a child. Immediately, Shlomie called a friend in America, and said, "A family here needs money for a *chasunah*. How about if I give $3,600 and you give the same?" The friend agreed.

They arrived at the wedding and Shlomie approached his friend, the *baal simchah*. Before wishing him *"Mazel tov"* he told him, "You're marrying off a child tonight, and someone in Yerushalayim needs money to make a *chasunah*. I'm giving $3,600 — how about giving the same?" The man agreed. Minutes later, an astounded Yerushalmi was called and informed that he would soon be receiving more than $10,000 for his child's wedding.[7]

Dimensions of Giving

HE DID NOT WAIT TO BE ASKED TO DONATE TO A CAUSE. WHEN someone informed him of a couple experiencing *shalom bayis* problems due to financial strain, he made an appointment to meet the husband and handed him some money.

Sometimes he would get involved in a situation after reading an advertisement in a *frum* publication pleading for help on behalf of a family.

Tsemach Glenn related: "I was sitting in Shlomie's office one day when a stranger walked in seeking a donation. The man enumerated multiple *tzaros* he and his family were enduring, enough to make any heart melt. Shlomie gave him $1,000. When the man left, he turned to me and said, 'I hope he was lying.'" Shlomie was very astute, and experience had taught him that while most

In Jerusalem at the wedding of the son of his friend Rabbi Yitzchak Porush (to the right of Shlomie).

---
7. Rabbi Yosef Gutfarb.

fundraisers are honest, a small minority are not. Despite the fact that he was not convinced that this man's story was true, he helped him generously on the chance that it was.

Chazal say regarding Moshe Rabbeinu: "He focused his eyes and heart to be distressed over them."[8] Shlomie was focused on the poor at times when others were not.

The day after Succos, he arranged to meet a well-known *gabbai tzedakah* on a quiet street in Jerusalem. There, he handed him a large sum and asked that he distribute it among the poor. Many involve themselves with helping the poor *before* Yom Tov, but how many people contemplate the fact that when Yom Tov is over there are many, poor and not so poor, who are in need of funds?

One Purim when he was somewhat inebriated, a *bachur* appeared at his *seudah* collecting *tzedakah*. Shlomie shouted, "Take whatever I have!" and he proceeded to empty his pockets, giving the boy $1,500. After Purim, the *bachur* called to ask if Shlomie wanted the money returned. Of course, he did not.[9]

At the Purim *seudah* with his brother-in-law Eli Cyperstein

---

8. *Rashi* to *Shemos* 2:11.
9. Eli Cyperstein. That Purim he cried tears of joy that Hashem had blessed him and his wife with good children.

Needs to Know Now

ON THE FIRST EVENING OF A VISIT TO ERETZ YISRAEL, HIS phone rang. The caller was in dire need of funds, and someone had given him Shlomie's number. "Can I come now to meet with you?" the man asked.

Shlomie replied that he was too exhausted from a hectic day to meet, but he could listen to the details over the phone. The man replied that he would prefer to wait until they met in person.

Shlomie replied with a touch of annoyance, "I want to know your problem. What right do you have not to share it with me now?"

The man proceeded to tell his story. Shlomie had one of his children bring him a check for a few thousand dollars. What this child did not know at the time was that Shlomie had told the man, "This is what I am sending you now. You'll be getting much more at a later date."

Rabbi Shimon Yanofsky asked Shlomie to help a *talmid chacham* with his daughter's wedding expenses. Shlomie asked, "How much do you need to raise?"

"Shlomie," Rabbi Yanofsky responded, "you know what it costs to make a wedding today."

"But tell me what your goal is," Shlomie responded. "How much do you need?"

"It makes no difference, Shlomie. Give me whatever you want to give."

This give and take continued until Shlomie withdrew his checkbook, signed a check, handed it to his friend, and said, "You fill in the amount."[10]

For Kollel Yungeleit

SHLOMIE UNDERSTOOD THE IMPORTANCE OF SUPPORTING *bnei Torah* who devoted their lives to the study and teaching of Torah. Over the years Heaven brought his way quite a number of

---
10. He filled in the sum of $1,000.

bnei Torah whom he helped substantially. When they were marrying off children, he would contact his friends and raise the funds to cover all wedding expenses. His involvement gave these *bnei Torah* the peace of mind to grow in their learning and service of Hashem without being distracted by the huge financial stress that is all too common today.

He became a major supporter of a Jerusalem kollel whose *rosh kollel* was an old friend from his high school days. He was excited and grateful to be supporting distinguished *yungeleit* who were sacrificing material comforts to devote themselves to Torah study in Eretz Yisrael. One year, before Pesach, he sent the *rosh kollel* a large sum with the instructions, "Put the money on the *bimah* and let everyone take."

Role Model

ONE OF THE GREAT PHILANTHROPISTS OF RECENT TIMES WAS, in Shlomie's eyes, a role model as to how a *baal tzedakah* should conduct himself. This man would regularly write *tzedakah* checks in the tens of thousands of dollars (and sometimes in the hundreds of thousands) at a time when such magnanimous giving was a rarity. Perhaps more important, it is well known that this man behaved with genuine humility, and that he accorded solicitors enormous respect, making them feel that he truly admires their dedication and mission.

"Maybe he can rub off on me?" Shlomie once told this man's nephew jokingly.

What Shlomie did not realize was that he himself was and is a role model of not only how to give *tzedakah*, but also how to give one's heart to the recipient as well.

Defining His Essence

HIS COUSIN YOSEF PERL REFLECTED:

Shlomie was a self-made man as far as his financial success was concerned. He came from a simple home and became a rich man. Very often, self-made men are quite arrogant, precisely because they see themselves as self-made. They take credit for their success, their money is the product of their keen business sense — at least that's what they think.

Shlomie had the opposite view. He viewed all his success as a gift from Hashem. Furthermore, he was convinced that the only reason Hashem blessed him with such success was so that he could give the money to those who needed it. This is why Shlomie had no ego and why he had such admiration for those askanim who solicit tzedakah for mosdos or individuals. To ask for tzedakah for others is not easy, but to give tzedakah? He loved giving to others, and to his mind, he was just giving them what was rightfully coming to them.

His neshamah became fused with the mitzvah of tzedakah. Tzedakah defined who he was. He was not a real estate mogul who dispensed tzedakah. He was a tzedakah dispenser who used real estate as his way to accomplish this mitzvah.

Siyata DiShmaya

SHLOMIE MERITED A SPECIAL *SIYATA DISHMAYA* WHEN IT CAME to giving *tzedakah*, as can be seen from the following incidents:

A Yerushalmi was desperately in need of funds to marry off one of his youngest children and asked one of his older children, "Zev," to travel to America for this purpose. "When you get to Brooklyn," Zev's father instructed him, "there is one Yid you should *not* visit — his name is Shlomie Gross. He helps my brother a lot, and I'm afraid that if I ask him for money, he might give my brother less."

In the airport at Lod, Zev was told that he would have to pay for one of his pieces of luggage. Before he could do so, a fellow passenger approached him and said that he would be happy to take the extra piece for him. Zev was very grateful to this stranger ... who introduced himself as Shlomie Gross.

On the plane, there was a mix-up with the seating. When matters were finally resolved, Zev found himself sitting next to Shlomie. Of course they talked, and Zev had no choice but to state the purpose of his trip. At the end of the flight, Shlomie took down his cellphone number and asked how long he would be in New York.

On a Motza'ei Shabbos shortly before Zev was supposed to return home, Shlomie called to invite him to join his family for *melaveh malkah*. After *bentching*, Shlomie took Zev to some Flatbush friends for money and added his own generous check. "I made twice as much that night as I had made in all my fundraising since my arrival," Zev recalled.[11]

Minchah Meeting

A YESHIVAH IN ERETZ YISRAEL FOR *BACHURIM* WHO REQUIRE individualized attention was in financial difficulty. The rosh yeshivah and a *gabbai tzedakah* involved with the yeshivah flew to New York; a meeting was held in an *askan's* Boro Park home. As sunset approached, the meeting was halted for *Minchah*. The *askan* decided to drive everyone to the famous Bobover beis midrash where *minyanim* are formed every few minutes — though he could have easily found a *minyan* closer to his home.

As the group entered Bobov, Shlomie, who was then in the year of mourning for his father, was leading the *davening*. When he finished, he greeted the *askan*, who was a close friend, and his guests, whom Shlomie knew. Previously, they had asked that he give a large contribution so that the yeshivah would bear his

---
11. Rabbi Yosef Gutfarb.

father's name. Shlomie had declined their offer, and they had not planned to visit him during this trip. Now, Shlomie invited them to come to his office after they had *davened.*

In the office, he told them, "I won't make the dedication, but I will give you a donation." And he handed them a check for a generous amount.

The *gabbai tzedakah* then mentioned a renowned organization that offers guidance to young couples. Shlomie wrote a check covering one month's budget.

The man then mentioned the case of an orphan who was a *chasan.* Shlomie handed him a third check.

A providential *Minchah* meeting had resulted in two *mosdos* and one family being helped in a meaningful way. And it was initiated not by the solicitors, but by a man who was inundated with requests for *tzedakah* on a daily basis but never felt that he had given enough.[12]

Torah and Chesed

THE MIRRER ROSH YESHIVAH, RABBI OSHER KALMANOWITZ, reflected:

> *Shlomie was totally unassuming. As much as is known about his great acts of tzedakah and chesed, no one will ever know the full extent of it, because he did so much quietly.*
>
> *He had a keen understanding of people, and part of his greatness in chesed was that he helped each person in a way that took the person's feelings and self-respect into account.*
>
> *And as he grew in chesed, so did he grow in his limud haTorah and attachment to Torah. The Chofetz Chaim comments on the words of Shemoneh Esrei's concluding*

---

12. Shimon Bertram.

berachah: כִּי בְאוֹר פָּנֶיךָ נָתַתָּ לָּנוּ ה' אֱלֹקֵינוּ תּוֹרַת חַיִּים וְאַהֲבַת חֶסֶד *(for with the light of Your countenance You gave us, Hashem our G-d, the Torah of life and a love of kindness).* When the Torah was given, Hashem opened all the Heavens and the Jewish people perceived that the Torah is the blueprint, the purpose of Creation. At the same time, they perceived that they must emulate Hashem by involving themselves with doing chesed, for the world could not exist were in not for the kindness of Hashem, Who sustains His creations constantly, even when they are not deserving.[13]

Shlomie personified this insight; as his efforts in and understanding of chesed grew, so did his connection to Torah.

"Do Me a Favor"

THE FOLLOWING ANECDOTE SPEAKS VOLUMES:

A Jew from New York fell on hard times and came to Shlomie for financial assistance. Shlomie gave him a generous check, and the man attempted to express his thanks. Shlomie interrupted him and said, "Don't thank me. Hashem gave me the money to give to you. But I have a favor to ask of you: If a year from now our situations are reversed and I am the who needs help, please help me."[14]

---

13. *Sefer Ahavas Chesed,* part II, ch. 1.
14. Overheard by Mr. and Mrs. Aron Cyperstein, who were in the next room.

8

A Man of Action

SHLOMIE WOULD COME TO HIS FRIENDS' HOMES, ONLY sometimes giving prior notice, to pick up *tzedakah* checks for whatever cause he might be involved with at that time. He let his friends know whether he was pleased with the amount they had given. No one took offense at this, because they knew that he gave generously, that there was no personal gain involved, and that it was his great heart that was driving him.

The love and respect others had for him made it hard for them to refuse his requests, especially when it involved a *mitzvah*. At a wedding, he was introduced to a man who had come to collect for himself; he was in desperate need of funds. Shlomie approached nine friends and ask each one to contribute $1,000. The man left the wedding hall with $10,000.

A friend recalled:

> *Once I called Shlomie about someone who desperately needed $1,500. He said, "I'll give half." I knew that he could have easily given the full amount, but he wanted*

others to share in the mitzvah. He wanted his friends to learn to give tzedakah easily and generously — an example that he set very well.

Rabbi Moshe Yechezkel Laufer, a *gabbai tzedakah* in America, grew very close to Shlomie and would call him regularly to ask that he share in his *tzedakah* projects. Once, Shlomie suggested that Rabbi Laufer accompany him on a business trip to Pennsylvania to discuss a *hachnasas kallah* case.

The sum of $25,000 was needed for the wedding. On that trip, Shlomie called 24 friends and acquaintances and raised $1,000 from each of them. He was elated to have involved so many people in the *mitzvah*. "I don't think he could have been more excited had he turned a million-dollar profit in a deal," Rabbi Laufer recalled. Later, Shlomie related that on that trip he had been saved from making what could have been a costly business mistake. "I have no doubt," he said, "that Hashem saved me in the *zechus* of the *mitzvah* we were busy with on the way there."

With Rabbi Moshe Yechezkel Laufer (left) and Sholom Brodt (to the right of Shlomie)

A *melamed* from Eretz Yisrael had married off a few children and was deeply in debt. During his previous visits to America he had developed a relationship with Shlomie. Now, while in the States, he was hospitalized after suffering chest pains. After doctors ruled out a heart attack and were confident that he would soon be on his feet, Shlomie addressed the next order of business. "How are we going to help him?" he asked his friends.

He called a meeting, wrote a large check, and placed it in the middle of the table, saying, "I can't do this alone." The meeting ended with pledges to completely pay off the man's debts.

An *askan* recalled:

> *One year before Yom Tov I ordered 100 suits for $55 each with the intention of distributing them for free to needy bnei Torah. I needed to raise the funds to cover the $5,500 bill.*
>
> *I approached Shlomie at a wedding and told him about my project. "I'll pay for ten suits," he said, and promptly wrote a check for $550. Then he rose from his seat and walked around the hall with me, introducing me and my cause to his friends.*
>
> *I left the hall with $5,500.*

Once, he walked into a friend's office and demanded, "Give me your checkbook." The friend complied and Shlomie promptly wrote out 12 checks for $180 each, for the benefit of a *gabbai tzedakah*. "You now have a new man on your payroll," he said in all seriousness. The friend accepted this demand, knowing that in all likelihood Shlomie himself was doing much more to help this individual.

There was another factor involved. Shlomie was well respected and had a great deal of *chein* (charm). Every one of his friends felt very close to him. It was simply hard to say "No" to someone you loved so much.

A Man of Action

Often he accompanied roshei yeshivah and *gabba'ei tzedakah* to friends to raise funds. One evening, he told his companion, "I want to *see* you smile." He was not content to bring this man the money he needed; his great heart could not be at peace until the man was genuinely happy.

"It's Not Your Problem"

HE WAS CLOSE WITH A YERUSHALMI WHO HAS SERIOUS HEALTH issues. When this man's daughter became engaged, Shlomie told him, "The burden [of raising the funds to pay for the wedding] is not yours." This happened close to Yom Tov when Shlomie visited Eretz Yisrael. After Yom Tov, before returning to the States, Shlomie arranged a parlor meeting in Jerusalem at which the necessary funds were raised.

Around seven years before his passing, an Israeli couple appeared in his office with their newborn son. They showed Shlomie that the baby could not see, but said that there was a costly surgery that could heal him. Someone had suggested that they seek Shlomie's assistance in raising the money.

He told them, "It was not necessary for you to show me the baby. I would have believed you anyway. I'm going to help you."

By the next morning, he had raised $100,000, and the surgery was performed. Six months before his passing, the couple came to the office with their child and happily showed Shlomie that their little boy was able to see.[1]

Rabbi Yisrael Friedman

SHLOMIE WAS VERY CLOSE TO RABBI YISRAEL FRIEDMAN, *Menahel* Emeritus of Yeshivah Chasan Sofer and a famous *gabbai tzedakah*. Their relationship began during Shlomie's short stint as a student in the Chasan Sofer elementary division, when he was sometimes sent to the *Menahel's* office. Rabbi Friedman

---

1. Mrs. Lena Kohn.

had done everything in his power to help Shlomie succeed, and Shlomie always felt a debt of gratitude to him.

Rabbi Friedman often raises funds for families who have no other way to access charity funds. Even in his advanced age, when his vision and mobility are limited, he makes the rounds of wedding halls collecting for the needy. When Shlomie would meet Rabbi Friedman at a wedding, he would go from table to table collecting on his behalf. If the total sum was not what Shlomie considered respectable, he would add a few hundred dollars of his own.

Sometimes he would tell a friend, "Rav Yisrael will be collecting at the wedding tonight. Make sure you bring along money to give him."

With Rabbi Yisrael Friedman (center) and Rabbi Yaakov Eliezer Schwartzman

If the friend forgot to bring money, Shlomie would say, "Okay, so I'll lend you money. How much do you want?"

For the Chofetz Chaim's Teachings

SHLOMIE WAS A SUPPORTER AND FRIEND OF THE CHOFETZ Chaim Heritage Foundation. Its director, Michael Rothschild, recalled:

> Shlomie and I were chavrusos in the Mir (Brooklyn) in 1982 and we stayed in touch after that. He was one of our organization's main supporters from the time of its founding in 1989 until his passing.

He came to every dinner and to the dedication of our new headquarters. When we had a sefer Torah written in memory of the Chofetz Chaim, he attended the hachnasas sefer Torah at the Kosel.

Each year before our annual dinner, he would come into his office and announce, "I paid for a table by the men and a table by the women. I want everyone to come as my guests. And tell your wives to come."

When I looked over my paperwork after his passing, I realized that his name was everywhere. There was not a list of askanim on which his name did not appear.

Whenever I had to be in Brooklyn for our organization, Shlomie's house was my base. He felt very bad that I had to do so much fundraising. He loved giving

Honored with *hagbahah* at the *siyum sefer Torah*

tzedakah, and he helped me raise funds whenever I asked him to.

Once, he agreed to accompany me to the home of a certain wealthy man. We called for an appointment a number of times, but the man was not available. Finally, Shlomie said that we should go and ring the doorbell without an appointment. He told me, "This is going to be very hard for me, but I'm going to be misgaber (prevail [over my reluctance to go])."

It was very easy to ask Shlomie for tzedakah. His eagerness to give, coupled with his exuberance for life and sparkling personality, made him unique.

The last time I saw him, I was about to walk out of his house when two "Yerushalmis" who had never met him rang the bell. I opened the door and they said to me, "Reb Shloime Gross?" I started to say, no, I was not Shlomie, but from behind me, a voice called out, "Yes, yes, he is Shloime Gross!"

Having made his joke, Shlomie then greeted his visitors warmly, invited them inside, and as always, treated them royally.

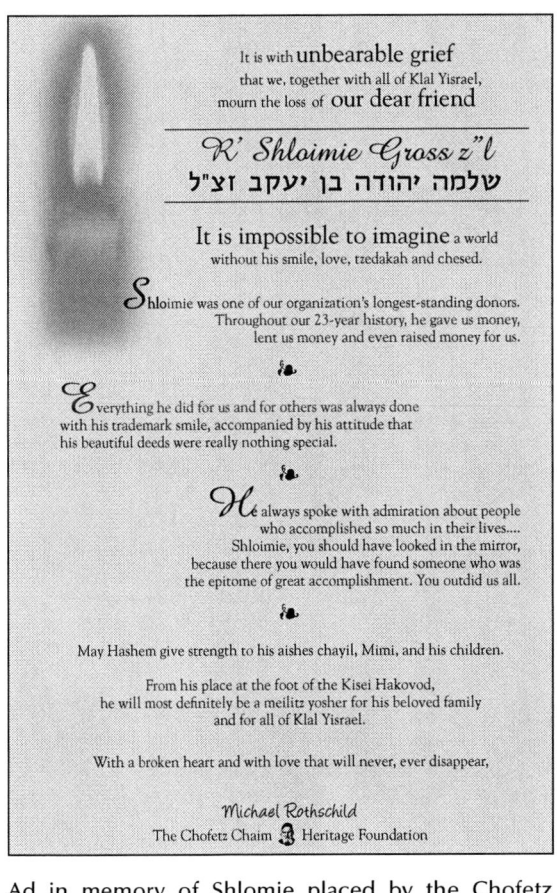

Ad in memory of Shlomie placed by the Chofetz Chaim Heritage Foundation in their annual journal

A Man of Action / 183

Refuah Resources

FOR YEARS, RABBI SHUKY BERMAN PROVIDED MEDICAL REFERrals and advocacy for people with serious medical issues. As his reputation grew it became impossible for him to respond to all requests for assistance. To continue his lifesaving work he needed to expand his operation.

Shlomie was approached by two of his close friends, Yosef and Kalman Tabak, who asked that he assist with initial funding to get the new organization off the ground. He agreed, and Refuah Resources was founded. Shlomie's involvement enabled the growth of Refuah Resources from a small operation that received a few dozen calls daily to an organization that fields approximately 200 calls a day, providing referrals for medical conditions both complex and routine, as well as support and advocacy for patients and their families.

From the time of the organization's inception until Shlomie's passing, he and the Tabaks would spearhead an annual parlor meeting to benefit Refuah Resources. More than once, Shlomie asked Rabbi Berman about the state of Refuah's budget. Whenever Shlomie sensed hesitation on the other end of the line, he would immediately organize another meeting.

A parlor meeting hosted by Shlomie was always a success. His conviction about the worthiness of a cause was compelling. Heedless of conventional propriety, Shlomie would announce his own generous contribution and in his trademark unreserved manner prevail upon his friends and business associates to do the same.

Shlomie did much more than give and raise money. Rabbi Berman relates:

> *As with everything else he did, Shlomie gave of himself as much as he gave of his money. I admired his love and concern for anyone who crossed his path. He would call me often on behalf of others who needed medical guidance and request that we get involved.*

He did not stop there. After the patient had been seen by a doctor, Shlomie would call me to hear the doctor's assessment. He was genuinely concerned about the patient and stayed on top of the situation.

Once, he called to say that an acquaintance of his was experiencing chest pains. We rushed the patient to a hospital and had the head of cardiology, a renowned name in the field, run a battery of tests. When I called Shlomie to tell him that all the test results were good and the patient was fine, he burst into tears.

Another time, he brought us a child from Eretz Yisrael who was diagnosed with a brain tumor. We had her flown to a medical center in North Carolina. One day Shlomie called me; he wanted me to accompany him to visit the girl and her father. It was in the middle of the week, but for Shlomie there was nothing out of the ordinary about selflessly giving up a day to lend support. We flew to North Carolina; our visit was a great chizuk to both the patient and her father. It also resulted in a kiddush Hashem, because the medical staff was quite impressed that we, who were not family, had made such a trip.

Over the years we formed a very close relationship; at Shlomie's funeral, I felt like I was one of the mourners.

For Every Good Cause

IT SEEMS THAT SHLOMIE WAS INVOLVED IN EVERY GOOD CAUSE, including those that are not well known.

An elderly Lubavitcher chasid from Eretz Yisrael visiting the States accepted the offer of a ride from Boro Park to Flatbush. In the car, he mentioned that he was on his way to two non-observant acquaintances whom he always helped to fulfill the mitzvah of *tefillin* whenever he visited there.

When the driver mentioned that he had a relative in Jerusalem named Aharon Gross, the chasid said excitedly, "Gross? Perhaps he is related to Shlomie Gross?"

"Shloime was his father — you knew him?"

"Yes, he sponsored a pair of *tefillin*."

For Shalom Bayis

HE WAS DISTRESSED AT WHAT HE PERCEIVED WAS THE EASE with which some couples opted for divorce. In a number of cases he worked at trying to save a marriage. In his straightforward way he would sometimes tell the husband, "Your marriage is not perfect? Tough! You have a wife and kids and you've got to make it work."

Shlomie got involved in a number of *shalom bayis* cases; in some, he was successful in bringing about a reconciliation between husband and wife. He would leave no stone unturned in trying to make peace. Once, he and a friend traveled some distance to discuss a couple's problems with a renowned Torah personality who was involved in the case. Shlomie's friend made a masterful presentation which impressed the *gadol* and pleasantly surprised Shlomie. On the way home, Shlomie repeatedly expressed his admiration for his friend.

Later, when Shlomie learned of a new *shalom bayis* case involving a young couple, he approached the husband's father to recommend his friend's services as a mediator. As his friend recalled, "I knew that there was no way this man would let me get involved with his child's problems. I would have been embarrassed to even suggest it. But Shlomie didn't care. He always wanted to help, and was never ashamed to say or do something no matter how remote his chances of success."

He also arranged therapy for some with emotional issues, directing them to the right psychologist, paying the fee when necessary, and following up to make sure that the therapy was achieving results. "His radar was always picking up problems, and when that happened he went into action," a friend recalled.

Mediator in Business

AMONG SHLOMIE'S PAPERS WAS THE FOLLOWING LETTER FROM a businessman who had been involved in a monetary dispute:

> *Dear Reb Shloime:*
>
> *It is with great appreciation and admiration that I sit down to write this letter of thanks. I thank you wholeheartedly for your efforts on my behalf and really on behalf of emes [truth] and shalom [peace]. The fact that a businessman such as yourself, with all sorts of responsibilities and demands on your time, tried — for the sake of shalom — to resolve this situation is a tremendous example of your generosity.*
>
> *It is very unusual and unique to find someone who would get involved the way you did; you truly personify "ohev shalom v'rodef shalom" [one who loves peace and pursues peace]. The intelligence with which you handled this matter as well as the fair and honest approach was refreshing, and I learned a lot from you. All your efforts were noticed and valued and helped me greatly. It was so impressive to me that you put in so much of your valuable time for someone you did not even know, and for this I am makir tov (grateful) to you.*
>
> *I am sure that you are the type of person who does acts of kindness constantly without even receiving a "Thank you" and you do not look for a "Thank you," but I very much wanted to communicate to you that what you did for me was truly appreciated and not taken at all for granted.*

For the Sake of Yeshivos

AN ISRAELI ROSH YESHIVAH RECALLED:

*Shlomie was involved with our yeshivah since its founding 17 years ago. He became one of our staunchest supporters, but he was much more than that. He was like a brother to me, and he didn't just give to the yeshivah — he **lived** the yeshivah.*

Once, he introduced me to a prospective supporter. He spoke to the person as if the yeshivah's finances were his responsibility, as if the man was doing him a personal favor by supporting the yeshivah.

I recall one of the first times he visited our new building. With his son Aharon right behind him, Shlomie raced up to the roof of the yeshivah with the excitement of a child. He stood gazing at the panoramic view and exclaimed, "Look! You can see the whole Yerushalayim from here!" He felt that such a spot was most appropriate for lomdei Torah.

On one of my visits to America, I joined Shlomie and his family for the Friday night seudah, and Shlomie walked me back to my lodgings. On the way, Shlomie pointed to a house and told me that a distinguished member of the Sefardic community lived there. Shlomie knew that I had a relationship with him and he felt that calling on him in his home would be a good idea. We had a very good visit.

Some time later, this man's son told me, "I learned a lot from Shlomie Gross. He was invited to a parlor meeting in Lakewood for a Sefardic kollel to which he had no previous connection. After the appeal was made, he was one of the first to announce his pledge. He's a person who gives and does so in a very unassuming way."

Another rosh yeshivah related:

> *We called a meeting of friends of our yeshivah to discuss our financial crisis. As the meeting dragged on, nothing seemed to be happening. Shlomie had not been involved in arranging the meeting, but was obviously troubled that it appeared headed for failure. He surprised everyone by announcing a large pledge — and others followed suit. The meeting was a huge success.*
>
> *That was his way, to make things happen.*
>
> *I heard about his passing as I was driving. I pulled over to the side of the road and cried.*

The respect he had earned in the community made it possible for him to assist yeshivos when they needed someone with clout, as a yeshivah administrator related:

> *I am responsible for covering our yeshivah's budget. It happened that someone wronged our yeshivah in a way that potentially could have caused it much harm. I was devastated. Feeling lost, I did what was only natural — I went to visit Shlomie.*
>
> *He listened to my story and said, "I know that fellow. I'm going to blast him the next time I see him. But right now, we have to undo the damage he's caused."*
>
> *He called a meeting, and as a result, the problem was resolved.*

Originality

AN ISRAELI ROSH YESHIVAH RECALLED:

> *I traveled to America when one of our loyal supporters was marrying off a child. Of course, I visited my dear friend Shlomie. He told me, "It would be a good idea if you would have breakfast delivered to the baal simchah's door the morning after the wedding. They will very much appreciate it."*

I had no idea whom to call to arrange such a thing — but I need not have worried. Shlomie called a dairy restaurant in the baal simchah's neighborhood, placed a generous order, and paid for it by phone. All I had to do was write the text for the card that would accompany the delivery. I attempted to reimburse Shlomie for the order, but he would not hear of it.

He made every favor seem natural, as if it was no effort at all on his part. And he never tarried; every time he thought of a way to help someone, he acted immediately.

Mechon L'Hora'ah

SHLOMIE WAS A SUPPORTER OF MACHON L'HORA'AH IN Monsey, a *beis din* and kollel dedicated to the learning and rendering of *psak halachah*. The Machon's Executive Director, Rabbi Berel Karniol, related:

Shlomie consulted the Machon's dayanim often, especially regarding business-related halachah. He valued the Machon's important work and was a devoted supporter.

Once, I asked him to accept an honor at our annual dinner. He was very reluctant. "I don't like sending out letters asking people to give money in my honor. Then they feel that they have to give." He did not mention the fact that he fled from any sort of honor.

But he had a solution. "Tell me, how much would you like to raise from honoring me?"

I named a figure. Shlomie took out his checkbook and wrote a check for the full amount. This was in addition to what he usually gave us each year.

Rabbi Karniol relating a revealing incident:

I was visiting him in his office on the day of the levayah of the Telshe Rosh Yeshivah, Rav Chaim Stein, zt"l. Shlomie asked me to drive him to Kennedy Airport to meet the funeral procession that was arriving from Lakewood, since he said he was not feeling well enough to drive himself.

We went to the levayah and then he asked if I could possibly drive him to Lakewood so that he could be menachem avel a noted philanthropist. I agreed. He said, "I can never repay you for what you are doing for me today. Promise me that your chesed will have no bearing on [our relationship regarding] Machon L'Hora'ah." Of course, I had no intention of using this mitzvah as leverage.

On the way, I asked Shlomie if this philanthropist was a personal friend or business acquaintance. He replied, "No, but whenever I raise money for tzedakah, he responds generously."

When we entered Lakewood, he asked me to stop whenever he saw a Yid walking. "Maybe we can give him a lift." He was always looking to do for others.

By the time we were ready to leave Lakewood it was dark. I had not eaten since breakfast, so I suggested we stop to buy some food. As we sat in the car eating, Shlomie mentioned that that day was Yom Kippur Katan (Erev Rosh Chodesh) and he was now breaking his fast.

Ramot Torah Schools

RABBI ABBA SWIATYCKI IS FOUNDER AND DEAN OF RAMOT Torah Schools – Tiferes Rivka, a network of nine schools in Eretz Yisrael educating some 1,000 children. The students are not *chareidim*; many are borderline religious and would be in public school if not for the existence of these schools.

Some 27 years ago, Rabbi Swiatycki was introduced to Shlomie. At a time when these schools were existing on $36 and $100 donations (the schools do not accept money from the Israeli government), Shlomie sponsored a year's tuition for a child — $800 at that time.

But Shlomie did much more than write a check. As Rabbi Swiatycki recalled:

> *Shlomie was a great baal tzedakah, but he was an even greater baal chesed. He helped me arrange our first parlor meeting, asked people to come, and formed a nucleus of supporters. He traveled out of the country with me on a fundraising trip.*
>
> *For a period of five years, he was the one I called if our American bank account lacked sufficient funds to cover that day's expenses. I would phone him and he would immediately wire the money into my account. There were days when he loaned us large sums to accomplish this. He did it with a smile.*
>
> *A few years ago, we found ourselves in deep financial trouble; $3 million of debt threatened to close down our schools permanently. A philanthropist agreed to give us half the money if we could raise the other half. Shlomie became my partner in raising the money.*
>
> *He opened doors for me. People liked him; he was everyone's "best friend." They enjoyed his company and were happy when he came to see them.*

With Rabbi Abba Swiatycki

He actually had a touch of bayshanus (shyness); he could not make someone uncomfortable by demanding money the person did not want to give. He was successful because he spoke from the heart, and his sense of humor put people at ease. He asked for large amounts and the person knew that Shlomie would give at least that much.

Largely thanks to him, we wiped out our debt. In his zechus, 1,000 children who might otherwise be educated as secularists are learning Torah and growing in their Yiddishkeit.

On Behalf of a Yeshivah

RABBI TZVI KAHAN, ROSH YESHIVAH OF YESHIVAH IMREI Noam in Jerusalem, enjoyed a close relationship with Shlomie. He related:

Gershon Barnett shaking hands with the Pshevorsker Rebbe at a meeting on behalf of Ramot Torah Schools. Behind them are Shlomie and Rabbi Swiatycki.

I come to the States during our bein hazemanim (intersession) to raise funds. On many of my visits, Shlomie would take me to wealthy friends.

Once, I asked him to accompany me to Manhattan in the middle of a workday to solicit a donation from a certain individual. When I arrived at Shlomie's office and saw how busy he was, I told him that I would go to Manhattan alone. But he would not hear of it.

Once, he wanted to help me by contacting a wealthy fellow whom he knew only casually. Each time he called, the fellow said that it was not a good time to come over. Finally, Shlomie said, "Let's go over without calling." We went to the house and at the door we found a package the mailman had left there. It was obvious that the man was not home. Such visits, where one goes without an appointment, can be very uncomfortable. A normal reaction would have been to be relieved and go home.

Rabbi Tzvi Kahan (left) with Rabbi Elya Ber Wachtfogel at the wedding of one of Shlomie's children

But Shlomie was not an average individual. Immediately, he took out his phone, called the man's cellphone, and said, "This is the mailman — I have a package for you." That joke was his way of opening a dialogue. He then introduced himself as Shlomie Gross and said that indeed, there was a package in front of the man's door, and he knew that fact because he was standing there with me to solicit money on behalf of my yeshivah. Nothing came of that visit, but Shlomie had given it his best shot, and later, he kept on trying.

Matching Funds

RABBI KAHAN CONTINUED:

During our yeshivah's building campaign, we hit a critical point. If we did not raise a significant sum quickly, there was a possibility that we would lose the beautiful tract of land upon which we planned to build.

Someone pledged a very large sum on condition that we found donors to match this amount. Shlomie was the first person I approached. "Now is the time," I encouraged him. I asked him to give one-third of the amount we needed, and I told him the name of the person from whom I planned to solicit the remaining two-thirds.

He agreed that it was a very crucial time for the yeshivah, but said that he could not give the amount I had requested. He pledged three-fifths of what I had asked of him (a very generous sum). He said that he could not give even that amount immediately, but that he would pay it out over time.

I asked him to please consider giving the full amount I had requested; it really was an emergency situation. He thought a bit and said that he would try to give the remaining amount, but was not committing himself. His "I'll try" was good enough for me to move on to the next step.

Together, we called on the other man and I asked him to pledge the remaining two-thirds. He said, "Right now I cannot give such an amount." We returned to him a second time. Motioning towards me, Shlomie said to the man, "Don't you see how much pressure he is under? We must help him — now."

The man replied that he really did want to help me, but there was a problem. He had recently invested a lot of money in a business venture, and so far it had not generated any profit. This was why he found it hard to give such a large sum at that time. "However," he said, "if a rav will tell me that I should give it, I will give it."

I suggested a certain rav, and he immediately agreed to let him decide the matter. That evening the three of us went to see the rav. Shlomie acted as my "lawyer." He presented my case well, with a combination of serious points and humor. The other man told the rav about the investment that was the cause of his reluctance.

The rav asked him, "Can you get out of this investment?"

"It doesn't look like it," he replied.

"Then," said the rav, "I have an idea. Make the Rosh Yeshivah a partner in your investment. You will do that by giving him his share right now — the sum that he has requested. And in exchange, the Rosh Yeshivah and his talmidim will daven for your hatzlachah (success)."

Shlomie was laughing from joy.

The man said that he wanted to speak with the rav privately. We left the room and Shlomie said, "Let's say Tehillim." We did.

The man emerged from the rav's study and said, "It's a deal."

The next morning, I went to the man's house and he gave me a check for the full amount. Later, Shlomie said to me, "Look — he's such a tzaddik! I'm not on his level." But I knew the truth, that it was a hard time for him, and he had really extended himself for me.

After three years, the man's investment began to turn a profit. This episode brought about a close relationship between me and this donor; at a later date, he presented us with another significant contribution.

At the time when the above story occurred, Shlomie requested of Rabbi Kahan that his involvement in this great undertaking remain a secret between them, and Rabbi Kahan honored his request. On the first Friday night after he returned to Jerusalem, Rabbi Kahan related the above story to his *talmidim* without revealing the names of the two benefactors. He told them of the "partnership" that the rav had suggested, and on his own, decided to include Shlomie in this partnership so that the *talmidim* would learn and *daven* on behalf of both men.

After Shabbos, Rabbi Kahan wrote a letter to his *talmidim*, in which he stated:

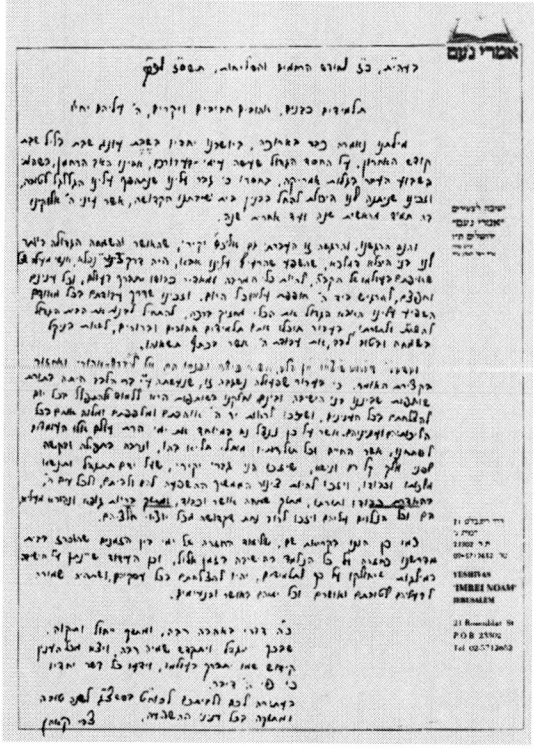

Letter that Rabbi Kahan wrote to his *talmidim* in which he asked that they learn and *daven* each day on behalf of their two great benefactors

It is my feeling, and I have conveyed this feeling to you, my dear ones, that the greatest aspect of our good fortune and happiness ... is that this great blessing (of funding which has made construction of our new building possible) has come through a wondrous "channel" — men of spirit whose whole yearning is to be agents for increasing and strengthening Hashem's glory in this world ... Thus, we have merited that through their service (of Hashem) with their material wealth, Hashem has conferred upon us His vessel of berachah so that we can

> begin building the great new structure that will be dedicated to Him and His Torah.
>
> I wish to remind you, my beloved talmidim, of what I said to you (on Friday night). The great deed of these two exalted individuals was predicated on a partnership between us — the bnei hayeshivah — and them. Our part of the deal is to learn and daven each day as a source of merit for their success in every endeavor ... that Hashem should be with them at every step ... and that they should merit much holy nachas from their offspring.
>
> In addition, the chazarah (review) program that has been established for bein hazemanim (intersession) ... will be a source of merit for these two men.

In a *hesped* delivered in his yeshivah following Shlomie's passing, Rabbi Kahan retold this story and revealed Shlomie's identity. He announced that the *chazarah* program of the forthcoming Pesach *bein hazemanim* would be dedicated as a source of merit for Shlomie's *neshamah*.

Shuvu

SHIMON LEFKOWITZ RELATED:

> A number of years ago the Shuvu school in Modi'in Ilit was faced with a crisis. The school had been evicted from its location, but the mayor had offered it another building. The problem was that the building required major, costly renovations and the school year was beginning soon. If the building could not be readied in time, these children would end up in public school.
>
> I was in Eretz Yisrael at the time. We hired a contractor and I assumed responsibility for raising the funds. As I prepared to return to the States, I was still far short of the sum that was needed.

Before leaving I went to see the mekubal Rabbi Dovid Abuchatzeira and told him of my dilemma. He said, "When you return to the States, ask the first person you meet to help you."

From Kennedy Airport, my first stop was a shul in Flatbush for Shacharis. As I left shul, I met Shlomie. Bearing in mind what Rav Abuchatzeira had said, I told Shlomie about the school. He replied, "I'll loan you whatever you need. I'll wire it immediately." He did not ask for any sort of note or guarantee of repayment.

That is how a school that is inculcating scores of Jewish children with love of Torah was saved.

Making Hashem Happy

IN 2001 SHLOMIE HOSTED A PARLOR MEETING IN HIS HOME TO benefit Nechomas Yisroel, an organization founded by Rabbi Avrohom Yaakov Pam which sponsors yeshivah tuition for children who would otherwise be attending public school.

Before the meeting Rav Pam told Shlomie:

Holding his son Nosson Tzvi as he speaks with Rav Pam at the Nechomas Yisroel parlor meeting.

Shlomie, let me tell you what you are doing by hosting the parlor meeting and supporting Nechomas Yisroel. You have the zechus of making Hashem happy. You see, Shlomie, each and every Jewish child is like Hashem's only child.

Greeting the Skulener Rebbe at the Nechomas Yisroel parlor meeting

The intense love that we have for our own children, and the feeling of appreciation that we have when someone helps our children, as intense as it is, does not come close to the love that Hashem has for every Jewish child. When you save a Yiddishe neshamah, and bring it back to Hashem before he or she assimilates, you are bringing one of Hashem's children back to Him.

Rav Pam would surely have been moved by the love, care, and concern that Shlomie showed for every Jew who crossed his path.

9

For Love of Torah

THOUGH SHLOMIE TRIED TO LEARN TORAH AS MUCH AS he was able to, learning for lengthy periods was a great challenge for most of his life. Nevertheless, he always had a deep appreciation for the greatness of Torah, its study, and its scholars.

Rabbi Avrohom Ausband, Rosh Yeshivah of Yeshivah Telshe Alumni (Riverdale), reflected:

> Aside from his incredible goodness, caring, and generosity, there was something else that made Shlomie so special — his complete hisbatlus (subservience) to talmidei chachamim. He was extremely close to the Mirrer Rosh Yeshivah, Rav Shmuel Berenbaum, and faithfully followed his every directive. And the same applied to the words of other talmidei chachamim whom he was close to.

When he was invited to a *melaveh malkah* in Brooklyn in honor of the late Telshe Rosh Yeshivah, Rabbi Chaim Stein, Shlomie said that he would come to drop off a check but could not stay.

He ended up staying for over an hour. "I was in an atmosphere of such *kedushah*," he explained, "I just couldn't leave."

One Purim, he was rather inebriated when he arrived at the home of a *talmid chacham* to whom he was close. Shlomie lay down on the floor and, ignoring the *talmid chacham*'s protests, kissed his shoes. In his uninhibited state, his total *hisbatlus* (subservience) to *talmidei chachamim* was revealed.

He was distressed when he flew business class and then discovered that a *talmid chacham* whom he knew was sitting in the coach section. To his mind, it was a lack of respect on his part to be seated more comfortably than a *talmid chacham* and benefiting from amenities that this man was not enjoying.

On one such flight, he pleaded with the scholar to switch seats with him, but to no avail. Another time, he met a *talmid chacham* in the airport who was to be on his flight. The person refused

With Rabbi Chaim Stein

Shlomie's offer to upgrade his seat to business class. During the flight, Shlomie came by a few times to check on the man and ask if there was anything he could do for him.

Rabbi Tzvi Kahan related:

> I traveled to America for the weddings of his children. At the end of his oldest child's wedding, Shlomie invited me to come to his house for breakfast the following morning. I arrived there at 9 o'clock, by which time Shlomie had already learned his usual hour with his chavrusa and davened Shacharis — after having gone to sleep in the wee hours of the morning.
>
> After we ate, he wrote a check for my travel expenses. I did not want to accept it. "For once, I can do something for you," I told him. But he was upset. "You have money to spare? If you don't take the check, I won't be able to handle it."
>
> Then we went for a walk. He had to stop in at a shoemaker, and I followed him inside. He asked that I remove my shoes so that they could be buffed. I protested that this was not necessary, but in a flash he was down on the floor removing my shoes and handing them to the shoemaker.

"I'll Come to Him"

RABBI BEREL KARNIOL RELATED:

> I wanted to bring gedolim to his home, as is commonly done, so that he would give a donation for their mosad. He was happy to give the money, but he insisted that he did not want to trouble the gedolim to come to him.
>
> When Rav Yitzchok Dov Koppelman, zt"l, of Lucerne was visiting America, I called Shlomie and said that I would bring the Rosh Yeshivah to his home. Who would not want such a gadol b'Yisrael to honor him with a visit?

For Love of Torah / 203

But Shlomie absolutely would not allow the Rosh Yeshivah make the effort. "I'll come to him," he insisted. Shlomie went to the Rosh Yeshivah, received his berachah, and gave a generous donation for his yeshivah.

A Word of Torah

THE MOMENT HE HEARD A VORT THAT HE PARTICULARLY enjoyed, he would call his son in Eretz Yisrael to share it with him.

The first three days of the final week of his life, Shlomie accompanied a relative on a business trip as a favor. On the plane leaving New York, Shlomie said that that day was the *yahrtzeit* of a friend's daughter, and they proceeded to learn together as a source of merit for her *neshamah*. In the course of their learning, his relative related a comment of the *Ohr HaChaim* that apparently

With Rabbi Don Segal

was at variance with a famous statement of Rabbi Chaim Soloveitchik. Shlomie became excited; as soon as the plane landed, he phoned his son, related the *vort*, and asked that he relate it to his Rosh Yeshivah, Rabbi Avrohom Yehoshua Soloveitchik, and call him back with the Rosh Yeshivah's reaction.

In commenting on the above story, Aharon Gross said, "That excitement for Torah was typical of my father."

Shlomie knew someone, a successful businessman, who in his middle age developed a thirst for learning and eventually completed all of *Shas* in depth. Shlomie expressed his envy of this man's accomplishments. "Look at the man's gemara; look at the notes in the margins! Look at how much work he put into it. I'm jealous." However, he was not the least bit jealous of someone else's magnificent house or luxury car.

When *bnei Torah* who were learning full time came to him for financial help, Shlomie conveyed his genuine feeling that they were doing what, in his heart, he truly aspired for: devoting many hours to the study and mastery of Torah.

His Uncle, R' Ben Zion

AS SHLOMIE GREW IN HIS APPRECIATION FOR TORAH AND ITS students, he became closer to his scholarly uncle, Rabbi Ben Zion Halpert. One day in 1999, it was suggested that Rabbi Halpert deliver a weekly *shiur* in *Tanach* with *Malbim*, in which he was fluent. Shlomie organized a small "*chaburah*" (study group) to meet in one of their homes each week. Restaurant food would be purchased for the occasion. The group would first eat supper together and chat, and then the *shiur* would begin. Rabbi Halpert's *shiur* was not strictly on *Malbim*; he would regale the group with *divrei Torah*, fascinating stories, and recollections of life in Europe before the war.

By this time, Shlomie enjoyed a close relationship with many rabbanim and roshei yeshivah. When such an individual from

Eretz Yisrael would visit the States, Shlomie would try to arrange to bring him to the *chaburah* so that he could be introduced to his uncle. Thus, R' Ben Zion, a *chassidishe Yid*, was introduced to the world of Lithuanian scholarship, and he enjoyed it immensely. The visiting rosh yeshivah would honor Rabbi Halpert and Shlomie by remaining for at least part of the *shiur*. For his part, Shlomie was ecstatic that he had brought honor and joy to his uncle and excitement to the *chaburah*.

Over the years since the *chaburah* began, Shlomie presented his uncle with gifts that were very meaningful: a leather-bound, gold-stamped set of *Tanach* with *Malbim,* and a leather-bound *siddur* with the *minhagim* of the *Magen Avraham*. Shlomie also brought Rabbi Chaim Elazar Reich, the *siddur's* compiler, to meet R' Ben Zion.

On a *shivah* call one day in 2004, Rabbi Halpert reminisced about life in Hungary before the war. The next day, he told his son Shuli, "I want to tell you something. *Ich vil gein aheim mit mayna kinder* (I want to go home — i.e., back to Hungary — with my children). But you cannot tell anyone except for your brother." He was then 80 years old and had never returned to his native Hungary since his arrival in America after the war.

That week, before beginning the *shiur,* Rabbi Halpert announced to the *chaburah*, "I want to inform you that I

Left to right: Rabbi Ben Zion Halpert with יבל"ח Nosson Tzvi Gross and Shlomie's uncle, R' Yidel Friedman

am planning to return to Nanash (his hometown), and I want the whole *chaburah* to come along!"

The *chaburah* was swept with enthusiasm, and no one was more excited than Shlomie. He loved learning about the history of European Jewry, especially when it related to his family. And he loved his uncle dearly, as his uncle loved him.

A few family members outside the *chaburah* joined them on the trip so they would have exactly a *minyan*. They spent two full days in Hungary on what was an inspiring journey.

An Insight From the Gaon

IN THE FALL OF 2011 SHLOMIE AND SOME FRIENDS JOURNEYED TO Lithuania and Poland to visit the cities that had been home to some of the greatest pre-War yeshivos and Torah communities. Late one night as they walked the quiet streets of Vilna, one of them repeated a thought from the Vilna Gaon that R' Ben Zion had told them:

The prohibition against murder is found in the *Aseres Ha-Dibros*. Its standard pronunciation is לֹא תִּרְצָח, with a פַּתַח under the צ. However, in the *taam elyon* which is used during the public Torah reading, it is pronounced לֹא תִּרְצָח with a קָמַץ. The Vilna Goan says that these variant pronunciations allude to a teaching of *Chazal*:

> What is the meaning of that which is written, "כִּי רַבִּים חֲלָלִים הִפִּילָה, For she has felled many victims ..."?[1] This refers to a *talmid chacham* who has not attained the ability to rule on halachic issues, but does so. [And what is the meaning of the end of that pasuk] "וַעֲצֻמִים כָּל הֲרֻגֶיהָ, ... and the number of her slain is huge"? This refers to a *talmid chacham* who has attained such proficiency but does not render halachic decisions. (In both cases, people err because they are not taught the proper halachah; the pasuk likens this to murder.)[2]

---

1. *Mishlei* 7:26.
2. *Sotah* 22a.

Said the Vilna Gaon: The פַּתַח of לֹא תִרְצָח refers to the first scholar, who is guilty of "murder" through the פְּתִיחָה, *opening,* of his mouth, when he should remain silent. The קָמַץ of לֹא תִרְצָח refers to the second *talmid chacham* who sins through the קְמִיצָה, *closing,* of his mouth when he should be opening it to render halachic decisions.

Those who knew Rabbi Ben Zion Halpert feel that this thought represents one of his frequent themes: When it comes to sharing one's Torah with others, one has to be honest with himself and not claim to be on a level of scholarship or piety which he has not attained.

The learning sessions with his uncle enriched Shlomie's life and further enhanced his growth as a *ben aliyah.*

Assisting Roshei Yeshivah

SHLOMIE'S REVERENCE FOR TORAH WAS EVIDENT IN THE WAY he extended himself to assist *talmidei chachamim* who turned to him for support of their yeshivos.

Rabbi Tzvi Kahan recalled: "On my visits to America, I often needed Shlomie's assistance. If he was in his office in the midst of business, he would ask me to come over. Much of the time, however, he insisted on coming to me."

Rabbi Uren Reich, Rosh Yeshivah of Yeshivah of Woodlake Village, recalled:

> *He would welcome you to his home late at night, when he probably was exhausted after a long and productive day. He greeted you with such a smile, with such simchah and warmth, as if you were his first solicitor that day. You felt that he was enjoying you more than you were enjoying him.*
>
> *The last time I went to him, he said, "I'll send you the checks tomorrow." Then he thought for a moment and said, "No, I'll write them out now."*

Rabbi Shlomo Feivel Schustal, Rosh Yeshivah of Yeshivah Torah Temimah, recalled:

> Ohel Rochel Leah is a very successful educational institution for Russian-immigrant girls, founded by my daughter. I would go fundraising on its behalf and invariably would visit Shlomie in his home. I cannot describe in words the manner in which he welcomed me into his home. He would speak with a blend of love and respect.
>
> A few years ago I became involved with raising funds for a kollel of outstanding yungeleit. A distinguished friend of the kollel drew up a list of potential donors and accompanied me. Shlomie was our first stop.
>
> We explained the kollel's situation to him and mentioned the large monthly budget. My companion suggested that this first time, when I was embarking on a new undertaking, Shlomie should cover an entire month's budget — and he immediately agreed.
>
> He began to write a series of postdated checks — until my companion stopped him. He suggested that this one time, Shlomie should give one current check for the full amount, and again, he agreed. I believe he did this because he felt it would be mechazek (encourage) me in this undertaking.
>
> After that, I would come to him once a year for the kollel. He did not match that initial contribution but always gave generously. Last Adar, I left him a phone message about coming over to see him. Then I met him two days before his passing. It was early morning, and he was learning with his chavrusa before Shacharis. He welcomed me to the beis midrash, and said that we would be in touch regarding my phone call. He understood without my telling him that it was regarding his annual contribution, and he wanted to take care of it. To our misfortune, this was not to be.

When Shlomie sat shivah for his father, I first learned of it on Friday afternoon, the last day for nichum aveilim. I called the house and asked that he wait for me. He did not need my visit. Throughout the week, hundreds of people, among them many distinguished roshei yeshivah, had come. I will never forget the manner in which he expressed his appreciation to me. He said that the visit meant a great deal to him, and that it was special of me to make time for this mitzvah on Erev Shabbos afternoon. It seems that he considered me a marbitz Torah, and therefore the visit was particularly meaningful to him.

"He Really Cared"

RABBI AHARON LOPIAN, ROSH YESHIVAH OF YESHIVAH LEV Aryeh in Jerusalem, had a close relationship with Shlomie. He related:

Shlomie really cared about you. When I would come to America for fundraising, Shlomie would "be on my case," calling me every day to ask whom I would be seeing that day. He wanted to make sure that my trip was successful. Sometimes he'd call to ask if I had eaten supper yet. On one occasion I was unable to rent a car. Shlomie arranged for me to borrow a different car for each week of my stay.

When he was preparing to visit Eretz Yisrael he would call me to ask if there was something he could bring me.

More than anything, I miss his nosei b'ol. His goodness was natural, but I believe that the way he felt another person's pain was something that he developed over time. It was incredible how he made someone else's trouble his very own. I witnessed him crying over the suffering of another Jew.

He would call me to ask about the yeshivah's financial situation. "How are you managing?" was his frequent inquiry.

Rabbi Aharon Lopian dancing with Aharon Gross at his *vort* in Jerusalem

He left a message on my phone an hour before he passed away, saying that he would be in touch either on Motza'ei Shabbos or on Sunday. To our misfortune, this was not to be.

"Whatever the Rosh Yeshivah Wants ..."

HE REVERED AND LOVED TORAH LEADERS TO AN UNUSUAL degree. As someone put it, "While Shlomie was physically imposing, whenever I saw him in the presence of *gedolim*, he was hunched over with utmost reverence, like a little child in awe of the giant standing before him."

A number of years ago the father of a large family in Eretz Yisrael was killed in a car accident. People close to the family were interested in establishing a fund to help provide support.

Shlomie was in Eretz Yisrael for Yom Tov at the time. He was approached by a brother of the widow and asked to spearhead a fundraising drive for the family. Shlomie replied that regretfully, he was too busy with too many other projects to get involved in another one. That same day, Shlomie went to wish a *"Gut Yom Tov"* to the Rosh Yeshivah, Rabbi Shmuel Auerbach, who knew that family well and was involved with helping them. When Rav Auerbach put forth the same request for Shlomie's involvement, he immediately agreed. He could not refuse the request of one of the *gedolei hador.*

As soon as he returned to America after Yom Tov, Shlomie arranged a parlor meeting in his house, and later helped organize similar fundraising events for this cause in other neighborhoods. A huge sum was raised.

The money was given to responsible trustees who placed the funds into a special account from which money could be withdrawn yearly for the family. However, there was a disagreement as to how the money should be used. The trustees, who were experienced in such matters, insisted on following their usual guidelines. The family wanted the monies used in a different way. Rav Auerbach agreed with the family.

One day, Shlomie received a phone call from someone close to Rav Auerbach who explained what was happening and said that the Rosh Yeshivah was not happy about the situation. Shlomie wasted no time in calling Rav Auerbach and telling him, *"Vos der Rosh Yeshivah vill, dos vet zein"* ("Whatever the Rosh Yeshivah wants, that is what will be"). To Shlomie it was unthinkable that a *gadol's daas Torah* should not be followed. Shlomie prevailed upon the trustees to bend their rules in this case.

Rav Shmuel Auerbach delivered a *hesped* at Shlomie's funeral in Jerusalem and made mention of this episode.

"Shloim'e!"

IT WAS SHLOMIE'S FRIEND YOSEF TABAK WHO FIRST INTROduced him to the gaon Rabbi Michel Yehudah Lefkowitz of Bnei Brak. On that occasion, the late Rosh Yeshivah conferred his *berachah* that Shlomie should "be *matzliach* (successful) in business and *matzliach* in learning." From Shlomie's facial expression it was obvious that he did not believe the second part of the *berachah* to be possible. Rav Michel Yehudah looked at him and said, "*Az men vill, ken men shteigen* (If one wants, he can advance in learning)." Shlomie was moved by these words; if Rav Michel Yehudah believed that he could *shteig,* then surely it was possible.

A friend recalled sitting at Rav Michel Yehudah's table when Shlomie appeared in the doorway. Rav Michel Yehudah rose to his feet, lifted his hands, smiled broadly, and exclaimed, as one would welcome an old friend, "*Shloime, vos machst du* (Shloime, how are you)?" The elderly, frail *gadol* then walked toward his beloved guest and kissed him.

Shlomie could sit with Rav Michel Yehudah for 45 minutes or longer, and one could see that the Rosh Yeshivah was truly enjoying his visitor's company.

Rabbi Eliyahu Mann often accompanied Shlomie on his visits to Rav Michel Yehudah. Once, when their conversation centered

With Rabbi Michel Yehudah Lefkowitz

around *tefillah,* Rav Michel Yehudah opened a *Sefer Mesillas Yesharim* and learned a relevant passage with Shlomie, reading each sentence slowly and explaining its meaning.

Another time, Rav Michel Yehudah opened a *siddur* and taught the meaning of *Yaaleh V'Yavo* (recited on Rosh Chodesh and Yom Tov). Tears welled up in the Rosh Yeshivah's eyes as he did this.

On a winter visit to Eretz Yisrael, Shlomie visited Rav Michel Yehudah. When they shook hands, the Rosh Yeshivah's hands felt very cold. Before the next winter, Shlomie paid to have the entire house insulated.

He enjoyed a close relationship with other *gedolim*. On a trip to Eretz Yisrael, he knocked on the door of the Kaminetz Rosh Yeshivah, Rabbi Yitzchak Scheiner. Rav Scheiner had already retired for the night, but when he heard who was at the door, he came out and warmly greeted him.

Excerpt of a letter thanking Shlomie for arranging
to have Rav Michel Yehudah's house insulated

בס"ד.

לכבוד ידידי היקר איש סגולה מאד נעלה מהמשכילים על דבר אמת מוקיר ורחים רבנן מעמודי הצדקה והחסד בדורנו, ומגדולי תמכין דאורייתא לסומדות התורה ולומדיהם

הרב רבי שלמה גרום שליט"א.

אחר דרישת שלומו הטוב בהערכה והוקרה מרובה.

באתי בדברים אלו להביע בפני מעלת כבודו שליט"א את רוב רגשות ההוקרה שאנו כל בני ביתו הקרובים של רבנו ראש הישיבה מרן פאר הדור הגאון רבי מיכל יהודה ליפקוביץ שליט"א מרגישים למע"כ שליט"א, ואת גודל התודה שאנו חבים לכם. על אשר בנדיבות לב מרובה מאד נטלתם על עצמיכם את כל עול הוצאות חשיפוץ והתיקון שעשו כעת בבית מרן רבנו שליט"א, אשר כפי הידוע למע"כ שליט"א כל הדבר הזה נעשה רק למען שמירת בריאותו של מרן רבנו שליט"א לפי הוראת הרופא, ולא נעשה דבר כדי להוסיף יופי והדר סתם, אשר מרן רבנו שליט"א בורח מזה כל ימיו, והוא כל השנים די לו בקב חרובין ממש.

מה רב זכותו שזכה להיות אושפיזכניה לצדיק אשר רז"ל הפליגו מאד בעניין זה, ודימוהו לזוכה לשרת במקדש ד'. וביותר כי כפי הידוע מרן רבנו שליט"א נשמר ונזהר כל ימיו לא לקבל ממון ואפילו טובת הנאה מזולתו, [וכפי הידוע כבר נשתבח בזה ע"י רבו בעל החזו"א זי"ע], ורק מע"כ שליט"א זכה עכשיו בזכות זו להנותנו משלו בנתינה מרובה זו באופן מיוחד ויוצא מן הכלל, לגודל הצורך בזה. בודאי רב מאד זכותו בזה.

Rav Elyashiv

ONE OF THE HIGHLIGHTS OF SHLOMIE'S VISITS TO ERETZ Yisrael was attending the daily Gemara *shiur* of the late *posek hador*, Rabbi Yosef Sholom Elyashiv. He became excited when telling someone that he planned to be at the *shiur*.

One Erev Yom Kippur, Shlomie and his son Nosson Tzvi were on their way to the Kosel when Shlomie's cellphone rang. It was Rav Elyashiv's *gabbai* calling, asking if Shlomie could come to the Rav's home. Of course, Shlomie came immediately. Rav Elyashiv asked that he help someone in need. Shlomie left the gaon's home with an additional *zechus* with which to be inscribed for a good year.

Once, a Yerushalmi Yid who regularly attended Rav Elyashiv's *shiur* was in America for a heart transplant. Doctors said that the surgery had to be done immediately, and because the man had no insurance, payment was required in advance. Rav Elyashiv was apprised of the situation; when he said, "Tell me whom to call," he was told, "Call Shlomie Gross."

A few minutes later the phone rang in Shlomie's office. "This is Yosef Sholom Elyashiv," the caller said, and he proceeded to

With his son Aharon on a visit to Rav Elyashiv

For Love of Torah / 215

explain why he was calling. He concluded by saying, "If you pay for this surgery, it will be as if his heart is your heart."

Shlomie was prepared to cover the cost of the procedure. However, he had one question. "How do I know that the person I am speaking to is really Rav Elyashiv?" Ever astute, Shlomie was concerned that a dishonest person might pose as the *gadol hador* in order to swindle him of a huge sum.

Rav Elyashiv responded that Shlomie was welcome to ask him questions in any area of *halachah*. That was sufficient for Shlomie to "close the deal." The surgery was performed successfully.

On a subsequent visit to Eretz Yisrael, Shlomie visited Rav Elyashiv and told him, "I sit at the Rav's *shiur* every day." He was alluding to Rav Elyashiv's comment that the patient's heart was like his own. Rav Elyashiv understood and laughed.

Letter from Rav Elyashiv to Shlomie requesting assistance for the man whose heart surgery was paid for by Shlomie. At the letter's conclusion, Rav Elyashiv wishes "Mazel tov" upon the forthcoming marriage of Shlomie's daughter.

Rav Chaim Kanievsky

SHLOMIE VISITED THE GAON AND TZADDIK RABBI CHAIM Kanievsky often. Each time as he prepared to enter Rav Chaim's study, Shlomie was obviously nervous. Once, his son Aharon asked him about this. He replied, "He can see right through me."

Rabbi Yosef Gutfarb of Jerusalem, who often accompanied Shlomie on his visits to *gedolim,* related:

> *The love with which he spoke about talmidei chachamim was something one rarely sees. The gedolim loved him with an ahavas nefesh. Rav Chaim Kanievsky enjoyed his visits so much, they would actually laugh together.*
>
> *As is well known, the Kanievskys own a chair that was used by Rav Chaim's great father, the Steipler Gaon, zt"l. Rebbetzin Kanievsky, a"h, would tell women who came to her for berachos to sit on that chair and recite Tehillim.*
>
> *Shlomie asked the Rebbetzin if this was Rav Chaim's idea. She replied that it was not Rav Chaim's, but Rav Chaim had said that she could use the chair in this way if she so wished. Shlomie then asked, in jest, if the Rebbetzin would rent the chair to him for $100,000 so that he could bring it to America. The Rebbetzin laughed heartily at this suggestion, and replied that the chair was not for rent. She then went to tell Rav Chaim about Shlomie's offer. Shlomie told them that for him it would have been a profitable venture. He would have charged $10 for the zechus of sitting on the chair and would have turned a profit in no time.*

Rav Chaim's *chavrusa,* Rabbi Eliyahu Mann, would accompany Shlomie on these visits. Once, Shlomie asked Rav Mann to ask Rav Chaim if one could recite the *berachah* "… Who has apportioned of His knowledge to those who fear Him" upon seeing Rav Chaim's father-in-law, Rav Elyashiv. This *berachah* is said upon seeing a *talmid chacham* of towering stature. The question was posed in the last year of Rav Elyashiv's life when he was not fully conscious.

Rav Chaim responded that a *berachah* could be recited even in Rav Elyashiv's situation. He then related that he recited this *berachah* on each of his bi-annual Chol Hamoed visits to his father-in-law. "But I always said it quietly at the doorway," he related, "because had I said it out loud, he would have thrown me out!"

For Love of Torah / 217

Shlomie then asked Rabbi Mann to ask Rav Chaim if one can recite this *berachah* upon seeing "the oldest son-in-law of Rav Elyashiv," meaning Rav Chaim himself. For a moment, Rav Chaim did not understand the question, but as soon as he did he responded, "A *berachah l'vatalah*" ("a worthless *berachah*"). Shlomie responded, "That means the Rav holds like Rav Elyashiv and not like the Chazon Ish." The Chazon Ish had said that if the generation believes that a particular *gadol* is so great that he is worthy of this blessing, then the blessing may be recited.

Visiting Rav Chaim. Rabbi Eliyahu Mann is next to Shlomie.

Rav Chaim replied, *"Ober nisht ven zei zenen opge'naart"* ("But not when they are deceived"). In his modesty, Rav Chaim felt that he had "deceived" our generation into thinking that he was greater than he truly is.

To Go or Not to Go

AS MENTIONED EARLIER, RABBI YOSEF GUTFARB WAS ESPEcially close to Shlomie. When Shlomie's daughter Tzipora became engaged, Shlomie told R' Yosef that he very much wanted him to be at the wedding. Rabbi Gutfarb's father, R' Ben Zion, is a renowned *talmid chacham* who has never left Eretz Yisrael. He was not in favor of his son leaving Eretz Yisrael to attend a wedding.

When Shlomie came to Eretz Yisrael before the wedding, R' Yosef, who often accompanied Shlomie on his visits to *gedolei Eretz Yisrael*, suggested that they pose this question to them. Shlomie loved the idea. R' Yosef brought along a digital recorder to preserve the *gedolim's* responses. In the end, he did not attend the wedding, but he did present Shlomie with a precious gift: a small book containing a transcript of the *gedolim's* responses.

The *gedolim's* responses varied, but clearly, all gave serious thought to R' Yosef's desire to attend the wedding as an expression of *hakaras hatov*.

Rav Elyashiv told R' Yosef that in light of the great *hakaras hatov* he felt towards Shlomie: "It is permissible and proper for you to make this trip, but you are not obligated to do so."

Following is the exchange with Rav Chaim Kanievsky:

(Rav Chaim's smile lit up his radiant countenance as he greeted Shlomie and lovingly blessed him upon the upcoming wedding.)

R' Yosef: Reb Shloime will, *b'ezras Hashem*, be celebrating his daughter's marriage in America. Inasmuch as I feel an enormous

With Rabbi Ben Zion Gutfarb

debt of gratitude to him, does this obligate me to attend the wedding?

Rav Chaim: If you will have to pay the airfare, you are not obligated to go.

R' Yosef: This is a question for Reb Shloime to answer.

(Rav Chaim turned to face Shlomie and with a smile asked him:) Are the traveling expenses his responsibility?

Shlomie: I will cover all expenses.

Rav Chaim (still facing Shlomie): If you will cover all expenses then he may attend the wedding — but he is not obligated to do so. "Everyone can be compelled to *go up* to Eretz Yisrael."[3] *Hakaras hatov* cannot obligate someone to *leave* Eretz Yisrael for *chutz laAretz*.

Shlomie (in jest): If I invite him to serve as *mesader kiddushin* would this obligate him to come?

Rav Chaim (smiling): You have no one in *chutz laAretz* to serve as *mesader kiddushin*?

Shlomie: I have a *mesader kiddushin*; I just want to know if he would be obligated to come *for siddur kiddushin*.

Rav Chaim: *Siddur kiddushin* is nothing more than a *kibbud* (honor). It is certainly forbidden to leave Eretz Yisrael merely for the sake of receiving a *kibbud*.

"Your Wife Needs You"

SHLOMIE PARTICULARLY ENJOYED THE RESPONSE OF RABBI Yitzchak Soloveitchik:

(R' Yosef explained that he felt great *hakaras hatov* to Shlomie and that Shlomie would pay the airfare.)

Rav Soloveitchik: When is the wedding?

R' Yosef: 3 Nissan.

Rav Soloveitchik: In the Pesach season, from Rosh Chodesh Nissan and on, one is required to be available at home to help

---
3. *Mishnah Kesubos* 13:11.

one's wife. It is forbidden for you to travel abroad when this will affect your wife.

R' Yosef: Baruch Hashem, I have been blessed with a true *eishes chayil,* and she does not ask me to help.

Rav Soloveitchik: Nevertheless, during times when there is pressure (i.e., in the days before Yom Tov), a husband must make himself available. It is forbidden for you to travel abroad at your wife's expense. One cannot express *hakaras hatov* at the expense of his wife and family.

Shlomie was excited that in this response, R' Yosef's wife's needs was the crucial factor. As someone who lived his life for others, this was particularly meaningful to him.

Rav Nosson Tzvi

SHLOMIE ENJOYED A SPECIAL RELATIONSHIP WITH THE LATE Rosh Yeshivah of Yeshivas Mir Yerushalayim, Rav Nosson Tzvi Finkel.

Rabbi Binyamin Carlebach, a Rosh Yeshivah at Mir and Rav Nosson Tzvi's brother-in-law, accompanied him on his trips abroad. He recalled, "We felt a *kesher nafshi* (soul connection) with Shlomie. He was a true friend."

Tzale Edelstein often hosted Rav Nosson Tzvi during his stays in Flatbush. He related:

> *When Rav Nosson Tzvi was our guest, Shlomie would come by in the morning and make phone call after phone call, trying to arrange appointments for the Rosh Yeshivah with some of his well-to-do contacts. Often, Shlomie would drive the Rosh Yeshivah to these appointments.*
>
> *As is well known, Rav Nosson Tzvi suffered from Parkinson's disease, which made these overseas trips extremely difficult for him. After a long day of fundraising, he would be thoroughly drained — and looked it.*

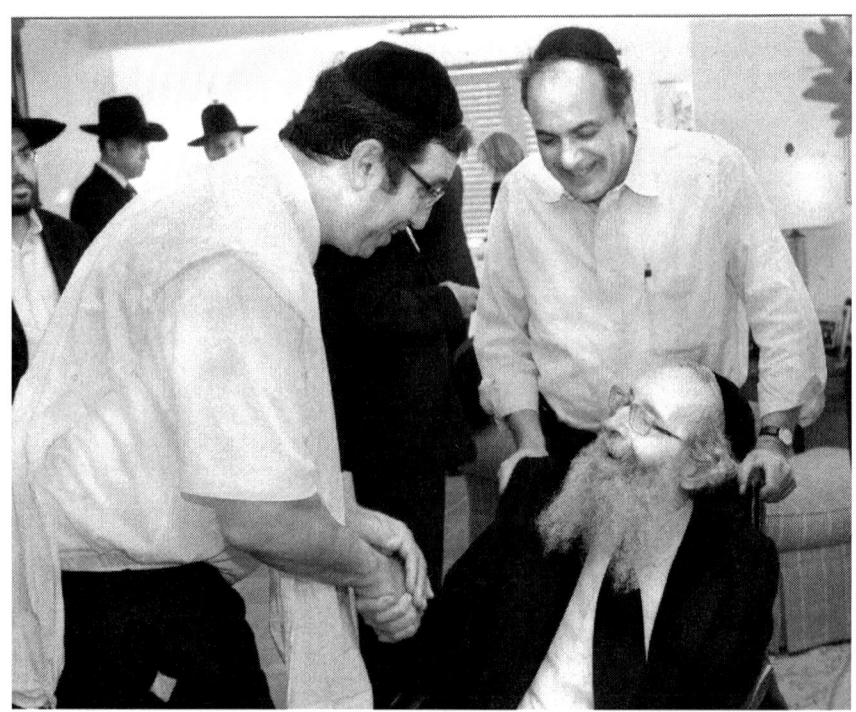

With Rabbi Nosson Tzvi Finkel in the Catskills. Tzale Edelstein is behind the Rosh Yeshivah.

> *Sometimes, Shlomie would come by at night and with his magic touch say just the right things to make Rav Nosson Tzvi smile.*

Mir's executive director, Rabbi Mordechai Grunwald, discussed their relationship:

> *There was a special love between Rav Nosson Tzvi and Shlomie, and I think it was because there were certain qualities that they shared. Rav Nosson Tzvi loved every Jew, and he strove to afford every ben Torah, of every type and background, the opportunity to learn in the Mir and develop into a talmid chacham. Shlomie had a huge heart, he loved every Jew, and he strove to help anyone who needed him.*
>
> *There was another quality they shared. Rav Nosson Tzvi, as great as he was, made everyone feel comfortable in his*

presence. And as incredibly busy as he was, when you needed him, he made you feel as if he had all the time in the world for you. Shlomie, too, as successful as he was, never talked down to anyone; to the contrary, he made you feel that you were his friend. And he had time for anyone who needed him.

That, I believe, is why Rav Nosson Tzvi's personality resonated so well with Shlomie. He felt attracted to this gadol who personified the very qualities that he strove for. They had a great love for each other.

Visiting Rav Nosson Tzvi with his son Aharon

Visiting Rav Nosson Tzvi with his son Nosson Tzvi

Rabbi Yosef Gutfarb became very close to Shlomie's son Aharon when the latter learned in Eretz Yisrael as a *bachur*. When Aharon became engaged, R' Yosef felt that he had to attend the wedding in America, but again, his father was opposed to the idea. His father agreed to accompany him to Rav Shmuel Auerbach for a ruling on the matter. After hearing both sides,

For Love of Torah / 223

Rav Shmuel turned to Rav Ben Zion Gutfarb and said, "*Er muzt foren*" ("He must travel [to the wedding]").

On the spur of the moment, R' Yosef asked the Rosh Yeshivah if he would write a "*Mazel tov*" letter to Shlomie. Rav Shmuel agreed. R' Yosef then went to many *gedolei Eretz Yisrael* who knew Shlomie and asked them for such a letter. He made a booklet of these letters and presented it to Shlomie upon his arrival in New York for the wedding.

When R' Yosef came to Rav Nosson Tzvi for a letter, he found the Rosh Yeshivah lying on a couch looking very weak. When R' Yosef explained why he had come, Rav Nosson Tzvi responded, "Ah, Reb Shloime, Reb Shloime!"

But he did not immediately agree to write a letter. He asked R' Yosef, "Does he help you personally?" R' Yosef replied that Shlomie had been enormously helpful to him. Rav Nosson Tzvi exclaimed with feeling, "*Ah, er helft* (he helps) *a yungerman, er helft a yungerman.*" Rav Nosson Tzvi told him to return the next day and he would give him a letter.

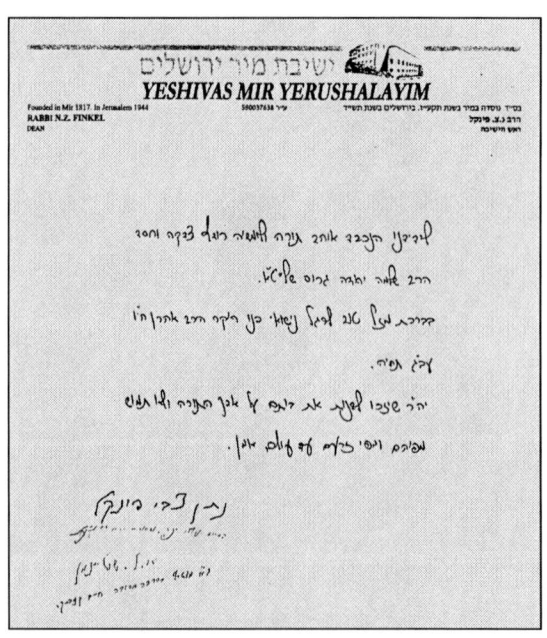

"Mazel tov" letter that Rav Nosson Tzvi dictated and signed in honor of Aharon Gross' marriage. Rav Yosef Sholom Elyashiv, Rav Aharon Leib Steinman and Rav Chaim Kanievsky later added their blessings and signatures.

But the next day, Rav Nosson Tzvi said that he was too weak to write the letter. He instructed R' Yosef to write the letter and Rav Nosson Tzvi signed it.

Rav Shmuel

SHLOMIE AND THE ROSH YESHIVAH OF THE MIRRER YESHIVAH in Brooklyn, Rabbi Shmuel Berenbaum, had a deep, mutual love for one another. Though Shlomie had learned in the Mir, their relationship only blossomed years later. His partner, Yossi Friedman, was a close *talmid* of Rav Shmuel; for a period of time, the Rosh Yeshivah would come to their office in the early afternoon (*beis hasedarim*) to learn with Yossi. At the same time, Shlomie was giving Rav Shmuel generous contributions for Mirrer Yeshivah and other important causes. It was during that period when his relationship with Rav Shmuel deepened.

This was some 20 years before Rav Shmuel's passing, when he was renowned as a *gaon* and *marbitz Torah* but had not yet assumed the role of *manhig Yisrael* to whom people streamed for advice and blessings. Shlomie recognized that when he was with Rav Shmuel he was in the presence of greatness, and he cherished his closeness to the Rosh Yeshivah.

Dancing with Rabbi Shmuel Berenbaum at his wedding

One morning Shlomie, then in his 20s, came into the office and excitedly said, "I was at Rav Shmuel's yesterday and he asked me to get him a drink from the fridge. I opened the fridge, and guess what? There was nothing in it except for a container of juice and a bottle of seltzer! Do you see how Rav Shmuel and his rebbetzin live? They don't need anything!"

Someone later commented, "Even at that period in his life, Shlomie showed a sensitivity for spirituality that was unusual. He was proud and excited to be associated with a *gadol* who had no need for any of the pleasures of this world."

Losing Sleep

SHLOMIE AND HIS PARTNER YOSSI BECAME ALMOST LIKE children to Rav Shmuel. The Rosh Yeshivah once confided in someone that on the night after his future son-in-law's *aufruf*, he had difficulty sleeping because of a business-related problem that Shlomie and Yossi were experiencing.

Rav Shmuel with his two "children" Shlomie and Yossi

The Mirrer Rosh Yeshivah, Rabbi Usher Berenbaum, related:

> *The love between my father and Shlomie was deep. Shlomie also felt a strong attachment to our yeshivah. He davened with us on Rosh Hashanah and always stood ready to help, visiting the yeshivah office often.*
>
> *Shlomie often visited my father at home; they would talk in learning and discuss other matters. Sometimes he would bring his son Aharon to talk in learning with my father.*
>
> *I had a brother (Rav Leibel z"l) who lived in Eretz Yisrael and passed away. When my brother's daughter was getting married in Yerushalayim, Shlomie came to the wedding to rejoice with my father and be mechazek the family.*
>
> *Shlomie and his partner Yossi Friedman visited my father in the hospital shortly before his passing. By that time, my father was unable to speak. When my father saw them, he smiled and waved. Seeing them brought him simchah.*

Shlomie's son Nosson Tzvi said, "Both my grandfathers passed away before I was born. Rav Shmuel was like a grandfather to me."

As the years passed, Shlomie grew in his own learning and, as mentioned, had a morning learning session which he rarely missed. Rav Shmuel, who was a living *sefer Torah* and was renowned for his *hasmadah*, demanded of those close to him that they have fixed, daily, intensive learning sessions. His *talmidim* knew that even if they donated millions to Mir, Rav Shmuel would not be satisfied unless they took their own learning seriously. Shlomie's love of Rav Shmuel and recognition of his feelings about learning were crucial factors in his personal growth.

At one point, Shlomie and his friends discovered that the Rosh Yeshivah was experiencing some personal difficulties. One afternoon, they took off time from work to visit him at the yeshivah.

Rav Shmuel with Nosson Tzvi Gross

The Rosh Yeshivah greeted them warmly: "*Vos tu'in azeleche groisse gedolim da* (What are such great *gedolim* doing here)?" The Rosh Yeshivah appreciated this visit from *talmidim* who were very dear to him. He reciprocated by utilizing it for what always warmed his heart and energized his soul — the study of Torah. They "spoke in learning" for more than hour.

"Come Now!"

A FRIEND RELATED AN INCIDENT THAT DEMONSTRATES THE unique relationship between Rav Shmuel and a select group of *talmidim*-turned-*baalei batim*:

> *I was driving in Manhattan when my phone rang. It was Shlomie calling from the home of my rebbi, Rav Shmuel Berenbaum, who was hosting a parlor meeting on behalf of his fund for needy bnei Torah in Eretz Yisrael. "Where are you?" Shlomie wanted to know. "The Rosh Yeshivah's waiting for you!"*

> *I explained to Shlomie that I was dressed for a summer outing, not an appropriate way to visit the Rosh Yeshivah. Shlomie responded by handing the phone to Rav Shmuel, after informing him of my reply. The Rosh Yeshivah told me, "Kum yetzt (Come now)!"*
>
> *A half-hour later, I parked my car and went up the steps to the Rosh Yeshivah's house. Shlomie was at the door with a big smile, waiting to greet me. He pulled me past the sea of black and white seated in the room and brought me to the Rosh Yeshivah, who said with a smile, "Ah, du bist da! (Oh, so you are here!)"*
>
> *Shlomie then lifted up the bottom of my pant leg and said to the Rosh Yeshivah, "Look how he comes here — he's not wearing socks!"*

In his last years Rav Shmuel suffered from a debilitating disease. On the night that his grandchild's wedding was being celebrated, the Rosh Yeshivah was in the emergency room of New York Methodist Hospital. Two *talmidim* who were at the wedding were asked to go to the hospital to see if there was any possibility of bringing Rav Shmuel to the wedding. At the emergency room, they were informed that the Rosh Yeshivah was behind a partition dressed in a hospital gown waiting to be examined. The *talmidim* requested of the Rosh Yeshivah's son to ask him if there was any chance that he would be able to come with them.

Rav Shmuel responded by insisting that one of them come behind the partition because he needed to speak with him. Seriously ill, unable to be at his grandchild's wedding, Rav Shmuel pounded his hand on his bed and exclaimed that an orphan from a distinguished Jerusalem family was a *chasan*, but there was no money for the wedding. "What are we doing to help him?" the Rosh Yeshivah asked his *talmid*.

Previously, Rav Shmuel had asked Shlomie to host a parlor meeting in his home for this *chasan's* benefit. Shlomie had felt he could not do it at that time for a variety of reasons. After that

For Love of Torah / 229

emergency room encounter, the *talmidim* told Shlomie about Rav Shmuel's distress. Rav Shmuel passed away shortly thereafter, and this final request that the Rosh Yeshivah had made of him was uppermost in Shlomie's mind. Instead of a parlor meeting, he and a friend made phone calls to close friends who also were close to Rav Shmuel. In one hour, they raised the entire sum.

There were times when Shlomie would hand Rav Shmuel a signed, blank check and say, "The Rosh Yeshivah should please let me know how much he made it out for."

Rav Leibel, z"l

SHLOMIE AND SOME OF HIS FRIENDS WERE VERY CLOSE TO Rav Shmuel's distinguished son, the late Rabbi Leibel Berenbaum. Rav Leibel had a feeling for *neginah* (song) and had a particular love for the song *"Ribono shel Olam"* made popular by Abish Brodt. When Rav Leibel took ill, Abish and Shlomie would visit him at Rav Shmuel's home and sing with him.

During that period, Rav Shmuel and his family spent Succos in Sea Gate in a home where the *succah* was easily accessible for Rav Leibel. On the night of Hoshana Rabbah, Abish, Shlomie, and a few others were invited to come and sing with Rav Leibel. They sang for over an hour. When they prepared to leave, Rav Shmuel, who was moved by the singing, said, "I'm already inviting you to come to the *seudas hoda'ah* (meal of thanksgiving following recovery from illness)."

Unusual Appeal

IN HIS ADDRESS AT A PARLOR MEETING IN SHLOMIE'S HOME TO benefit the Mirrer Yeshivah, Rav Shmuel turned to his host and said, "Shlomie, there will come a time when you will dedicate the cornerstone of the Mirrer Yeshivah. People will ask, 'Who paid for this building?' and they will be told 'Shlomie Gross.' 'Who is that?' they will ask. 'You don't know?' they will be told. 'He is Aharon Gross' father.' (Aharon was then in high school.)

Rav Shmuel continued, "Nu, Shloime, with such a son, you have to learn more. Accept upon yourself to learn another hour a day!"

Some of those present were sure that Shlomie would agree to the Rosh Yeshivah's request, simply because it was uncomfortable not to do so. But Shlomie's integrity was such that he absolutely would not make a commitment that he might not honor. He sat silently and did not respond to Rav Shmuel's "appeal." It was probably the only time he ever declined a request from his beloved rebbi.

On the way home from a skiing trip with his children, Shlomie drove by the Mirrer Yeshivah. "Kids, you had a *geshmak'e* time today?" he asked. The children all agreed that they did. "Who do you think had a better time today — us or Reb Shmuel, sitting and learning? ... I'm telling you that for sure, it was Reb Shmuel."

Rav Shmuel speaking at a parlor meeting which Shlomie and his son Aharon (second and third from right) attended

For Love of Torah / 231

This was the message he would impart to them: although he spent only a small part of his day in the beis midrash, he knew that there was nothing greater, and nothing that could be more pleasurable, than *limud haTorah*.

Shlomie's younger daughter, Tzipora, became engaged shortly before Rav Shmuel's passing. Her *vort* was scheduled to be held on what turned out to be the night following Rav Shmuel's funeral. Shlomie and his wife cancelled the *vort*; it was not rescheduled.

"A Man on Whom to Rely"

IT HAPPENED THAT THE MENAHEL OF A CERTAIN YESHIVAH WAS experiencing a problem. It was felt that Shlomie could help resolve the matter if he would make a commitment to do so. The *menahel* arranged a meeting with Shlomie and one other person in Rav Shmuel's office.

After some discussion, the matter appeared resolved. However, the *menahel* wanted a signed commitment from Shlomie that he would do his share. To this request, Rav Shmuel responded with a story:

Shlomie speaking at the Mirrer Yeshivah dinner in 1989 at which he was honored as "Alumnus of the Year." Sitting alongside the podium are the Mirrer Roshei Yeshivah, Rabbi Shraga Moshe Kalmanowitz and his brother-in-law Rav Shmuel.

When the Mirrer Yeshivah was in Shanghai during the Second World War, a non-Jew's typewriter was stolen. The man accused the gaon Rabbi Leib Malin of being the culprit.

Rav Leib was summoned to the local police precinct. A policeman who lived in the same building as Rav Leib spoke up. "I know this man," he said. "He is someone upon whom you can rely. It is impossible that he is the thief."

The police chief accepted the policeman's words and Rav Leib was released.

Smiling, Rav Shmuel motioned toward Shlomie and told the *menahel,* "Shloime is someone upon whom you can rely. His word is good. Nothing more is necessary."

10

A (Not So) "Regular Guy"

H E WAS *MURAM MEI'AM* (HEAD AND SHOULDERS ABOVE everyone), an unusual *baal chesed*, a special person. But everything about him was very natural; as far as he was concerned, his *tzedakah* and *chesed* were no big deal, nothing to make a commotion about." This is how Shlomie was described by a friend of many years.

He had no airs about him; despite his wealth and *askanus* (involvement in community issues), the respect and admiration he had earned, and his immense popularity, Shlomie viewed himself as a "regular guy." He had no ego; he was not the least self-conscious and had no difficulty doing things that lesser men would have considered beneath their dignity.

It is common for businessmen to take pride in their successes. Shlomie was different. He never took credit for his business success. When he completed a major deal that resulted in huge profit, his attitude was, "Why me? What did I ever do to deserve such *hatzlachah*?"[1]

---
1. Kalman Tabak.

A friend related:

> For a number of years, Shlomie would pick me up at Rav Schorr's shul each morning after Shacharis to drive me to the Manhattan bus. If he had gone to a bris that morning, he would prepare two bagels-and-lox sandwiches for me — and nothing for himself. If he had gone to a vort on the previous night, he would bring me a full plate of cake. Not that I ever asked for these things; he just had this tremendous desire to do for others in any way possible. He was not embarrassed to walk around the sweet table at a vort, looking for the particular pastries that he thought I would most enjoy.
>
> Every morning when he came to Rav Schorr's shul — the shul where he davened every Shabbos, and of which he was a leading member — he invariably needed to get out of his car to speak to someone there. Often, he would pick up any garbage that littered the area. Upon entering the building, he would go over to the wastebasket near the sink that contained discarded paper towels, lift his foot high, and press down the pile to make room for more.

Rabbi Avrohom Schorr with Aharon Gross at his wedding

> As we drove to the bus stop, he would be on the lookout for a car that might be headed to Manhattan so that maybe I could get a comfortable car ride instead of going by bus. He would honk to get the driver's attention, roll down the window, and ask on my behalf. I would have been uncomfortable doing this myself, but Shlomie had no problem doing it.
>
> And on frigid winter mornings, he would insist on my waiting in his car at the bus stop until the bus arrived.

The average adult would probably be embarrassed to be seen walking around at a *simchah* making himself a platter of the most delectable pastries. Such concerns were non-existent in Shlomie's mind. He was not the least bit concerned that others might look down at what he was doing or think less of him. To his mind, there was no reason to feel self-conscious when engaged in an act of kindness for someone else, especially if that "someone else" was his close friend.

Nothing was beneath his dignity. When the shul floor was littered with cake crumbs following a *kiddush*, it was Shlomie who got down on his hands and knees to clean up the mess. When someone else's son vomited in shul, Shlomie washed him off and then cleaned up.

A friend related:

> Shlomie learned every weekday morning at Khal Bais Avraham (Rabbi Halberstam's shul). When he arrived each morning, he would clean the tables of any coffee spills and take out the garbage. Sunday morning, he would take all sefarim that had been left lying around after Shabbos and return them to their proper place in the bookcases. It didn't take him very long; he was quick with everything he did. Whenever there was a snowstorm, Shlomie was the one who shoveled a large area of the sidewalk so that the shul would be accessible to everyone.[2]

---
2. Tzale Edelstein.

Fun on Deposit

ONE SUMMER, ONE OF SHLOMIE'S CHILDREN HAD AN IDEA. "Let's collect all the soda bottles and cans in White House Estates and cash them in for five cents apiece!" Many parents would have responded, "What for? It's not worth the effort." Many parents, especially affluent ones, would have been embarrassed to have their children make such a collection. Shlomie's reaction? "Great idea!" — and he would even be an active participant.

He announced after *davening* at White House Estates: "We are collecting soda bottles and cans. Just leave them outside your bungalow and we will pick them up."

Soon after, on a vacation trip to a hotel, Shlomie could be seen accompanying his children on their trek around the hotel grounds, collecting bottles and cans.

His Equals

ON HIS VISITS TO GEDOLEI ERETZ YISRAEL, HE WAS OFTEN accompanied by Yerushalmi friends and occasionally by *yeshivah bachurim* he knew. He would never go inside alone to speak to

the *gadol*, leaving his companions outside. He always insisted that whoever accompanied him be allowed to come in with him. He also gave his companions the opportunity to speak with the *gadol*.

His brother-in-law Aron Cyperstein recalled:

> *Sometimes, the presence of a wealthy person — especially if he is very involved in community matters — can be intimidating, even if he is a relative. You might think twice before disagreeing with his opinion, and you would be very careful how you speak to him. With Shlomie there was no such thing. While we all admired and respected him, we never felt the least bit intimidated by him. He was the most regular, down-to-earth fellow, had a great sense of humor, and was a pleasure to be with.*

A few years ago, an Israeli magazine published a feature article on "100 great *baalei tzedakah* in *Klal Yisrael*." Shlomie was among the 100. When someone showed him the article, he reacted with genuine disgust. "I only hope my kids don't see this," he said.

Visiting Rabbi Chaim Greineman in Bnei Brak

"You Trust Me?"

A FRIEND WOULD OFTEN KEEP LARGE SUMS OF CASH AT HOME for *tzedakah* purposes. He related:

> *One evening, on what must have been a night of many meshulachim, Shlomie came over to borrow some money — he had run out of cash. I gave him a wad of bills, mentioned that I had no idea how much money it was, and told him to take whatever he needed. As I walked out of the room, he said with genuine surprise, "You trust me with so much money? How will you know how much I'm taking?" I replied, "Of course I trust you! What's the question?"*
>
> *I could not get over his humility. Here was a man whose integrity was well known, and he was surprised that a good friend would trust him with his money.*

Contrast the above with the following anecdote related by another friend:

> *I was involved in an investment that required a sizable sum which I did not have at the time. I approached Shlomie, who told me that he had an account with the amount I needed. He offered to go with me to the bank and sign me on as a partner in the account.*
>
> *I could not believe it. "Shlomie, do you realize that I could just empty the account and there would be no way to prove that it was really your money?"*
>
> *"I'm not worried about it," he replied.*
>
> *The broker who managed the account tried to talk him out of it, but he would not be dissuaded. There was nothing he would not do for a friend.*

And though he did so much for everyone, he never expected anything in return, as his friend Volvi Elbogen related:

> *One year before Rosh Hashanah, Shlomie was going through a hard time in a business-related matter. I bought*

him a gift, a silver honey dish, as a small gesture to lift his spirits. I was moved by how genuinely appreciative he was. And once again, I gained insight into how special he was. He was a man who just gave and gave. Yet he was very grateful when a friend gave him something relatively small, for he felt that nothing was coming to him. Anything he received was more than he deserved. Such humility! It was mind-boggling.

Without Recognition

HIS HUMILITY WAS APPARENT IN OTHER WAYS. WHEN A NEW shul opened in his neighborhood, Shlomie called a friend and asked that he join him there for *Kabbalas Shabbos* to "be *mechazek* the rav." Later, he dedicated that shul's *ner tamid* in memory of his father, but did not place his own name on the dedication plaque. He did this in other shuls as well. He always preferred to have his good deeds go unnoticed.[3]

His family has a video of a chassidishe Rebbe's *tisch* at which Shlomie was brought to sit on the dais. At the first opportunity, he jumped off the stage and blended in with the crowd.

Rabbi Tzvi Kahan of Jerusalem recalled:

> He never wanted any honor for his support. He would come to visit our yeshivah but never wanted to be taken around as is common when a philanthropist comes to the mosad that he supports. He wanted to be מֵצִיץ מִן הַחֲרַכִּים, to peer through a window without being noticed.
>
> Once, when he arrived in the midst of our simchas beis ha'shoeivah, I wanted to bring him into the center circle to dance with the rabbanim, but he absolutely refused. He was content to stay on the perimeter, where he would not be the object of everyone's attention.

---
3. Volvi Elbogen.

There were some young people, potential donors, whom Shlomie did not know, but they knew of him. He would drive with me, three-quarters of an hour each way, to talk with them about our yeshivah. These visits were important in garnering their support; Shlomie was very happy that he helped the yeshivah in yet one more way. His humility was such that it never entered his mind that perhaps these young men should be visiting him, and not the other way around. He was truly unique.

"My Friend, Shlomie"

A YOUNG MAN RECALLED:

As a twelfth-grader, I accompanied Shlomie's son to his parents' house on Purim as we made the rounds collecting tzedakah in Flatbush. Shlomie enjoyed my humor and said he would take me out to lunch after Purim. He did, and that is how our relationship began.

Getting to know him changed my life, because he taught by example that in essence, all Jews are equals. We are all Hashem's children, and therefore we should never look down at anyone.

He treated me, who was young enough to be his son, like an equal. That is why I had the nerve to do something that was somewhat outrageous.

I was on my way to learn in Eretz Yisrael for the very first time. I flew from my hometown to New York, and from there I had a flight to Tel Aviv. When I landed in New York, I was informed that my flight would be delayed by about eight hours.

Someone drove me to Flatbush, and now I had seven hours until departure. What should I do? Where should I go?

I called my friend, Shlomie Gross. How did I muster the nerve to call this wealthy fellow, whom the whole world ran after for their tzedakah and other needs? I felt that he was my friend.

It was a good move on my part. Shlomie drove over to where I had been dropped off and took me to a classy restaurant for dinner. He said to me, "You're going to Eretz Yisrael to learn; you need to go in a good frame of mind." He bought me some nosh for the trip and gave me spending money. Then he called his worker, Carlos, and had him drive me to the airport.

A young fellow who lives in Flatbush told me that he would walk a certain way to shul because that way he was likely to bump into Shlomie, who always made him feel like a million dollars.

"They're All Mine!"

THERE IS A RENOWNED *CHASSIDUS* IN ERETZ YISRAEL THAT IS a very popular place for anyone who wants to experience true *simchas Yom Tov*. On Succos the *chassidus* welcomes outsiders for their nightly *simchas beis hasho'eivah*, but on Shemini Atzeres they do not allow outsiders for *hakafos* due to lack of space.

One year, some 30 *bachurim* were waiting outside this beis midrash, hoping to be allowed in somehow, but the door remained locked from inside. Then Shlomie arrived. When the *gabbai* heard that Shlomie Gross was outside, he opened the door and invited him in. Shlomie motioned to the *bachurim* around him and told the *gabbai*, "Zei zenen aleh mayna!" ("They are all mine!") The *gabbai* laughed and allowed everyone to enter.

Painful Honor

HE WAS HONORED BY FOUR YESHIVOS WITHIN A SPAN OF five years. People did not understand him. Wasn't it embarrassing to ask the same circle of friends to give money in his honor many times in quick succession?

As one friend put it, "Being honored was painful to him. He was very uncomfortable speaking in public. His acceptance speech upon receiving his reward was, 'Thank you very much,' or 'Thank you for coming.' But he did it, because he was willing to suffer discomfort to help a yeshivah or organization."[4]

At the *sheva berachos* of the son of a distinguished *rosh kollel*, Shlomie was honored with reciting one of the *berachos* following *Bircas HaMazon*. Shlomie was so upset with this honor that he told a friend he was sorry he had attended.

Hand-Delivered

THE PARENTS OF A *KALLAH* WHOSE WEDDING WAS ABOUT TO take place did not have the money they needed for the *simchah*. Shlomie told an *askan* who was raising funds for the wedding, "I'm in for a thousand." When the person asked if he could come by to pick up the check, Shlomie replied, "I know where you live; I'm going to put the check through your mail slot."[5]

His friend Avrohom Colman related:

> On my visits to New York, we would sometimes drive around together. Shlomie would make a stop for two minutes to drop off a check at someone's house. I would ask him what it was all about. He didn't talk about all the chesed he was involved in, but if I asked him he would answer me. Invariably, such checks were for people marrying off children, someone having problems with medical expenses, a widow ... I learned a lot about tzedakah just by being around him.

---

4. For one of those dinners, many *mosdos* and *gabba'ei tzedakah* sent in ads in Shlomie's honor for the dinner journal. After the dinner, Shlomie paid all outstanding balances for those ads.
5. Rabbi Moshe Grossman.

Special Treatment

ONE YEAR, SHLOMIE SPEARHEADED A FUNDRAISING CAMPAIGN for a Jerusalem family which raised some $80,000. On his next trip to Eretz Yisrael, Shlomie took along the money, in checks, to bring to the family. When questioned about the checks at Kennedy Airport, he explained what they were for. Airport officials believed his story but said that in order to take that much money out of the country, he was required to be an official courier. This information was entered into their files, and from then on, every time he returned from an overseas trip he was taken to a room in the airport and questioned. On subsequent return trips from Eretz Yisrael, he would send his wife home from the airport ahead of him in a taxi while he went through this process, which lasted 45 minutes or more. He showed no sense of discomfort or embarrassment.

How could a man of stature, a world-class *askan* who rubbed shoulders with prominent men in the community and was a frequent visitor to *gedolei Yisrael,* not be humiliated by such treatment? The answer is that in Shlomie's mind, he was no one special, just a regular guy. And if this was the price he had to pay to help someone in need, it was certainly worth it.

Wrong Man for the Job

HE WAS READY TO HELP EVERY YESHIVAH AND ORGANIZATION, but he admitted that his personality sometimes worked against fundraising success. When a distinguished rosh yeshivah called to ask if Shlomie could make a parlor meeting in his home for his yeshivah, he replied, "I'm really the wrong person for this. A parlor meeting should be hosted by someone who will feel embarrassed if it's a failure. That way, he will try his hardest to guarantee it will be well attended. With me, I won't feel embarrassed if only two people show up. I'd feel bad for the *mosad,* not for myself.

These things just don't bother me."[6]

As his family and friends report, when Shlomie was involved in a parlor meeting, his pre-event phone calls and active participation at the event were usually what ensured its success. But it was never done for personal pride.

A Fair Exchange

A FRIEND RELATED:

> One morning I walked into shul for Shacharis and removed my hat to put on my tallis. Someone told me, "Ari,[7] you're still wearing your shlof kappel (yarmulka for sleeping)." I had forgotten to change my yarmulka when I got out of bed. The one I was now wearing was oversized and quite strange-looking.
>
> Shlomie darted over from the other side of the beis midrash, removed his yarmulka, and tried to switch with me. Apparently, he was perfectly comfortable walking around looking ridiculous.
>
> But I didn't let him switch.

A Lesson for Life

WHEN A FRIEND NEEDED HELP TO PAY FOR HIS CHILD'S wedding, he could count on Shlomie. Friends would often express their gratitude by honoring him with reciting a *berachah* at the *chuppah*. At one such wedding, he was announced as "a *mechutan* from the *chasan's* side."

A friend related:

> A few days before I was to marry off my oldest child, Shlomie asked me, "So how are you paying for this wedding?" I told him the truth: "I have no clue." I struggle to

---
6. Willy Beer.
7. Not his real name.

make ends meet and I did not have the money that I was supposed to bring with me to the wedding hall.

"I'm bringing money to the wedding," Shlomie said. He brought $5,000 and also had some friends contribute toward the wedding expenses.

A few years later, Shlomie was marrying off his oldest child, Adina. I happened to have a surplus of funds at the time, which was highly unusual for me. When I arrived at the wedding hall, I went straight to the caterer's office, handed him an envelope with $5,000, and told him, "I'm Shlomie Gross' cousin [which was not true]. This is towards his bill tonight." The caterer accepted the money, asked me if I wanted a receipt, which I did not, and my mission was accomplished.

The next afternoon Shlomie rang my doorbell, holding a bag which I later discovered held $5,000. "Shlomie," I said, feigning surprise, "what are you doing here the day after your daughter's wedding?"

"Are you a meshugena?" he demanded. "What's the meaning of this, paying for part of my wedding?"

From his pocket, he withdrew a photograph of myself in the caterer's office and explained that the wedding hall had a video camera that had caught me in the act. "Now take back your money," he said, holding out the bag.

But I was not ready to accept it. "Shlomie, tell me, how did it feel when you found that someone had paid for part of your daughter's wedding?"

"Horrible," he replied.

"Right, it felt horrible. That's how it feels when someone else pays for your child's wedding. It's not like, 'Wow, my wedding is all paid for!' even when the other person does it in the best *derech hakavod* (most honorable way) possible. It's not a good feeling to be a taker.

"Shlomie, I'm not taking the money back. I want you to hold on to it and remember for the rest of your life how painful it is to receive money, even from a good friend such as yourself who gives it with all his heart. I think that the next time you're going to help someone make a wedding, you're going to do it with a different feeling."

Shlomie made no further attempt to return the money.

How many people of Shlomie's stature would have accepted such a lesson? One would have expected him to respond, "Okay, you taught me a nice lesson. Now stop being ridiculous and take your money back."

But Shlomie, the humble giant and good friend, did not see it as belittling to keep the money if this would help him to internalize the lesson. Perhaps he also felt that it would make his friend feel good to have used his money to convey this lesson.

And undoubtedly, he had ample opportunity to return the money in the years that followed.

The Key to Good Middos

IN HIS FAMOUS ETHICAL LETTER, *RAMBAN* WRITES OF *ANAVAH*, humility: "This sterling quality is the finest of all *middos tovos* (positive character traits)." *Sefer Tomer Devorah* sees humility as the key to attaining all good character traits.

Shlomie's genuine, deep-rooted humility allowed his personality to shine in many other ways as well.

Gratitude

HE NEVER EXPECTED ANYTHING IN RETURN FOR THE COUNTless favors he did, and shrugged off attempts to thank him. But if someone did him a favor, his gratitude was boundless. This was especially true if someone helped his children.

On the last Purim of his life, at his brother-in-law's Purim *seudah*, he stood up in the middle of the meal and went to visit a young *talmid chacham*. That person had been involved with Shlomie's older son, Aharon, during his years in high school and beis midrash, and Shlomie's gratitude to him was boundless. Nevertheless, other men of Shlomie's stature might not have been as quick to visit someone much younger than himself as a way of saying "Thank you." Not Shlomie. In his mind, he was a "regular guy" going to rejoice with a *talmid chacham* to whom he felt enormous *hakaras hatov*.[8]

When the above-mentioned *talmid chacham* and Shlomie would meet, Shlomie would tell him, "No words," meaning that no words were sufficient to express his *hakaras hatov*. Upon Aharon's engagement, a bottle of wine was delivered to this *talmid chacham's* home along with a card on which was written: *"No words."*

Dancing with Aharon at his *vort* in Jerusalem

Rabbi Binyomin Povarsky of Jerusalem recalled:

> *It happened that someone Shlomie knew was arrested in Eretz Yisrael on trumped-up charges. Shlomie asked me to do whatever possible on that fellow's behalf. I spent one day in a Tel Aviv court and was not successful, though eventually the charges were dropped. For the rest of his life, Shlomie could not do enough for me.*

---

8. Eli Cyperstein.

When I would travel to America, he would send his worker, Carlos, to pick me up at the airport. He insisted on lending me one of his cars, along with its E-Z Pass, GPS, and other amenities.

In the fall of 2011, Shlomie went with a group to Eastern Europe to the places that had been the great Torah centers of the pre-war Lithuanian Torah world. I did not even know that such a trip had been scheduled, but Shlomie knew that it had always been my dream to visit those places. In addition, it had been arranged for my father, shlita,[9] to come on that trip. Shlomie called me up and told me that he had already signed me up for the tour, and of course, he would be paying my way.

He once told a friend that he was on his way to a yeshivah dinner in Monsey to "stop in for a couple of minutes." The friend

With Rabbi Berel Povarsky on their trip to Lithuania

---

9. The Ponovezher Rosh Yeshivah Rabbi Berel Povarsky.

did not understand. Travel an hour and a half each way to be at a dinner for a few minutes? To Shlomie, the answer was simple: "My son learned in that yeshivah."

His friend Avrohom Colman related:

> *From Shlomie I learned the meaning of hakaras hatov. I met him once at Palm Springs, where we and our wives had gone for a brief vacation. We davened at the local Chabad shul. The morning that he was to leave, Shlomie handed the gabbai a check. It dawned on me how right he was. These people were performing a priceless service, making it possible for us to daven with a minyan three times a day while on our vacation. Since then, I've made it my practice to leave a check.*

He was a wonderful boss to his devoted worker, Carlos, who worked for him for many years. On many overseas trips, Shlomie would visit the airport's duty-free shop to buy Carlos a gift.

Carlos was a loyal worker, but often there was no work for him. Someone once asked Shlomie, "Why do you keep him? You probably could do without him."

Shlomie replied, "He took care of my father in his final years. He was devoted to him. For that, I keep him."[10]

An employee recalled:

> *Carlos once drove me somewhere and for 25 minutes raved about what an unbelievable person "Sol" was. I thought to myself, "When Shlomie's time comes, Carlos can deliver a hesped."*
>
> *Carlos told me that once, Shlomie sent him to the Bronx to pay the superintendents their salaries, forgetting that it was Carlos' holiday. Carlos carried out his mission; only later did Shlomie realize his mistake. He called Carlos and apologized profusely. Until Shlomie*

---

10. Rabbi Moshe Grossman.

passed away, he would call Carlos every year on that holiday to apologize for what had happened.

Hakaras hatov is a Gross family trait. Mrs. Tsivia Yanofsky, a former assistant principal at Masores Bais Yaakov, recalled: "When the girls graduated twelfth grade, Mr. Gross came down to the school to thank the teachers for their roles in his daughters' development.[11] I saw this *middah* in the girls themselves. Upon graduation, one of the daughters gave me a beautifully inscribed book that I treasure to this day."

A Shabbos of "Thank You's"

THE SHABBOS *SHEVA BERACHOS* FOR SHLOMIE'S ELDEST child, Adina, was held in a hotel. Many of the *gabba'ei tzedakah* with whom Shlomie was close, as well as others whom he had helped over the years, were invited. At each *seudah* there were many speeches. Everyone wanted to express his feelings of gratitude to Shlomie and his wife.

Each time someone would get up to speak, Shlomie would leave his seat at the head table and take a seat

With his *mechutan* Reuven Kaufman

---

11. When his younger daughter, Tzipora, became engaged to Eli Kaufman, Shlomie asked Rabbi Yosef Gelman, Dean of Masores Bais Yaakov, to take him around the school beginning with the youngest grade, so that he could thank each teacher who had contributed to his daughter's development.

directly in front of the speaker, looking at him and smiling throughout the speech. It looked a bit strange, as if Shlomie were drinking in the accolades being heaped upon him.

Many of the guests, however, had something else on their minds. The roster of speakers was far too long, and the *seudos* dragged on and on. Before *shalosh seudos*, some people approached Shlomie to complain.

"You don't understand," he told them. "These people feel bad enough that they have to come to me for help. The least I can do is to give them a chance to say 'Thank you.'"[12]

Seeing the Good

"WHO IS THE MAN WHO DESIRES LIFE, WHO LOVES DAYS TO *see good? Guard your tongue from evil* …"[13] A rav who knew Shlomie well applied this verse to him. He was a gregarious fellow, the "life of the party." But he did not speak negatively of others.

As the years passed and he became ever more spiritually attuned, his mundane conversation underwent a change. A friend related:

> The last years of Shlomie's life we got together much less frequently. When we did see each other, we would sit down to shmooze. Sometimes I wanted to make him laugh by sharing a cute story about someone we both knew. Truth be told, the story sometimes could be considered lashon hara. Years ago, Shlomie might have let me tell the story and enjoy a good laugh. But not in his later years. As soon as he sensed where the story was headed, he tactfully changed the topic.

---

12. Shimon Kaplowitz.
13. *Tehillim* 34:13.

Another friend recalled:

> *Shlomie avoided lashon hara and he did not want it spoken in his presence. But he never said, "Stop the lashon hara." He would employ his humor or find some other way to steer the conversation elsewhere.*[14]

A related quality was his ability to separate the deed from the person. He could become extremely upset with something that someone did, but this did not affect his love and concern for that individual.

Rav Avraham Pam would stress the importance of not speaking critically of groups of Jews or the Jewish people as a whole. To engage in such talk is to invite Heavenly indictment of our people. Shlomie was someone who only wanted to hear good said about Jews, and he would grow upset when the opposite was spoken.

His *ayin tov* (positive view) extended to the Torah projects he supported. One Israeli *mosad* refused on principle any funding from the Israeli government. A friend argued that since it was soliciting funds that it could have easily acquired from the government, it did not deserve their support. Shlomie disagreed. "This *mosad* does very good work, and that's all that counts."

Someone once remarked to Shlomie that he would never give a donation to a certain yeshivah where he had been a student because they had sent him away. Shlomie replied, "I give donations to yeshivos that sent me away even if I only lasted there a week. After all, they kept me for a week!" And he added, "You know, if I *didn't* give money to yeshivos that threw me out, I'd be a very wealthy guy!"

To "Fargin"

THE MITZVAH OF *AHAVAS YISRAEL* REQUIRES US TO REJOICE IN another's success as we would over our own. This is not as simple

---

14. Kalman Tabak and other friends who shared this observation.

as it sounds. People are quick to sympathize when their neighbor suffers a loss, *r"l,* but often they are not as quick to rejoice over his *simchah.* Envy creeps in, making it difficult if not impossible to share in his joy. To *"fargin,"* a Yiddish term that defies translation, means to be truly happy when someone else has attained something that we wish for ourselves.

A friend related:

> *People are often reluctant to share their successes with others because they are afraid of awakening jealousy. Shlomie had the ability to fargin.*
>
> *I am blessed with a son who is a metzuyan (outstanding). Shlomie often expressed how happy he was for me, how excited he was over my son's development. When we began to seek a shidduch for my son, Shlomie kept cautioning me not to "settle" for someone who would not appreciate his qualities — as if it were **his** son we were discussing.*

During the *shivah,* someone told the family: "It is common for people not to *fargin* the rich. They are jealous of their wealth and think to themselves, 'Why is he rich and not me?' I don't think anyone thought this way about Shlomie. Everyone was able to *fargin* his money because they knew that he wanted to share his money with others and make others happy."

Sensitivity

ONCE, HE WAS STANDING WITH OTHERS WHEN A MAN approached them for *tzedakah.* He poured out his tale of woe, mentioning a number of difficulties he had undergone, including the fact that he had recently suffered the loss of a child. One of the people interjected, "Why are you mentioning that? It has nothing to do with your asking for *tzedakah.*"

Shlomie was distraught at the question. True, the passing of a child did not make the man more destitute, but what did that matter? This was a man in pain, and he was expressing it. To ask such a thing was hurtful and insensitive.

Shlomie took the poor man aside, spoke with him for ten minutes, and handed him a large donation.

His friend Dr. David Kreiser related:

> On a visit to Eretz Yisrael, the two of us spent part of a day busy with the mitzvah of bikur cholim. First we went to visit a rav who was hospitalized with whom Shlomie was very close. I wanted to wait outside, so Shlomie handed me his cellphone. I felt like a secretary; the phone did not stop ringing.
>
> Then we went to visit my uncle, the Ponovezher Rosh Yeshivah, Rav Dovid Povarsky. This was shortly before Rav Dovid passed away. He was hospitalized and on oxygen. Only one person at a time was allowed in. Shlomie told me to go in. Rav Dovid could not speak, but he recognized me and motioned with his hands. It was the last time I saw him.
>
> When I left the room, I asked Shlomie if he wanted to go in. "No," he replied, "he is weak and I don't want to bother him. I only wanted to come here so that you would have a chance to see him."

Once, someone who was experiencing financial trouble asked him for a loan. Shlomie was not happy lending him money because he felt that the man's lifestyle was too lavish, but nevertheless, he granted him the loan. When the due date arrived and the money was not repaid, Shlomie went out of his way to avoid meeting the borrower so as not to make him uncomfortable.

Savlanus

THE VILNA GAON WRITES THAT MAN'S PRIMARY PURPOSE IN this world is to perfect his *middos*. Shlomie invested great effort towards overcoming the flaws in his nature. He toiled to acquire the trait of *savlanus* (tolerance and patience). He was very happy to share his money with others, but sometimes he was disturbed by the recipient's attitude.

With a smile, he would hand the person a donation, but the man was not happy. He had heard that Shlomie Gross was capable of giving larger amounts, and he wanted more. But Shlomie felt that for this person, what he had given *was* a proper amount; he did not want to give more. The man would become insistent, even a bit brazen, hoping that Shlomie would cave in. As Shlomie put it, "Some people would prefer to get more money with a frown than less with a smile."

At first, he needed to muster every ounce of self-control to refrain from lashing out at such people. As the years passed, he worked on being a *savlan* and learned to not become upset over such audacity. He was, after all, a *tov ayin*; he excelled in seeing the good in others. And he knew that usually, these people acted as they did out of financial desperation.

He once remarked, "For me, giving *tzedakah* is not a *nisayon* (test); I love to give *tzedakah*. Having *savlanus*—that's a *nisayon*."

In his final months, his schedule allowed him ten minutes between his morning learning session and *Shacharis*. During these minutes, *gabba'ei tzedakah* would line up to solicit contributions. One fellow, whom Shlomie knew well, would bring a number of collectors on a single morning. Once, he asked Shlomie, "How many am I allowed to bring at one time?" Shlomie replied with a smile, "As many as you want."

Seeking Forgiveness

ONCE, A RAV WAS DELIVERING AN ADDRESS AT A BAR MITZVAH celebration when Shlomie walked in. Being the personality that he was, his entrance to a gathering where his friends were present usually created a stir, and this time was no different. After concluding his words, the rav approached Shlomie and told him,

"I want you to know that all the noise your entrance caused really disturbed my train of thought."

The next day, the rav's doorbell rang. It was Shlomie. "I've come to ask *mechilah*," he said. "And if you're so upset with me that you're not ready to grant *mechilah*, I'm prepared to give $25,000 to any cause you name — just please be *mochel* me."[15]

Rabbanim were not the only ones to whom he was quick to apologize. In Shlomie's office, if ever he felt that he had spoken somewhat harshly to an employee, he would apologize. Once, a secretary went on vacation and, due to a misunderstanding, returned a day later than was expected. Shlomie was not happy about this. After she returned, Shlomie told her, "I hear that you were told I was unhappy that you came back a day later than I thought you would. Don't worry about it. And I apologize that I even got upset."

A number of his friends expressed the same feeling: "The last thing in the world Shlomie would want to do was hurt someone's feelings."

A Blending of Qualities

IN THE FOLLOWING INCIDENTS, SHLOMIE'S OUTSTANDING *middos*, generosity, and love for *talmidei chachamim* come together:

One day, Shlomie's friend Dovid Langer received a phone call from the Mirrer Rosh Yeshivah, Rabbi Nosson Tzvi Finkel. Rabbi Gedaliah Sheinin[16] was coming to the States to raise funds and Rav Nosson Tzvi asked that Mr. Langer "take him around."

Rav Nosson Tzvi had one more request. At that time, Shlomie's cousin Yosef Perl, who lives in Eretz Yisrael, was in America undergoing treatments.[17] Rav Nosson Tzvi suggested that Yosef

---

15. Jack Friedman.
16. Rosh Yeshivah of Yeshivah Kesser Torah in Jerusalem.
17. See *"One Mitzvah Leads to Another"* in chapter six.

accompany them on their fundraising visits. "This will be a *zechus* for him that he should have a *refuah sheleimah*," the Rosh Yeshivah said.

Yosef suggested that their first fundraising stop should be at Shlomie's office. Shlomie was intimately involved with Yosef's situation and visited him every day. He was shocked when Yosef appeared as part of this threesome, especially since Yosef had undergone a treatment that day and looked tired and drawn. Shlomie asked Mr. Langer, "Why is he here?"

"Because Rav Nosson Tzvi said he should come along and felt it would be a *zechus* for him," was Dovid's reply.

Shlomie was upset. He felt that if the Mirrer Rosh Yeshivah would have seen how Yosef looked, he would not have requested that he accompany them. "Take Yosef home right now and see that he gets into bed right away," Shlomie said. He motioned for them to leave and did not give a donation.

An hour later, Dovid's phone rang; it was Shlomie. He apologized for having "thrown" his friend out of his office. "I feel bad about what happened. I meant well, but I still feel bad. Please be *mochel* me."

Later that day, Dovid received a phone call from the Chief Rabbi of Rechovot, Rabbi Simchah HaKohen Kook. He was about to return to Eretz Yisrael from a fundraising trip for Yeshivah Meor HaTalmud, which his late brother had founded. "Dovid," Rav Kook said, "take me to someone, anyone, for a donation before I leave."

Because of Shlomie's phone call a few hours earlier, there was no question in Dovid's mind whom they should visit. Soon they were in Shlomie's office. He received his friend warmly and was introduced to Rav Kook for the first time. It was the beginning of a close relationship. (When Shlomie passed away a few years later, Rav Kook was in America, in another state, preparing to return to Eretz Yisrael. He changed his plane ticket so that he could stop off in New York to fulfill the mitzvah of *nichum aveilim*.)

Shlomie later met with Rabbi Sheinin, gave him a generous donation, and made phone calls to others on his yeshivah's behalf. That was the beginning of a close relationship.

In Rabbi Sheinin's words:

> *Shulchan Aruch states that a very high level of tzedakah is that of "matan b'seiser" (charity given in secret) — when the donor and recipient do not know each other's identity.*[18] *Shlomie took tzedakah-giving to a unique level — he was the donor but acted as if he was the recipient.*
>
> *He was a supporter of my yeshivah and he helped me personally. When he would visit Eretz Yisrael, he would call up and say, "Reb Gedaliah, perhaps I could come over for a cup of coffee?" Or on an Erev Shabbos, "Perhaps I could taste the cholent?"*
>
> *I know that he did not need my coffee or cholent. He wanted me to feel that **I** was giving **him** something, that he was the recipient and I was the giver.*

The Missing Necklace

SHLOMIE AND RABBI ELIYAHU MANN[19] FIRST MET THROUGH AN incident at a Kennedy Airport lounge, as related by Dovid Langer:

> *When I accompanied Rav Mann to the business class lounge (since his economy ticket had been upgraded), I saw Shlomie and his wife, who were on their way to Eretz Yisrael. I approached Shlomie alone and told him, "I would like to introduce you to Rav Eliyahu Mann, who will be on your flight."*
>
> *Shlomie replied that he was with his wife on his way to Eretz Yisrael and did not feel it was a good time to be making a new acquaintance.*

---

18. See *Shulchan Aruch, Yoreh Deah* 249:7.
19. See Chapter Nine, *"Rav Chaim Kanievsky."*

While I was standing there, Shlomie's wife suddenly realized that an expensive necklace she thought she had been wearing was missing. Shlomie suggested that she retrace her steps. Perhaps she would find it on the floor. Mrs. Gross acted on this suggestion and walked out of the lounge.

As soon as she left the room, Shlomie called his daughter Tzipora at home, told her what happened, and said, "Mommy's not going to find the necklace. I don't want her to be feeling bad about it when she should be enjoying the trip. So listen to what we're going to do. Call Mommy's phone in about three minutes and tell her that you found her necklace on the kitchen floor. She'll think it fell off in the house. I'll get another necklace to replace it."

Shlomie's wife came back empty-handed, his daughter called, and Mrs. Gross happily told Shlomie the "good news" that the necklace was found at home. The story seemed to be over.

I returned to another area of the lounge; from that vantage point, I had a clear view of where the Grosses had been sitting. I noticed something shiny under the seat where Mrs. Gross had sat. I thought it might be a chewing gum wrapper, but just to be sure, I went over to look. It was the necklace.

I happily handed it over, but from the look on Shlomie's face, I could see that he was not happy. He thought that I should have put the necklace in my pocket and given it to him when his wife was not present. Now, she knew what had really happened, and she asked him, "Why did you tell Tzipora to say that?"

Shlomie replied truthfully, "Because I didn't want the loss of the necklace to ruin your trip. I did it for your good."

His wife understood, and Shlomie was no longer upset with me. He gave me a kiss and said, "Thank you so much."

I responded, "I want two favors in return. I want you to meet Rav Eliyahu Mann, and when you're in Eretz Yisrael, I want you to visit a widow whose story is particularly tragic."

Shlomie agreed to both requests. On that flight, he spent some time conversing with Rav Mann, and they became close. Rav Mann often accompanied Shlomie on his visits to Rav Chaim Kanievsky and other gedolim.

Rabbi Mann recalled:

When I arrived at the wedding of one of his children, Shlomie hugged me like a brother. Someone said to me, "You must be related to him!" That was Shlomie, pure ahavah (love) and achvah (brotherhood).

With Rabbi Eliyahu Mann

The pasuk says חִכּוֹ מַמְתַקִּים וְכֻלּוֹ מַחֲמַדִּים, *The words of his palate are sweet and he is all delight.*[20] *Of Shlomie I say,* חִכּוֹ מַחֲמַדִּים וְכֻלּוֹ מַמְתַקִּים, *The words of his palate were a delight and he was all sweet! I would refer to him as "der zisse Shloime (the sweet Shloime)." How I miss him. It is a different world without him.*

Once, I was in his office shortly before I returned to Eretz Yisrael. He asked me to take a few shirts for a poor person. It is not uncommon to send money for the poor. But for someone of his status to go out and buy a few shirts for someone in need? That is quite unusual.

---

20. *Shir HaShirim* 5:15.

11

Helping Our Youth

Our outdoor bell buzzed and I looked at the camera to see who it was. It was a fellow who looked to be in his older teens, wearing a bright-colored sweatshirt with the hood pulled over his head. I thought he was from one of the Bronx tenements our company owns.

I was wrong. He was a troubled teen from a frum home whom Shlomie had reached out to.

I watched this boy return to the office time and again, and I was amazed at the transformation. The many hours of love, attention, and heart that Shlomie invested in him changed his life.

(Mrs. Chana Fonfeder, a secretary in Shlomie's office)

AFTER SHLOMIE'S PASSING, A FORMERLY TROUBLED TEEN who has since found his way back as an observant and productive Jew told Mrs. Mimi Gross, "I owe Shlomie my life; he understood me and was able to help me straighten myself out." She replied, "He was able to relate to you so well because he had his own struggles to deal with as a teenager."

Mitzvah observance was never an issue for Shlomie, but his difficulties in the classroom and restless nature did not augur well for a successful future. This, along with his great heart, allowed for a unique relationship between him and many a troubled teen.

He gave his heart and soul for kids at risk. He would take them skiing, horseback riding, find them jobs, and inject some joy into their lives while encouraging them to maintain a proper lifestyle.

When he became involved with such boys, he took full responsibility for them, working with them personally, providing them with money, and, if they turned their lives around, sending them off to yeshivah. In some cases, this meant paying their airfare to Eretz Yisrael or tuition to the yeshivah most suited for their individual needs.

Environmental Control

THERE WAS AN ARAB WHO OWNED AN ESTABLISHMENT IN Flatbush that was a hangout for Jewish teenagers. Shlomie invested much time and money until finally the owner agreed to close his doors.

One summer in Monticello, someone opened a club that became a hangout for secular Israelis and kids at risk. Reports of the goings-on there were not good. Someone suggested that if clean-cut adults would come to the club, this would make the teenagers uncomfortable and the place would no longer serve as a hangout.

One evening, Shlomie and a couple of friends entered the place and began walking around. The proprietor approached them and said, "I want you to leave." One of the group responded, "We came to enjoy the club." Moments later, they were surrounded by five husky bouncers. Shlomie stood his ground despite the bouncers shoving him.

That evening, one of the kids at the club challenged him. "So you're ruining our fun, but what are you doing *for* us?" Rather than be angered at the boy's brazenness, Shlomie took his words to heart. He befriended the boy, and found him a job and a place to live. Slowly but surely, the boy returned to the proper path and even began a daily learning session.

Following the confrontation at the club, a meeting was held, and the proprietor was given a sum of money; he agreed to vacate the premises. Shlomie and his friends then reopened the establishment on Motzaei Shabbosos, where they had a *melaveh malkah* with dancing, and a game room.[1]

Nipped in the Bud

HIS KEEN PERCEPTION SAVED AT LEAST ONE BOY IN THE NICK of time.

On a trip to Eretz Yisrael, Shlomie met a friend's son who had been learning there for two years. Shlomie sensed that the boy was not learning very much and was in low spirits. Upon his return to the States, Shloimy contacted the boy's parents and apprised them of his assessment, which confirmed what they had suspected from speaking with the boy by phone. "I'm going back to Eretz Yisrael in a month," Shlomie told them, "and I'll look into it further."

His next trip convinced him that the boy had to return to the States. He called the parents and suggested that they bring him home and seek employment for him. "Will the *yentas* (gossipers)

---
1. Binyomin Berry.

talk about him when they find out about this?" the parents asked Shlomie.

"Yes," Shlomie replied, "for a day. Then they'll find someone else to talk about."

The day after the boy's return, Shlomie found him a job. That job led to another, and ultimately the boy, now a young man, became very successful at his profession. He felt very good about himself, and little by little, began to study Torah again. Inspired by the grand *Siyum HaShas* in MetLife Stadium during the summer of 2012, he undertook the study of *Daf Yomi* in Shlomie's memory.

An American *bachur* in Eretz Yisrael was not learning well and was feeling wholly unsuccessful. Shlomie was apprised of this; on his next visit to Eretz Yisrael, he visited the boy and invited him to spend the day with him. For Shlomie, it was a typical day on such a trip: a visit to Rav Chaim Kanievsky and other *gedolim*; visits to yeshivos; a restaurant stop for lunch, and more. The boy returned to yeshivah that evening exhilarated, and his learning improved.

With Rabbi Chaim Kanievsky on his way to see Rabbi Shmuel Berenbaum, who was on a visit to Eretz Yisrael

A "kid at risk" whom Shlomie took under his wing went off to Eretz Yisrael to learn and returned to a Torah life. When he came back to America, he began working by day and learning with a *chavrusa* at night. After Shlomie passed away, this boy called Shlomie's cousin, Shuli Halpert, crying. A friend who had been with him in that yeshivah had returned to the States too soon and was sinking again. This boy wanted to raise money for his friend's tuition so that he could return to yeshivah in Eretz Yisrael.

This was the fruit of Shlomie's efforts on behalf of many a lost soul.

"I Just Talk to Him"

ONCE, HE WAS ASKED TO TRAVEL FAR FROM NEW YORK City to try to influence a boy who had abandoned Torah observance. After the initial meeting's success, he traveled often to meet with this boy, took him to ball games, and drew him close. Ultimately, the boy returned to yeshivah. Someone asked Shlomie, "How did you do it? You have no *kiruv* training!"

"I just talk to him," was his reply.

He was correct. He "just talked to him," but the language he used was the language of the heart, a heart that was bursting with love for every Jewish soul.

When someone asked him why he invested so much effort in helping boys whose lives had taken a wrong turn, he replied, "I could have ended up like them."

One boy recalled:

> *At one point in my life, I felt it was all over. I was in despair. I called up Shlomie and cried. He asked, "Where are you? I want to meet with you." At one point, he said, "I am not going to sleep until you come to my house and we take care of this problem."*
>
> *I finally came very late at night. We sat in his car. I was crying and crying. "Shlomie, I'm done, I'm finished."*
>
> *"There is no reason to cry," he assured me. "Don't worry about it. We'll make a few phone calls. Don't let your emotions take over. When you get past it, you will laugh at the problem."*
>
> *He was right.*

One such *bachur* said:

> *Once, I was shmoozing with some friends when the question was asked, "Is there anyone whom you aspire to be like?" I replied, "Yes, Shlomie Gross; he was so good to me. Meeting him was a big turnaround in my life."*
>
> *I loved going to his office. He made me feel really good and he had such a good sense of humor. Being around him, I always felt relaxed and calm.*

Tough Love

SHLOMIE'S METHOD OF DEALING WITH TROUBLED TEENS CAN best be described as "tough love." They knew that he loved them. He understood them and would do anything to help them put their lives together. Toward that end, he made certain demands of them and held them accountable when they did not fulfill those demands.

He would sometimes hire these boys to work for him. When one boy missed work one day, Shlomie told him, "You're not getting paid for the day you missed, and the next time you don't show up for work without calling, you'll lose two days' pay for each day you miss."

This boy recalled something else:

> *Often, he would take me places in his car. Sometimes we would stop for soda and chips. If he was out of small bills, I would pay for him. "I owe you $1.35," he would tell me, or whatever amount it was. It was a joke: $1.35? Do you know how many thousands of dollars he spent on me since I first met him? And besides, the job he hired me for was not really a position he needed filled. It was just his way of keeping me in a good environment until I was ready to move on. So **he** has to owe **me** $1.35?*

> But he always paid me back to the penny, and I know why. This was another way of teaching me to be responsible. If you borrow money, you've got to pay back.

Another boy recalled:

> At one point, I was seeing a therapist and Shlomie was paying for it. One day, I called to say that I would be stopping by to pick up a check for that day's session.
>
> It was a warm summer day and I was wearing a tee-shirt and shorts. This is how I walked into his office. He took one look at me and then ignored me for five full minutes. I was sitting right in front of him, but it seemed as if he didn't see me. I took out my phone to keep busy. I knew something was wrong. Then he jumped up, leaned over from the other side of his desk, and said, "What are you wearing? Shorts and a tee-shirt?"
>
> Then he gave me $500 and said, "Have a good day."
>
> I knew what message he was conveying to me: "Yes, you've been living this lifestyle for 10 years, but that doesn't mean you have to walk around dressed in such an undignified way."
>
> Today, I live in an out-of-town community where just about anything goes. But I'm not like everyone else. Even when I take out the garbage, I don't walk out in flip-flops and a tee-shirt. That's because Shlomie taught me self-respect. I take this lesson with me every day.

"He Changed My Life"

ANOTHER *BACHUR* RECALLED:

> Shlomie changed my life in many ways. A turning point was when he taught me the meaning of responsibility.
>
> One summer, he made a deal with me. I wanted to join a camp that would be doing some traveling in the States

during July, but the price was expensive. Shlomie told me, "I'll pay for it, but on one condition. I don't want you hanging around the streets during August. If you promise to get a job for August, I'll pay for your camp in July." I agreed.

In June, I did something that really upset my parents. Shlomie called me up and told me, "If you don't call up your parents and apologize, our deal is off." I called, and the call ended with our relationship better than it had been in quite a while.

I enjoyed the trip in July and Shlomie found me a job for August. But I found the work boring, so after a week or so I stopped showing up for work. A couple of days later, I got a phone call from Shlomie. He sounded angry.

"I don't get it," he said. "I get you a job and then you stop showing up? I'm sick of playing games with you. Either you show responsibility, or we're through."

I hung up the phone and said to myself, "This is the first person who understands how I operate, that I play games with people."

He had seen right through me. He shook me up. I realized that I had better start showing some responsibility. I called him a few days later and apologized for not keeping my part of the deal, and he accepted my apology.

Our wonderful relationship continued until his passing.

Straight Talk

SHLOMIE WAS A "STRAIGHT SHOOTER." HE SPOKE HONESTLY and from the heart. In dealing with troubled youth, he had no hidden agendas; this was a key factor in his success, as one *bachur* recalled:

I was a lost soul, far from my family both literally and spiritually. Then one day, I received a message that Shlomie Gross was coming to see me. He had to travel quite a distance for this meeting. I was not happy about it. I knew that he was friendly with my parents, and it was obvious that this was why he was coming to see me. But I could not stop him from coming.

The first thing that impressed me about him was his forthrightness. As soon as I accepted his invitation to come into his car, he told me, "I'm here because I care about your parents and they are in a lot of pain right now. I want to bridge the gap between you. Now you may be thinking, 'What do I get out of this?' So I'll tell you: I have money, and I'm willing to help you with my money. And I don't mean by making deals like if you put on tefillin, I'll give you such-and-such. Of course I would like you to be religious, but I'm not going to use money to get you there. If I help you, it's with no strings attached."

His honesty continued during that first meeting when, on the way to a restaurant, he made a stop at a clothing store. He said, "If you'd like to buy some clothing, I'm happy to pay for it. But not the kind of clothing that will make your parents upset."

I had never met a man like this before. I had great respect for him after that first meeting. I remember thinking to myself, "I would like to be like this man."

We stayed in touch. Through Shlomie, I began to reconnect with my parents and ultimately, I returned to yeshivah.

Gesher L'Yeshivos

IN 2007, HIS COUSIN SHULI HALPERT FOUNDED GESHER L'Yeshivos, an organization that was founded to guide parents to the best yeshivah for their child. As time passed, it also reached out to kids at risk and children with family problems, and helped children get accepted into yeshivos.

There were times when Shuli and his colleagues had determined that a certain yeshivah was best suited for a particular boy, but the yeshivah was not willing to accept him. Shlomie usually knew either the rosh yeshivah or someone closely affiliated with the yeshivah, and would make the effort to have the boy accepted. His "sales pitch" was as important as his checkbook when placing these phone calls. He would say, "I am sure that this yeshivah is the best place for this *bachur*; you have to accept him. And I would like you to call me in one month and tell me if this was a good idea or a bad idea. If the boy is not conforming, I will personally go after him and make sure that he does well." And he kept his word.

Shlomie and his office colleagues developed a reputation among the community of kids at risk as people who wanted to help them. Once, a teenager who was a total stranger walked into the office and begged them to save him; he had reached rock-bottom and wanted desperately to turn himself around. Today, he is learning well for a good part of the day in an established yeshivah.

With his cousin Shuli Halpert (center) and Rabbi Usher Friedman

Straight From the Court

AFTER ONE BOY COMPLETED A DIFFICULT YEAR IN YESHIVAH, he could not return there the following year. His parents applied to seven yeshivos for the following year, but he was not accepted to any of them. The first day of school was rapdily approaching; this boy needed to be accepted somewhere, quickly.

Shuli Halpert was contacted by someone in Mesivta Rabbi Chaim Berlin, who said that the yeshivah was prepared to accept the student, but only if the Rosh Yeshivah, Rabbi Aharon Schechter, would give his approval.

Shlomie had a close relationship with the Rosh Yeshivah. When Shlomie was contacted, he told his cousin, "No problem. I'll be at the tennis court at 2. Meet me at the Rosh Yeshivah's house at 3:30." Shuli said that he would bring along the boy, his *rebbi*, and an influential person.

With Rabbi Aharon Schechter

A few minutes later, Shuli called Shlomie again. "There's a problem. I don't see how the Rosh Yeshivah will accept the boy without meeting him, and the boy refuses to come. He locked himself in his room and is crying that he can't get in to a yeshivah."

"If necessary," Shlomie replied, "I'll bring the Rosh Yeshivah to him."

Shuli and his two companions, all wearing suits and ties, arrived early in front of the Rosh Yeshivah's home. A few minutes later, Shlomie arrived. He rang the doorbell of a neighbor whom he had never met and asked to borrow a hat and jacket so that he could look presentable when visiting the Rosh Yeshivah — without an appointment. However, the neighbor could not be of help. Shlomie then proceeded to knock on the Rosh Yeshivah's front door. Someone opened the door, Shlomie entered, and then knocked on the door of the Rosh Yeshivah's study. The Rosh Yeshivah opened the door, looked at the group before him, and said with a smile, "Shlomie, I see that some very important people are here." He invited them into his study.

It was obvious to the other three men in the room that the Rosh Yeshivah and Shlomie had a very warm relationship. For 45 minutes they engaged in friendly conversation. The boy was accepted into the yeshivah.

"Tell the boy," the Rosh Yeshivah said, "to be at the *menahel's* office tomorrow morning at 9 o'clock, and not to worry."

The next morning, the parents were shown into the yeshivah's financial office while the boy was brought to the Rosh Yeshivah, who took him into his office privately and said, "From today and on you are my *talmid*. Anything that you need, come to me."

More Than Just a Boss

IT WASN'T ONLY "KIDS AT RISK" WHOM SHLOMIE WORRIED about. When a *bachur* who had left yeshivah needed a job, Shlomie gave him one. But as the young man recalls, Shlomie was not only concerned that he do his work:

> *I was managing some of his buildings, and he would call me every morning. "Where are you? Are you at work yet?"*
> "I'm on my way to the Bronx. I'll be there soon."
> "Did you daven yet?"
> "I'll put on tefillin in a little while."

"That's not good enough. Go daven."

He would do this day after day, calling me each morning to find out where I was. I finally realized that he wasn't concerned whether or not my work was getting done. He wanted to make sure that I davened every day with a minyan.

He also kept tabs on my learning, that I kept my seder with my chavrusa. And every once in a while, he would suggest that perhaps I would one day return to yeshivah.

Like a Son

ONE OF THE BOYS WHO WAS VERY MUCH INFLUENCED BY Shlomie eventually went to Eretz Yisrael to learn. When Shlomie's son Aharon was getting married, Shlomie flew the *bachur* to the States for the *aufruf* and wedding. On the way to a suit store with the *chasan*, Shlomie stopped by the boy's house. "You need a suit or hat for the wedding? Come along, it's no big deal."

This *bachur* recalled:

When Shlomie came to Eretz Yisrael, his son Aharon called me. "I'm picking up my father at the airport. Why not come along?" I came, and when we got to Yerushalayim, Shlomie said that he wanted to see my yeshivah. He even wanted to see my dorm room, like any father would.

He once called my rebbi at 3 a.m. New York time to discuss my progress. My rebbi told me, "I never met a man like this in my life. He really cares about you."

I would visit his son-in-law and daughter, Meir and Adina Kaplowitz, often. Once, Meir invited me to a siyum, and I came. At the end, his wife said to me, "If you want to make a siyum, call me and I'll make the same kind of seudah for you."

When I was almost finished the masechta our yeshivah was learning, I called her. "Great," she said, "my grandfather's yahrtzeit is coming up. We'll make the siyum l'ilui nishmaso (in his memory)."

Around the time of the siyum, Shlomie called me. "Thank you so much for making the siyum in my father's memory," he said. "You should know that I wanted to fly in for the siyum, but I just could not work it out."

Last year he came to visit me at my yeshivah. It was during seder. He came in to the beis midrash, sat down, and learned with me. The family told me that when he would come to his children's kollelim, he would not come inside, but would peek in from the outside. But he came inside to learn with me. After seder, he took me out for dinner. That was the last time I saw him.

On Purim, a week before he passed away, I called him. I gave a whole speech in which I thanked him for all that he did for me. I told him, "I look up to you."

He took an interest in me. He taught me responsibility. He really cared for me. He changed my life.

12

Family Man

I was privileged to observe how, despite other responsibilities and distractions, Shlomie placed his family's needs and desires above everything else. His pride in all of you was something to behold, and you should all know how happy you made him ... one phone call from any of you and he would light up like a light bulb.

(from a letter by Eli Karman,
a friend of Shlomie, to the family)

AS IS OBVIOUS FROM THE PREVIOUS CHAPTERS, Shlomie was an extremely busy person. He was partner in a thriving real estate business and spent much of his day dispensing *tzedakah* and helping others in a variety of ways. There were many individuals who viewed him as their "best friend" because of the special relationship he had with them.

And yet, there was no more devoted father. He was deeply involved in the lives of each of his children, and this devotion continued even after they married and established their own homes.

Though he was concerned for the needs of every person that crossed his path, his first concern was the needs of his wife and children.

A *mechanech* who is close to one of the children said:

> *Never did I see such love and devotion of a father to his children. There was nothing, absolutely nothing, that Shlomie would not do to help ensure his child's success in yeshivah. And I'm not talking about spending money. I mean giving of his time — time to make sure that his child was in the yeshivah that suited him best, to ensure that he was in the shiur most suited to his growth, to determine that all his material needs were cared for so that nothing would interfere with his yegiah (toiling) in learning. I never ceased to be amazed by this.*

When one of his daughters was in seminary in Eretz Yisrael, she told her parents that she had not found a host to join for the second day of Shavuos.[1] In his daughter's words, "My father was broken. How could such a thing be? He did not rest until he found a host for the Yom Tov meals."

His children were always on his mind. One Motzai'ei Yom Tov, Shlomie was with a friend when he suddenly took out his cellphone. "Maybe my daugher in Eretz Yisrael is still up," he explained, "and I can ask her how her Yom Tov was."

His daughter Adina Kaplowitz related:

> *When we were first married and were living in Eretz Yisrael, my father frequently sent us packages with things that we needed. At some point, he decided that he was spoiling us, and the packages stopped.*
>
> *But being the loving father that he was, he could not stop completely. When someone from his office was*

---

1. Those who live in Eretz Yisrael observe Shavuos for only one day, as mandated by the Torah. The second day, which is a rabbinic enactment, is observed by those residing outside the Land.

> going to Eretz Yisrael, my father would put together a package containing one treat for each of his children. For each child he sent the specific item that he knew that child enjoyed.

The children reciprocated by trying to be the best they could, not just because this is what one should do, but because they felt their parents' intense love and wanted to please them.

Rabbi Yisroel Garfunkel, who is very close to Shlomie's older son, Aharon, commented, "Shlomie lived for his children — and so does his wife. And that is why these children are the way they are."

A Wait in the Cold

AHARON GROSS RECALLED AN INCIDENT THAT ILLUSTRATES his father's sensitivity:

> My father was driving me somewhere one afternoon when I received a phone call from a close friend who wanted to discuss something very personal. I felt that it would be proper to speak in privacy, so I began to tell my friend that I would return his call later. But my father immediately understood the problem and said, "Aharon, you continue talking — I'm getting out of the car so you'll have privacy." I wanted to tell my father that this was not necessary, but he did not give me the chance. He had already pulled over to the side of the road and alighted from the car, and he stood outside in the bitter cold until the phone call was completed.

Focus on Chinuch

WHEN THE CHILDREN WERE SMALL, MRS. GROSS TOOK their younger daughter Tzipora to the doctor. When they returned home, Tzipora was given a treat for her good behavior. Her sister Adina, all of six years old, said, "Mommy, you're doing like Yaakov (Avinu) when he gave Yosef the *kesones pasim* (special tunic) and made his brothers jealous of him!" Shlomie was so proud that his daughter had absorbed this lesson she had learned at school, and had applied it, that he called her principal, Rabbi Gelman, to share the *nachas* with him.

On the night of *bedikas chametz*, the Gross children would hide a piece of bread in every room. Once, Shlomie searched a room and announced that he had not found any bread. His young daughter responded, "Tatty, I didn't put any *chametz* there because there *already is* a big piece of *chametz* — the television!" Her teachers had taught her that television is an abomination and should be disposed of like *chametz*.

Another parent might have been upset at his daughter's way of lecturing him, but Shlomie was proud of her. And eventually, he and his wife got rid of the television.

With Aharon　　　　　　　　　　With Nosson Tzvi

When one of his daughters needed extra reading practice, it was suggested that during summer vacation she complete the reading of the entire *Sefer Tehillim*. When she accomplished this, Shlomie suggested to his wife that she be rewarded immediately. The next day she was taken to a mall where she picked out a necklace as a prize.

With his children

As the children were growing up, they were not pampered or provided with amenities that wealth usually brings with it. Their home was not one of opulence and indulgence.

Shlomie spoke daily to his three married children in Eretz Yisrael. If one was dealing with an issue where he felt his hands-on involvement was needed, he would hop on a plane for a 12-hour visit. Nothing was too difficult if his children needed him.

But he understood that there is a fine line between parental devotion and excessive involvement bordering on meddling. Once, after providing guidance to a married daughter, he said, "But remember: Your husband is #1. He has to agree with what I'm telling you."

Fatherly Love

RABBI AHARON SCHECHTER RECALLED THAT OFTEN HE would see Shlomie walking down Avenue L with his youngest child, Nosson Tzvi. Their love for one another was obvious.

As mentioned in a previous chapter, in his last years Shlomie joined two friends for a Friday-night learning session in *Minchas*

Chinuch. Even on a late Friday night in the summer, he would bring Nosson Tzvi along so that he could watch his father learn. Often, the boy would curl up and fall asleep. When the learning ended, Shlomie would wake him up and take him home.

One year at the Toldos Aharon *simchas beis hasho'eivah* in Jerusalem, both Shlomie and six-year-old Nosson Tzvi were not feeling well. Shlomie lifted his son onto his shoulders and began walking back to his apartment in Rechaviah. Knowing that Shlomie was not feeling well, his brother-in-law Avi Szenberg offered to carry Nosson Tzvi part of the way, but Shlomie insisted on carrying his child the entire way home.

An Israeli friend recalled:

> *My wife and I flew to America to attend the wedding of one of Shlomie's children. During the week of sheva berachos, Shlomie insisted on taking us to Manhattan, where he took us to parks, on a horse-and-buggy ride, and to stores of interest. In between entertaining us, he ran into banks to take care of business.*

With (right to left) the Toldos Aharon Rebbe, Shlomie's *mechutan* Shimon Kaplowitz, and son-in-law Meir Kaplowitz

One of the stores we visited was a huge toy store. Shlomie emerged from the store carrying a big stuffed animal for Nosson Tzvi. I still recall the smile on the boy's face when his father presented him with the gift. And to Shlomie, bringing a smile to anyone's face, especially his own child, was what life is all about.

Teaching by Example

HIS DAUGHTER TZIPORA RELATED:

When it came to applying for seminary, I had my mind set on a particular one. When I was not accepted there, I was upset, and my father literally lost sleep over it. He knew that I was looking for a ruchniyus experience, which that seminary offers, and it bothered him very much that they would not accept me.

He made many phone calls to people of influence whom he knew personally. But it did not help. I was not accepted to that seminary.

On a visit to Eretz Yisrael months after my being rejected, my father and I were in a hotel lobby when the menahel of that seminary walked by. To my shock, my father greeted him in a friendly way, and they had a nice conversation. When the menahel walked away, I asked my father how he could be so friendly to him. I knew that I still bore resentment.

My father responded that the man had made a mistake in not accepting me, but he was not a bad person. And my father added that if I was not accepted by that seminary, it was from Hashem, and I would surely be successful at the seminary that I would be attending.[2]

---

2. Shlomie continued to give *tzedakah* to the *menahel* when he came to his office to collect from time to time.

> *The following year, my father came to Eretz Yisrael to visit me and make sure that I was happy and that things were going well. He called me often. And he did things to add to the spiritual experience of that year.*
>
> *I know that he paid seminary tuition for some girls who could not afford it. It would not surprise me if he paid for girls who attended the seminary that I could not get into.*

Nosson Tzvi, who was 11 at the time of his father's passing, recalled:

> *We would walk down the street, a walk that normally takes me and my brother-in-law 15 minutes. With my father it took over a half-hour, because every time he would meet someone, he would stop and say, "Hi! How are you doing?" Even if he didn't know the person, he made believe he knew him. I would always ask my father, "Who is that man?" and often he would say, "I don't know; he's a Yid."*
>
> *Sometimes my father was taking me somewhere and we made a stop on the way to drop off an envelope with tzedakah. There were times when someone was making a vort for their daughter and my father was bringing them money for the wedding. Other times, there were people from Eretz Yisrael who had come to America and my father would go to where they were staying to drop off an envelope for them.*

Shlomie would speak of Purim as a *groisse avodah* (day of great service of Hashem).[3] He would rejoice with family and friends, dispense *tzedakah,* and raise funds for causes close to his heart. But closest to his heart was his family, and therefore he always made time to take Nosson Tzvi and his friends collecting for their yeshivah on Purim day.[4]

---

3. See Chapter Thirteen.

4. In the last years of his life, Shlomie's wife suggested that with three married children living in Eretz Yisrael, they should spend Purim there. Despite his being very family oriented, Shlomie would not do so, because he knew that many

As busy and as exhausted as Shlomie was after a long day, he made time to learn with Nosson Tzvi on weeknights and especially on Shabbos.

A neighbor recalled: "I would watch Shlomie and Nosson Tzvi in the morning waiting for the carpool to come to bring Nosson Tzvi to yeshivah. They wouldn't just stand there waiting; they would play basketball or football until the car arrived."

When asked what lessons could be learned from his father, Nosson Tzvi said:

Shlomie and his wife with their grandchildren

> *My father was geshmak. He knew how to mix ruchniyus (spiritual matters) with gashmiyus (material matters). He wanted me to learn well, but he also gave me good incentives to encourage me to do well.*

A family friend recalled: "Nosson Tzvi came to our house for Shabbos and we could not get over how he helped my elderly father. He assisted him with his coat and held his hand as they walked to shul. And this is a boy who never saw his grandfathers."

But he did see a father and mother who were selfless.

---

tzedakah collectors, both young and old, were counting on his being home.

Their Role Model

SHLOMIE LOVED SURPRISING OTHERS WITH GOOD THINGS, especially his family. When his children were planning to spend summer vacation in the States, he planned with them on making their arrival a surprise for his wife.

The first year Aharon was learning in Eretz Yisrael, he was eating breakfast one morning in the yeshivah's dining room when he looked up to see the smiling face of his father.

In the words of his daughter Tzipora Kaufman:

> *My father's devotion to our mother and to us, his children, was something incredible. He did not want to spoil us, but he wanted to make sure that our needs were taken care of. And most of all, he wanted us to grow in ruchniyus (spiritually). He would look at a situation and say to himself, "Will this help my children to grow or not?"*
>
> *When we went on family trips, he maximized the time, using it not just for physical enjoyment but for an opportunity for growth.*
>
> *He was our baal eitzah, our keen advisor on any sort of matter. I knew that if I had a problem with something, I could just pick up the phone and he would give me the best possible advice.*
>
> *He would not advise his married children unless they sought his advice, which was often. And he taught me and my sister that all final decisions were between husband and wife, and that a husband's opinion must be respected. Once, when my father was not completely happy with something we were planning to do, he told me, "Your husband is a chashuva (distinguished) person; if he feels this is the right thing, he must have a good reason."*

As Shlomie's children grew spiritually, it seemed that he said to himself: "I'm going to have such wonderful, spiritual children and grandchildren and remain the same guy as before? No way. I also have to grow."

A close friend since childhood said, "He made great strides in *ruchniyus*, surpassing us all — I don't know how he did it. But I know one thing — the spiritual growth of his children had a lot to do with it."

But the converse was true as well. As Shlomie's children watched him become ever more spiritual, they wanted to emulate him.

Rabbi Moshe Aharon Rosengarten[5] reflected:

> *Dovid HaMelech says: "Praiseworthy is the man who fears Hashem, who greatly desires His mitzvos. Mighty in the land will his offspring be, a generation of the upright who shall be blessed."*[6] *The Midrash comments: "[Who greatly desires] His mitzvos, and not the reward for His mitzvos."*

With Rabbi Moshe Aharon Rosengarten (left) and Rabbi Zilberman

---

5. *Rosh Kollel* of Kollel Tiferes Tzvi in Jerusalem and a close friend of Shlomie.
6. *Tehillim* 112:1-2.

> *Beis HaLevi explains that while it is an accomplishment to do mitzvos with the intent of receiving reward, there is an inherent danger in such an attitude. When one's children see that one performs good deeds with an ulterior motive, they may be inclined to seek gratification from behavior that is not a mitzvah. However, when one's intention in doing mitzvos is purely for the sake of Heaven, then he can be assured that his children will follow in his footsteps.*
>
> *Shlomie was such a person. He did chesed and gave tzedakah without any thought of reward, certainly not in this world. He fled from honor as from a fire. He desperately did not want recognition for all the good that he did. And his children took note of that. They admired him, and as he grew spiritually they strove to grow as well.*

As with everything else, Shlomie never took credit for the way his children are. He once turned to a rosh yeshivah and asked, "How was I *zocheh* to such children?"

A House of Torah

WHEN HIS OLDEST CHILD, ADINA, WAS ABOUT TO BECOME engaged, he called a close friend in Eretz Yisrael before Shabbos and left a message: "I know it's already Shabbos by you, but I want you to know that my daughter is becoming a *kallah* to a *bachur* from Brisk!" His joy knew no bounds.

He derived enormous *nachas* from seeing his sons develop into true *bnei Torah* and his daughters into young women who married budding *talmidei chachamim*. His older son and a son-in-law studied in a highly regarded kollel in Eretz Yisrael of which Shlomie had been a long-time supporter. Shlomie would refer to this kollel as "the best investment I ever made."

When Shlomie came for a visit, he told the *rosh kollel*, "I don't want to walk into the beis midrash [where everyone will notice me]. Take me to the *ezras nashim* so that I can peek through the curtain and *shep nachas* from my son-in-law."

Shlomie stood behind the curtain of the women's section, watching and listening as his son-in-law delivered a *chaburah* (i.e. an informal *shiur* on a Talmudic topic). He cried tears of joy from beginning to end.

The highlight of his day was the daily 15-minute learning session by phone with his son Aharon, who lives in Eretz Yisrael. Shlomie would sit in his office in late afternoon, while in Jerusalem it was close to midnight.

Aharon became engaged on the second day of the new *zman*. Shlomie's son-in-law was in America but returned to Eretz Yisrael for the *zman* knowing that he would miss his brother-in-law's *vort*. Rather than feel bad that his son-in-law would not be in attendance, Shlomie rejoiced over his devotion to his learning.

The Gross children are fortunate to have a mother who continues to inspire them with her appreciation for Torah and its primacy. Aharon Gross related:

In the Judean Desert. Left to right: Shlomie with sons Nosson Tzvi and Aharon; sons-in-law Meir Kaplowitz and Eli Kaufman; and grandson Avraham Yaakov Kaufman

Family Man / 289

The vort following the engagement of my sister Tzipora to Eli Kaufman was cancelled because of Rav Shmuel Berenbaum's passing. The chasan was coming to my parents for Shabbos. I was learning in Yeshivah of South Fallsburg at the time. It is common for the kallah's brother to be home for Shabbos when the chassan is there, and this seemed especially important in light of the vort's cancellation.

When I spoke with my mother that week she said, "You don't have to come home for Shabbos. I told Eli that with this being the week of Rav Shmuel's petirah, you probably want to be mechazek (strengthen yourself) in limud haTorah."

Family portrait taken at the wedding of Aharon and Rivki Gross

A Caring Son

SHLOMIE'S *KIBUD EIM* KNEW NO BOUNDS. ONE YEAR, HIS mother accompanied the family to spend Succos in Eretz Yisrael with Shlomie's married children. After Yom Tov, Mrs. Gross was scheduled to fly back home a day before the rest of the family. Though she was capable of flying alone, Shlomie was not pleased with this arrangement. He drove his mother to Ben Gurion Airport and walked her as far as security would allow. There he met a young chassidic man who was to be on the same flight. Taking $2,000 out of his pocket, Shlomie said, "My mother is flying business class. Take this money and upgrade your ticket to business class. Sit near her and make sure that she has everything she needs."

Yitzchak Waldman serves as *gabbai* in Khal Tiferes Yaakov where Shlomie davened and which he dedicated in his father's memory. He related:

> *For a number of years, Shlomie's mother davened in our shul on Rosh Hashanah. Each time that she did, Shlomie would come to the shul before Yom Tov and try out the various types of chairs that we have in the women's section. He was looking for the chair that his mother would*

With his mother and son Aharon

find most comfortable. When he finally decided on the right chair, he would ask me to set it aside for his mother.

I recall him approaching the baal tefillah before Rosh Hashanah and singing a niggun. "My mother likes this niggun," he told the baal tefillah. He did not ask the baal tefillah outright to use the niggun. But he wanted the baal tefillah to know that if this niggun was as good as any other, it had the added benefit of bringing his mother pleasure.

Extended Family

SHLOMIE WAS A BELOVED UNCLE TO HIS NEPHEWS AND NIECES, and a rock of support to the adult members of his extended family. As his brother-in-law Avi Szenberg put it:

Shlomie was like a rechargeable battery; he seemed to have an endless amount of energy and patience. I could call him ten times in one day for various reasons. He was always patient and ready to help; whether it was money, changing a tire, or some sound advice, Shlomie was always there for us.

I was once called at the last minute to host a parlor meeting because the original host had to cancel. I knew that my wife and I could get our home set up and take care of the food — but we had no idea how to draw the crowd that would ensure its success. So I called Shlomie, and of course, he brought the crowd.

Shlomie found the time to balance his familial obligations, his work, and his kindness to friends and countless others.

A nephew related:

When we were kids, Uncle Shlomie took us skiing. For me it was the first time and for his kids it was the second.

We kids were nervous. My uncle said he would show us how to go down the slope, a small one. Down he went;

On a skiing trip with (left to right) his son Aharon and nephews Dovid Sosowsky and Avigdor Cyperstein

at the bottom he stumbled and fell. He got up laughing. "You see? There's nothing to be afraid of." He had an instructor give us lessons that day, and we had a great time.

In the car on the way home, my uncle told us that he had to catch a plane to fly to the wedding of a friend's child. As we approached Newark Airport, he pulled over to the side of the road. Moments later, a taxi pulled up and out stepped his trusted worker, Carlos, whom we all knew. Shlomie got into the taxi and headed to the airport, while Carlos got behind the wheel of Shlomie's car and drove us home.

Another time, Uncle Shlomie took us to a local shul where Shlomo Carlebach was performing. It was a frigid night; when we left the shul, we kids complained about the cold. My uncle noticed a parked limousine with a chauffeur behind the wheel. He offered the chauffeur a few dollars and we quickly piled into the limousine for the four-block drive home.

The years passed. When I was an experienced driver, he would lend me one of his cars. One night, I parked the car in Manhattan. When I came back to the spot, the car was gone. At first I thought it had been stolen, but then a policeman showed me a sign that I had overlooked. I had parked illegally, and the car had been towed.

I went down to the pound to pay the fine and retrieve the car. To my dismay, the registration was not in the glove compartment; without it, I could not get the car back. I had no choice but to awaken my uncle at 2 in the morning. He was not the least bit upset at me. "What do you need ... what do you need?" he asked me groggily. Soon the registration was faxed and I was able to drive home.

A niece expressed her feelings after his passing:

I could not believe it when I learned of all the chasadim he was involved in, all the individuals and families he helped so much. Where did he have time for all that? He was our "Uncle Shlomie," the one who, when we were small, would lift us up high and seat us on top of our Savta's refrigerator so that we could touch the ceiling. He was always there for us when we needed him, visiting often and brightening our lives.

Direction for Life

HIS NEPHEW AVIGDOR CYPERSTEIN RECALLED:

When I was in yeshivah in Eretz Yisrael, I would talk with my uncle by phone on a daily basis. When he would come to Eretz Yisrael, which was often, he always made sure to meet with me, take me around to the gedolim he visited, and have some serious conversation.

When I began to look for a job, he hired me to work for him. I'm sure he gave me that job to prepare me for the future, and the truth is, virtually every experience I had while working for him, I've been able to apply to my work at other positions. He taught me how to relate to a boss, to people, to clients.

And I learned a lot about my uncle from watching the tzedakah meetings that went on in his office on a daily basis.

Once, we made up to speak about something personal after office hours. When I got there, two other men showed up to discuss something. My uncle told me that he needed a few minutes with these men and directed me to an adjoining office where I was to wait for him.

I could not hear every word of their conversation, but it was clearly about the need to raise a lot of tzedakah funds quickly. Shlomie told his visitors, "We're not leaving here until we raise $150,000. I'm giving [a certain sum]. What are you giving?" The men responded and my uncle then got on the phone, asking people to pledge large sums. He continued to make phone calls until his goal was met. Only then did our meeting begin.

Outside the office he was my uncle, but in the office he was my boss and he had expectations that I knew I had to fulfill. But though he was my boss, we talked about things outside of work as well. You could talk to him about anything. He was always there for me, to listen, to advise. We could rehash the same issues over and over again. He would never tire of talking about what I needed to talk about.

Even after I moved on to another field of employment, he kept in close touch with me, seeing how I was doing in the business world and in my Torah study. "How is it going with your chavrusa? Come over and let's schmooze." Whenever I came by, it was a rewarding conversation for me.

In the weeks before he passed away, he called me a number of times. "Go to Savta [Bubby Cyperstein, who *lives a few blocks from her daughter, Shlomie's wife] for Shabbos and come with her for the Shabbos seudos."*

The arrangements were finally made, but on Thursday my Aunt Mimi called to say that she was not feeling well and it would not be a good week to come. I was asked to come the following week. I decided to keep my plans of coming to my Savta that week, spend a quiet Shabbos with her, and come back the following week to join my aunt and uncle.

Before Shabbos began, Savta told me that Aunt Mimi was feeling better and we would be going there for the daytime seudah. We were there for hours. Uncle Shlomie was at his best, captivating us with his stories and sense of humor. It was wonderful.

I was sure that I had "been yotzei" (i.e. fulfilled my obligation for) my Shabbos invitation with that delightful seudah, and I was not planning to return for the following Shabbos. But the following week I received a phone call from my uncle. "You're coming for Shabbos just as we made up — right?" I came, and I am very grateful that I did.

How many people would have made that phone call, making sure that I would come again? I think the average person's attitude would have been, "He came already; there's no need to have him come a second time." But my uncle was different. He was always thinking about everyone else.

When Shlomie's family was still young, they spent one Pesach with extended family in Florida. The women went early to make Yom Tov preparations. Shlomie, his young son Aharon, and his brother-in-law Avi Szenberg flew to Washington, D.C., where they would get a connecting flight to Florida. However, upon arriving at Dulles Airport they discovered that through some glitch, only two seats on the flight were available for them.

"Avi," Shlomie said, "you take Aharon on this flight. I'll find my way later."

As Avi later reflected, "It really didn't make sense. Shlomie should have gone together with his son and I should have flown on a later flight. But to Shlomie it made a lot of sense. Because to him, all that mattered is that the other person be taken care of. He was constantly thinking of others, not himself."

In the words of his cousin, Shuli Halpert:

> *We were 20 first cousins, and Shlomie was the youngest. Yet he made room on his shoulders to carry every one of us no matter what the issue was. Shlomie was always there for us. If I had to describe what Shlomie Gross was to the family, I would sum it up in two words: absolutely irreplaceable.*

13
Final Days

IN THE DAYS AND WEEKS BEFORE HIS PASSING, SHLOMIE was at his peak in distributing *tzedakah* and performing acts of *chesed*.

A friend related:

> *Around a month before his passing, I was involved with a hachnasas kallah campaign on behalf of a family Shlomie knew well. I approached him and asked for a large sum. Shlomie told me that it was hard for him to give so much at that time, but that he would think about it. A week or two later, he gave me the sum I had requested.*
>
> *Then, a week before his passing, I was informed that this same family was in need of money for a reason unrelated to the wedding. I felt that I could not approach Shlomie again, after he had given an amount that he had said was hard for him.*
>
> *However, someone else involved with this family did approach him. Shlomie responded by asking the man, who is well-to-do, "So how much are you giving?" The*

Shlomie and Rav Nosson Tzvi Finkel in Mir Yerushalayim, Motza'ei Yom Kippur 5772. By the next Yom Kippur, both had ascended to their place in Gan Eden.

man thought for a few moments, then responded, "Five thousand dollars."

"And I'll match it," Shlomie replied. The man then contacted the family with the good news that he would be bringing them $10,000.

Purim

PURIM BEGAN ON A WEDNESDAY NIGHT, TEN DAYS BEFORE Shlomie passed away.

On Purim evening Shlomie accompanied a distinguished *talmid chacham* from Eretz Yisrael to raise funds for the network of *chadarim* that he heads.

Shlomie had made a parlor meeting for this cause a month before Purim, which a certain friend had attended and where he had given generously. The man therefore could not hide his surprise when Shlomie and his companion walked into his house on Purim seeking another donation.

Shlomie understood his friend's reaction and said, "I know, I know, you really don't have to give anything now." Then Shlomie grabbed his friend's lapel and said, "This is not for him, this one is for me. Do it for me." Shlomie named a figure and his friend promptly wrote a check for the amount. Shlomie hugged and kissed him.

Following is an excerpt of a letter sent to the family by Rabbi Meir Krawiec, a *maggid shiur* who also heads a *bein hazemanim* learning program, Yeshivas Abirei Lev:

> *Though I would only meet Reb Shloime z"l a few times a year, each time was special; a warm word, a kiss, and always a generous hand. His concern and care for every Yid was something I have never seen.*
>
> *Some time ago, Reb Shloime heard about a bachur I knew who was going through a difficult period and was no longer a complete shomer Torah u'mitzvos. He sent me close to $2,000 to hire a mentor who would draw the boy close and look after him. When I would speak with Reb Shloime on the phone, his concern for this bachur was enormous. He was ready to do anything to save his neshamah.*
>
> *This past Purim, I met Reb Shloime when he was already out of his house, about to enter his car. He saw me, ran back into the house, got his checkbook, and wrote out a very generous check (for Yeshivas Abirei Lev).*
>
> *Then I told him that the bachur whom he had worried about had made a huge turnaround and was now fully observant. I told Reb Shloime, "This is your work; you brought him back." He brushed aside the comment as if he had done nothing.*

Following is an excerpt from a letter by Rabbi Yaakov S. Marcus of Yeshivat Or HaTorah:

> *I met Shlomie on Purim night and asked if I could see him after Shacharis in the morning regarding a donation*

for our yeshivah. Of course he answered positively, so I and my 11-year-old son davened at Rav Schorr's minyan that morning.

We happened to seat ourselves at Shlomie's table for davening. I sat alongside Nosson Tzvi, my son sat opposite me, and Shlomie sat near my son in the aisle. Nosson Tzvi turned to me right before the reading of the Megillah and with sweetness and respect asked if I would like to follow along with him in his kosher megillah. Of course I accepted his offer, and closed my Chumash. Then Shlomie turned his chair so that he was sitting alongside my son, handed him the rolled-up side of his Megillah, and said to him, "Come hold it; we'll look in together." I could not help but notice that while the reading was in progress, Shlomie actually put the Megillah in front of my son and leaned over in order to see!

After Shacharis, Shlomie learned with Nosson Tzvi at the Avos Ubanim program and, without interrupting his learning, dispensed tzedakah with respect to those who approached him. This was a lesson to me as well.

A kollel *yungerman* from Kollel Tiferes Tzvi in Jerusalem had come to the States for a *simchah*. On Purim he raised funds for a needy *talmid chacham*. He called Shlomie before Purim to ask if he could come on Purim for a donation. Shlomie told the *yungerman* to call him on Purim morning and they would meet.

But in the morning Shlomie could not come to the phone, and the *yungerman* did not leave a number where he could be reached. He did not think that people of Shlomie Gross' stature return calls to solicitors — especially on a busy day like Purim.

He did not know Shlomie.

When Shlomie realized that he had not been available as promised, he phoned the young man's *rosh kollel* in Eretz Yisrael to ask if he knew of a phone number where the *yungerman* could be reached. The *rosh kollel* did not know how to reach him.

Final Days / 301

Meanwhile, the *yungerman* decided to go to Shlomie's house and ring the bell. He had his family in the car, and on the way his baby daughter cut her finger on a *gragger*. He rang the bell and Shlomie's wife opened the door. Seeing the bleeding child, she quickly ushered the family inside and tended to the child's wound. After it was properly bandaged, Mrs. Gross said, "So now tell me why you really came!"

The *yungerman* stated the purpose of his visit. Mrs. Gross called Shlomie, who was also out fundraising, and he asked that she write a generous check.

"Where Are You?"

RABBI YOSEF MAYER RELATED:

> My last encounter with Shlomie was by phone. Abish Brodt makes a kumzitz on the second night of Purim; it's something I look forward to every year. This past Purim, I strained myself, running around Brooklyn to raise

Donning a spoduk at his last Purim *mesibah*.
Rabbi Avrohom Schorr is seated next to Shlomie.

desperately needed funds. By the time the second night came, I was thoroughly exhausted and collapsed into bed. I did not have the strength to attend the kumzitz.

At around 11:30 p.m. my phone rang. "Where are you?" Shlomie wanted to know. "How come you're not by Abish?" He knew how much I enjoyed Abish's singing. I told him I was too exhausted to come and hung up.

Three minutes later, the phone rang. It was Shlomie. "If you're too tired to arrange for a car, how about if I come pick you up?"

He was a true friend.

Another friend recalled:

On Purim night, after the kumzitz was over, a few of us went to the Purim mesibah of a certain kehillah. We were standing in the back, far from the head table, when one of the gabbaim spotted Shlomie. He came over and invited him to come to the front near the head table. Shlomie replied, "I'm not going unless you can find a place for my friends as well."

The next day, Shlomie spoke by phone with his *mechutan*, Moshe Feuer.

"How was your Purim?" his *mechutan* wanted to know. "*Baruch Hashem*," Shlomie replied. "But it's not a *leichta zach* (simple thing), Purim; it's a big *avodah* (i.e. it takes effort to utilize the day properly)."

Moshe knew that Shlomie had helped a *talmid chacham* in his fundraising that day. "How was business?" he asked.

"It was *k'dai* (worthwhile) for what one person gave," was Shlomie's response.

"I know how much you gave," his *mechutan* replied in jest. "But what about everyone else?"

Shlomie was not in a joking mood. "It's not a *leichta zach*," he repeated. "It's a big *avodah*."

The week of Shlomie's passing, a renowned rosh yeshivah in Eretz Yisrael married off a child. Shlomie sent a sizable sum towards the wedding expenses. The rosh yeshivah thanked Shlomie but said that all expenses were already covered, so he was returning the money. Shlomie laughed and told him, "Please do not return the money. It can be used for other needs."

A friend related:

> *I married off a child at the end of Adar. Shortly before the wedding, Shlomie called and told me, "You're making a wedding soon; I'm sending you a check." I protested that it was not necessary, but Shlomie would not hear of it. He knew I could use the money, and he was sending it.*
> *The check arrived the day after he had passed away.*

The Gemara states that though a person does not know what the future holds in store, he may have a premonition *("mazlei chazei")*.[1]

Two nights before he passed away, Shlomie was visited by a friend who often accompanies *gabba'ei tzedakah* on their fundraising visits. Shlomie would often tell him, "It's hard to collect. I am *mekan'e* (jealous of) you. I wish I could do what you are doing." On this night, Shlomie kissed him on his forehead and said, "Continue doing what you are doing."

Thursday

ON THURSDAY, SHLOMIE CONTACTED A FRIEND FOR WHOM he had purchased an apartment as an investment a while ago. Though they saw each other daily, there were a few important papers that for some reason he had not yet given him. That day he gave them to him.

Thursday night, 22 Adar, Shlomie met with a renowned rosh yeshivah on behalf of a *bachur* whom he had helped guide toward full-time learning. The Rosh Yeshivah accepted the *bachur* into

---
1. *Megillah* 3a.

his yeshivah; as of this writing, he continues to grow in Torah and *avodah*.

He also attended a meeting that night with two respected *askanim* regarding an important *klal* matter.

There was something else Shlomie had to take care of that night, as a friend related:

> On the last night of his life, I received a call from Shlomie; he wanted to come over to speak to me. He sat down and said, "You're upset at me over something."
>
> First I tried to deny that this was so, but he did not accept my denial. Finally, I told him that he had made a comment that I found personally offensive.
>
> He felt terrible. The last thing he would want to do is hurt someone. "I'm so sorry, so very sorry. I had no idea that what I said was hurtful. Please forgive me." Of course, I forgave him.
>
> I am very grateful to Hashem that He allowed us to have this meeting before Shlomie passed away. Shlomie and I were so close; I loved him so much. I would have felt terrible had we not ironed things out.

During that meeting, Shlomie ignored the ringing of his cellphone — except once. It was a call from a *bachur* with Down Syndrome who had come to Shlomie's home on Purim night as he did every year, collecting *tzedakah*. Shlomie felt bad that he had not been home for him. When the *bachur* called that Thursday night, Shlomie said that he would come to his home that night with a check, and he did.

Friday

THE LAST DAY OF HIS LIFE BEGAN, AS USUAL, WITH HIS EARLY-morning learning session with Rabbi Avrohom Aharon Levy. His *chavrusa* explained a *machlokes Rishonim* on the topic they were learning in *Masechta Chagigah* and Shlomie toiled to fully understand the *machlokes*.

That morning, Shlomie went to a *gabbai tzedakah* and paid a balance from *tzedakah* that the *gabbai* had distributed on his behalf.

Later that morning, Shlomie was approached by a Russian immigrant. The man explained that he had been laid off from work and was in need of cash to pay for his family's basic needs. He was not asking for a donation. He wanted to borrow $400.

Shlomie handed the man $400 and the man handed him a postdated check for that amount. As soon as the man was out of view, Shlomie tore up the check.

Later that morning he reminded a close friend to make good on his *tzedakah* pledge to a yeshivah.

Rabbi Chaim Yitzchak Cohen of Jerusalem related:

> *I had an appointment with Shlomie in his office at 11 o'clock that morning, to receive a contribution for my tzedakah fund. In the past, he would give me a series of postdated checks. This time, without explanation, he gave me one large check for the full amount.*

Less than an hour before he passed away, Shlomie called a friend to ask if he knew of a ride to Lakewood for his mother.[2]

In early afternoon, on *Erev Shabbos Parashas Parah,* 22 Adar, Shlomie suffered a massive heart attack and died.

His Rav, Rabbi Avraham Schorr, noted that regarding the mitzvah of *parah adumah* Hashem says, "It is a decree that I have decreed and you have no right to question Me."[3]

The heartrending funeral at Khal Tiferes Yaakov was held on Motza'ei Shabbos and was attended by a very large crowd.[4]

---

2. Rabbi Mendel Bromberg.
3. Cited by *Rashi* to *Bamidbar* 19:2.
4. *Hespeidim* were delivered by (in order of appearance): Rabbi Ben Zion Halberstam, Rav of Khal Bais Avraham; Rabbi Dovid Olewski, Rosh Yeshivah of Mesivta Bais Yisroel D'Ger; Rabbi Avrohom Aharon Levy, *maggid shiur*, Mesivta Tiferes Elimelech; and Rabbi Avrohom Schorr, Rav of Khal Tiferes Yaakov.

At the funeral, Rabbi Aharon Schechter, Rosh Yeshivah of Mesivta Rabbeinu Chaim Berlin, was offered a chair but refused to sit. After he had escorted the *niftar* for one block, the person accompanying him suggested to the venerable Rosh Yeshivah, out of concern for him, that they had walked enough. "I'll tell you when it's enough," the Rosh Yeshivah responded, and continued walking until the hearse sped away.

The *niftar* was brought to Kennedy Airport to be flown to Eretz Yisrael for burial. At the airport, Shlomie's mother, Mrs. Rivka Gross, asked one of his friends to take her home. They drove in silence for a while, until Mrs. Gross said, "Shlomie … he was so young, only 52 years old … But Hashem does not make mistakes."

At the funeral at Shamgar Funeral Home in Eretz Yisrael, also attended by a huge crowd, the distinguished *maspidim* shed bitter tears.[5] Young Yerushalmi children were crying. When someone asked them how they had known the *niftar*, they responded, "*Shloime? — Alle kenen Shloime!* (Shloime? — everyone knows Shloime!)."

Posters announcing Shlomie's funeral in Jerusalem

---

5. *Hespeidim* were delivered by (in order of appearance): Rabbi Shmuel Auerbach, Rosh Yeshivah of Yeshivas Maalos HaTorah; Rabbi Berel Povarsky, Rosh Yeshivah of Yeshivas Ponovezh; Rabbi Yitzchak Scheiner, Rosh Yeshivah of Yeshivas Kaminetz; Rabbi Ben Zion Gutfarb, *Mashpia,* Kehilas HaMasmidim; Rabbi Avrohom Schorr, Rav of Khal Tiferes Yaakov; Shlomie's close friend and business partner Yossi Friedman; his sons-in-law Meir Kaplowitz and Eli Kaufman; and his older son, Aharon Gross.

Men and women, old and young, wept bitter tears of deep personal loss. A Yerushalmi applied the words said regarding Aharon HaKohen, *"They wept for Aharon ... the entire House of Israel."*[6]

Rav Schorr applied the verse *"Is not Ephraim the son who is most precious to Me? Is he not a delightful child, that whenever I speak of him I remember him more and more? Therefore, My inner feelings yearn for him ..."*[7] Shlomie, he said, was a *delightful child*, a mature, growing person who remaining fun-loving until the end. *I remember him more and more* — we remember his incredible accomplishments and cry over all that he would have accomplished had he been permitted to live longer.

The grave on Har HaZeisim

The funeral continued on to the Mirrer Yeshivah[8] and from there to Har HaZeisim where Shlomie was laid to rest next to his father-in-law, R' Nosson Tzvi Cyperstein.

---

6. *Bamidbar* 20:29.
7. *Yirmiyahu* 31:19.
8. *Hespeidim* were delivered by: Rabbi Aryeh Finkel, Rosh Yeshivas Mir – Brachfeld; Rabbi Yehoshua D. Turtzin, Rav of Kehilas HaPerushim; and Shlomie's brother-in-law Eli Cyperstein.

14

Mourning the Loss

FOLLOWING ARE EXCERPTS OF *HESPEIDIM* DELIVERED AT the funerals in New York and Eretz Yisrael, as well as others given at gatherings at the conclusion of *shivah* and *sheloshim*.

Rabbi Shmuel Auerbach[1]

HE WAS THE FIRST FOR EVERY DAVAR SHEBIKEDUSHAH (sacred endeavor), such warmth, such passion. He received every poor person with wisdom and warmth; he was a pillar of chesed.

Rabbi Berel Povarsky[2]

THIS IS A LOSS THAT HAS AFFECTED ALL OF KLAL YISRAEL. The ways of Heaven are hidden from us.

---
1. Rosh Yeshivah of Yeshivah Maalos HaTorah in Jerusalem.
2. Rosh Yeshivah of the Ponovezh Yeshivah in Bnei Brak.

The Midrash says that when a person leaves this world, the Ribono shel Olam says to the Heavenly angels, "Go and see what people say about him."

Shloime: What shall I say about you? The Ribono shel Olam is saying: "See what kind of people I have in My world." Such a precious soul, such a great heart, such a nosei b'ol im chaveiro (one who shares in his friend's burden). He was someone who loved the Torah and its students. Whenever we met, he wanted to hear Torah …

He did so much good for people … Shloime, you accomplished so much in your short life.

You fulfilled the mitzvah of וְאָהַבְתָּ לְרֵעֲךָ כָּמוֹךָ *with everyone you met.*

Reb Shloime was an adam gadol.

Your loss has affected the entire Torah world.

When one of his talmidim passed away, Reish Lakish delivered a hesped. "My beloved has descended to His garden, to graze in the gardens and to pick roses."[3] Reish Lakish was saying that he thought he knew his talmid. But the Ribono shel Olam, Who had chosen him as the rose to pluck from this world and take to Himself on High, knew him better. He knew of qualities that this talmid possessed of which Reish Lakish was unaware.

In Heaven now, thousands upon thousands of angels created through your good deeds are now accompanying you to the Heavenly Throne.

Rabbi Yitzchak Scheiner[4]

WE ARE ASSEMBLED HERE TODAY TO ESCORT ONE OF THE great people of our generation to his final resting place. He was one of those rare individuals who lived not for himself but for others.

---
3. Shir HaShirim 6:2. See Shir HaShirim Rabbah 6:4.
4. Rosh Yeshivah of Yeshivas Kamenitz in Jerusalem.

We have just heard two great roshei yeshivah (Rav Shmuel Auerbach and Rav Berel Povarsky) speak about the deceased like one would speak about a brother who passed away. And that is exactly how I feel, and how I'm sure everyone here feels. Reb Shloime was everyone's best friend, and everyone felt this way. And now we have lost our best friend.

The Ponovezher Rav[5] once said that when he would not get a response upon knocking on the door of a wealthy man to solicit funds, he would have mixed emotions. On the one hand, he did not get the money he needed. On the other hand, he was relieved that he did not have to endure the discomfort of asking the man for money. There were no mixed emotions when knocking on Shlomie's door. He made every visitor feel so at ease, and he was such a pleasure to talk to, that it was truly disappointing when he was not home.

In discussing the death of a certain Tanna, Chazal offer a mashal: Once there was a king who came to observe as the workers tended his vineyard. He noticed that one worker was particularly diligent. The king desired to draw this worker close, so he had him stop working and took him for a stroll. At the end of the day, he gave this worker the largest payment, though he had worked less hours than the other workers. The king explained to the workers, "This man accomplished more in his few hours than you accomplished while working the entire day."[6]

How appropriate is this mashal to Shlomie, who accomplished so much in his short lifetime. He loved Hashem with all his heart. He loved the Torah with all his heart. He loved every Jew with all his heart.

I attended the wedding of one of his children. Every rosh yeshivah, every meshulach, every poor person was his main guest at the wedding. He spent more time with them than with

---

5. Rav Yosef Shlomo Kahaneman (1886-1979).
6. Yerushalmi Berachos 2:8.

his other guests. He was an ish hachesed in the fullest sense. He was a chad b'dara, unique in the generation.

And now they have taken him Above, where they need such people with great ahavas haTorah and ahavas chesed. But here on this world there is a tremendous void, and it is everyone's obligation to fill this void — and it is not an easy task. Everyone who knew him, who loved him, and was loved by him has the holy duty to continue his great work.

Rabbi Ben Zion Gutfarb[7]

REB SHLOIME WAS TAKEN AWAY SUDDENLY. HAD HE BEEN sick, all the batei midrash around the world would have been filled with people davening, "Send a refuah shleimah to the friend of all of Klal Yisrael."

He pursued tzedakah and chesed in the fullest sense. He was "rodeph," he ran after opportunities to help others.

Often, when a poor man comes to ask a rich man for assistance, he has to think about how to present his case, what to say to find favor in his eyes. Sometimes, he has to send an intermediary to plead on his behalf. With Shloime there was no such thing. He received every poor man with great warmth and respect. He was the friend of every rosh yeshivah, every poor man, every broken soul. Every sort of mosad from all communities was close to his heart.

Where does one find a wealthy man to whom every poor man relates like a brother?

מַה יָּפוּ פְעָמַיִךְ בַּנְּעָלִים בַּת נָדִיב (lit. How lovely are your steps in sandals, O daughters of nobility).[8] Chazal say that נָדִיב refers to Avraham Avinu, the pillar of chesed.[9] The Chiddushei HaRim interprets the beginning of the verse this way: פְעָמַיִךְ refers to

---

7. Mashpia, Kehillas HaMasmidim in Jerusalem.
8. Shir HaShirim 7:2.
9. Succah 49b.

a פַּעֲמוֹן, bell, and בַּנְעָלִים refers to a מִנְעָל, lock. Thus the verse means: "How beautiful is the bell that is locked within you, daughter (i.e. descendant) of Avraham." Sometimes a bell of kedushah, of mighty deeds, pounds within one's heart, but is locked, for no one knows about it.

Shloime accomplished many great deeds, but they went almost unnoticed because he did them quietly, in a very natural way. One deed was done and then on to the next one, and no one had to know about it.

His ahavas Yisrael was a semblance of that of Rav Levi Yitzchak of Berditchev. I was once with him at the kever of Shimon HaTzaddik, where a man was davening and crying. Shloime handed someone a few hundred dollars and asked him to give it to this man.

Rabbi Tzvi Kahan[10]

I ALWAYS KNEW THAT HIS TZEDAKAH AND CHESED ENCOMpassed worlds, but I did not know to what extent. At his funeral here in Eretz Yisrael, there was a huge crowd of those whom he had personally assisted: roshei yeshivah, roshei kollelim, and private individuals all crying out in pain.

All these people were his good friends. I had thought that my relationship with him was unique. But then I heard more and more people expressing the same feeling! His heart was big enough to encompass everyone.

We had many earnest conversations. He wanted to know what were his obligations regarding tzedakah, and we discussed other areas of avodas Hashem. His asking מַה חוֹבָתִי בְּעוֹלָמִי (What is my obligation in this world?) was real. He was sincere through and through.

When we began to plan our new building, he was very excited. He wanted to give, and he wanted to get others to give

---
10. Rosh Yeshivah of Yeshivah Imrei Noam in Jerusalem.

as well. His face would shine when someone gave generously. When he heard that one of our supporters had given more than he had given, he said, "He is a tzaddik; halevai (if only) I would give like he gives."

At his funeral, I rode in the hearse together with his rav, Rav Avrohom Schorr. When Rav Schorr told me what percentage of his earnings he gave to tzedakah, I exclaimed, "Oy, Shloime! You did not tell me the truth! You always claimed that others were greater baalei tzedakah than you, but in fact, you were the greatest."

Rabbi Avrohom Schorr[11]

THE GEMARA SAYS THAT THUNDER WAS CREATED TO straighten out the creases in a person's heart.[12] Reb Shloime's passing is more than thunder; it is a lightning bolt. He was the ultimate merachem al habriyos (one who is compassionate towards others).

The Ribono shel Olam went looking for a neshamah whose passing would affect every member of Klal Yisrael, a lightning bolt to the heart of every one of us. He searched and searched and found one precious neshamah whose passing would affect everyone in a very personal way.

The pasuk says 'וְיוֹדוּ שָׁמַיִם פִּלְאֲךָ ה, The heavens will acknowledge Your wonders, Hashem.[13] Rashi uses the word פֶּלֶא, wonder, to describe someone who acts contrary to his natural inclination.

The Heavens are now rejoicing with the פֶּלֶא, wonder, that was Shlomie. They are saying, "Look at what this person has accomplished in his 52 years. Look at his mitzvos, Torah, chesed, and mesiras nefesh. In Shamayim now there is a tumult for this neshamah, a פֶּלֶא.

---
11. Rav of Khal Tiferes Yaakov, Brooklyn, N.Y.
12. *Berachos* 59a.
13. *Tehillim* 89:6.

Shlomie is still with us because he will always remain before our eyes as a shining example of someone who succeeded in overcoming his nature in many different ways. He was constantly growing — and we can be sure that he will ascend from level to level in the Next World.

The Yam Suf split, says the Midrash, when it saw the coffin of Yosef HaTzaddik. Sfas Emes explains that Yosef overcame his nature in fleeing Potiphar's wife. Therefore, the Yam Suf went against its nature and split.

Shlomie overcame his nature in the way he helped others, in the level in which he gave tzedakah, in the way he studied Torah daily for 25 years, in the way he did not bear a grudge when someone wronged him. And Hashem rewarded him with the greatest reward that one can receive in this world — children who, like their parents, want to ascend the ladder of Torah and avodas Hashem.

He was a true hatznei'a leches, as he walked modestly with Hashem, not publicizing his amazing spiritual growth. Only those closest to him knew how he was working on himself, perfecting his middos and overcoming his nature in many areas.

There are all kinds of chesed and baalei chesed. Some take care of tzedakos for widows, some care for the sick, some help yeshivos, but here was a person who was an ish ha'eshkolos, who encompassed within himself every form of chesed. He was a gabbai tzedakah for every cause, doing the job of many gabbaim. There was no particular area of need that was his "cup of tea"; he was involved with everything. And it didn't matter what kind of person came to him; he helped everyone.

Shloime! Remember your family from your place in Shamayim, your eishes chayil and your wonderful children.

Remember your many, many yedidim (friends).

You are bringing with you all your tzedakos and chasadim, the kids at risk whom you saved ...

... *and we are going to try to follow in your ways on this world. May you plead before Hashem for all of Klal Yisrael.*

Rabbi Avrohom Aharon Levy[14]

THE GEMARA RELATES THAT WHEN RAV YOCHANAN PASSED away, the maspid began: "This day is as difficult for the Jewish nation as the day when the sun set at midday."[15] This metaphor refers to one who leaves this world in the prime of his life, at the height of his powers.

Shlomie can be likened to the sun in many ways. The sun shines in every corner of the world; it gives warmth to everyone. There was not a person who met him who did not feel his love, a love that he conveyed with all his soul. He never said a bad word about anyone.

The *pasuk* says וְזָרְחָה לָכֶם יִרְאֵי שְׁמִי שֶׁמֶשׁ צְדָקָה וּמַרְפֵּא בִּכְנָפֶיהָ, *But a sun of righteousness will shine for you who fear My Name, with healing in its rays.*[16] Shlomie healed many souls, with his tzedakah, with his empathy; he made them feel that their distress was truly his own. He was a protector like the sun; people felt soothed by his involvement in their troubles.

In Shlomie's view of life, a "good day" was when he helped to give money and raise money for someone in need, or if he was on the phone all day long helping to get a child placed in yeshivah. He did not enjoy his real estate work because he never looked at it as if **he** were the one accomplishing — all his success was Hashem's.

He was a master at sensing what each person needed. He would take one needy fellow to an expensive restaurant, another to the shvitz (sauna), another he took horseback riding.

---

14. *Maggid shiur* in Mesivta Tiferes Elimelech, Brooklyn, N.Y., and Shlomie's *chavrusa* for the last 25 years of his life.
15. Moed Katan 25b.
16. Malachi 3:20.

There were times when he gave tzedakah way above what even he could afford. He told me that he did this with the emunah that "לְוּוּ עָלַי וַאֲנִי פּוֹרֵעַ (borrow on My account and I will repay)."[17]

Shlomie had a tremendous appreciation for Torah. Sometimes, when a person excels in a particular area, he views that concept as the most important, the pinnacle of achievement. Shlomie excelled in chesed, yet he had a clear perception of the primacy of Torah, that יְקָרָה הִיא מִפְּנִינִים וְכָל חֲפָצֶיךָ לֹא יִשְׁווּ בָהּ (It [the Torah] is more precious than pearls, and all of your desires cannot compare to it).[18]

Most people are unaware of the great effort he invested in his own avodas Hashem. In the week he passed away he traveled out of state on a two-day chesed trip. The morning after he returned he was at his gemara for his early-morning seder as usual.

He never missed. He toiled to gain clarity in the sugya (topic).

This past Elul, he decided to add to his daily learning. He had tremendous aspirations to grow spiritually. He would daven like a child talking to his elder.

He felt great admiration for talmidei chachamim. He never called roshei yeshivah to ask that they come to his children's weddings. (He would simply send them an invitation out of respect.) "I should bother them to come?" was his attitude. He did not use his great support of Torah as a means of enhancing his simchah with their presence. When they came, he appreciated it, but he felt bad that they had made the effort.

He was extremely humble. Whenever I arrived late for our seder, he would use the time to clean the tables of any garbage. He was very humble in the way he viewed his own accomplishments. He would look at what others accomplished and say, "Look at how much he learns; look at how much tzedakah he gives."

---

17. *Beitzah* 15b.
18. *Mishlei* 3:15.

He didn't feel he was anyone special. He was always looking to become better. Just last week he was saying that he was working on his savlanus (tolerance), not to get upset when solicitors were not happy with the amount he gave and pressed him to give them more.

In 25 years, I never heard him use the word "shnorrer" (beggar).

The last couple of weeks he outdid himself in tzedakah and chesed — in a quiet, unassuming way.

His nachas was seeing his children grow in their middos tovos, in their hasmadah (diligence in study), in their being bnei Torah.

The Gemara states: "Hillel obligates the poor."[19] *If a poor person would come before the Heavenly Court and claim that his poverty made it impossible for him to study Torah, he would be told, "Were you any poorer than Hillel? If he was able to learn Torah, then you could have done the same."*

Shlomie obligates us all. He came from a regular home, was a very lively boy, and to a large degree was a self-made man. By nature he had no "zitzfleish" (ability to sit still). He forced himself to sit and learn diligently every day without fail. Each year he undertook a new kabbalah (resolution in spiritual matters) — and he kept it. This is how he grew from year to year.

Many of his friends said, "I never saw anyone change that much."

The Chofetz Chaim said that when a person ascends to be judged, the judgment parallels his way on this world. If he dealt with others with strict judgment, then he will be judged that way. If he treated others with compassion, that is how he will be judged.

Shlomie — we once spoke about what you would say when you would come before Hashem's Throne. You said that your

---

19. Yoma 35b.

words would be, "Ribono shel Olam, You are the Av HaRachaman (Compassionate Father), You know what rachmanus means." Shlomie, on this world you were the biggest rachman. Go before Hashem and plead for your wife. Just the other week you told me she is such an eishes chayil that she stands behind you in all that you do. Plead for your mother, for Nosson Tzvi, for your other children. Please don't forget us, and we will try to go in your ways of chesed.

Shlomie's son, Aharon Gross

A FEW YEARS AGO ON THE SEDER NIGHT, WE WERE ASKING the Mah Nishtanah, *"Tatte, ich vil dir fregen di fir kashas."* And he burst into tears, as he mentioned a family who had just lost their young father.

The morning after my sister's wedding, my rosh yeshivah (who had been there) asked me, "What did you see at the chasunah? I'll tell you what I saw. The tables were dancing, the chairs were dancing." Everyone was rejoicing to such a degree with my father because his ahavas Yisrael for everyone was very real.

Many people have come over to me to say how much they enjoyed meeting my father and speaking with him. Whatever a person needed — money, a good word, some chizuk — my father was there. But he never had the attitude that "I'm doing something great right now." To him it was simply the natural thing to do; to his mind, he deserved no credit for it.

A little boy in Williamsburg was killed by a bus and my father went to the funeral and nichum aveilim. A man called my father and asked, "What are you doing going to Williamsburg — you know them?" My father answered, "No, but if such a thing happened you have to go." He didn't think to himself that he might feel uncomfortable going to people whom he does not know. His attitude was, "It's the right thing, so I have to go."

Rav Eliyahu Mann[20] *told me that a chassidishe woman in Eretz Yisrael lost her husband at a young age and there was no one to bring the child to a chassidishe cheder for his chalakah (upsherin). My father brought the child for his chalakah. He did not consider that he might feel out of place.*

He lived only for others, wanting nothing for himself.

But let's not forget: My mother gave so much strength to my father. And my father gave so much strength to my mother.

No matter what time he went to sleep, no matter how he was feeling, he would arise in the morning with such gevurah (inner strength), ready for his learning seder before davening.

When I would come home from Riverdale for Shabbos, we would learn the sugya I was learning in yeshivah. He thundered with the kol Torah as we learned together.

We live in a world where there is tremendous focus on gashmiyus (materialism). He was very removed from that. When was the last time he ate a normal meal during the week? He had no time for that. He lived in a higher world.

The last really meaningful conversation I had with him was on Purim (by phone, when I was high). I must have told him ten times, "Tatty, you have no idea how much I love you." Then I told him, "Ta, if we felt the love for Hashem like we feel for each other, then no nisayon (spiritual test) would be difficult to overcome."

And my father responded, "Ah, it's not an easy avodah, Aharon, it's not an easy avodah."

Tatty! Go before the Kisei HaKavod and beg that we should merit to have true ahavas Hashem, true bitachon, so that we can continue to shteig (grow spiritually).

Look, Tatty. Everyone is crying. The whole world is missing your greatness. May Mashiach come soon, bimheirah v'yameinu, amen.

---

20. Confidant and *chavrusa* of Rav Chaim Kanievsky, with whom Shlomie had a close relationship. See Chapters Nine and Ten.

Reflections

RABBI BEN ZION HALBERSTAM IS THE RAV OF KHAL BAIS Avraham, where Shlomie learned and *davened* every weekday morning. In his words:

> *Shlomie was not just a baal tzedakah. When he saw that someone needed financial help, he became involved in that person's total situation. It was as if he asked the person, after handing him tzedakah, "Do you have a wallet in which to put the money? Do you have a suit in which to put the wallet? Do you have a coat to wear over the suit? Do you have a means of transportation with which to get back home?" No detail escaped him.*
>
> *Anywhere that chesed needed to be done, Reb Shloime was there. He was the one who made sure that a friend's simchah ran just right; he was there to help a person who had gotten into trouble; he was involved in every important cause.*
>
> *And when he did chesed, he made the other person feel that he was doing him the favor by allowing him to help. And in a sense that's the way it was. Because Reb Shloime derived great pleasure from bringing pleasure to others. When he bought an expensive pair of gloves for someone, he was so happy to make the other person happy.*
>
> *He learned and davened in our shul for 25 years. This distinguished Yid took out the shul's garbage every morning. When it snowed, he was there at five in the morning to shovel so that by the time men began arriving at six, the paths had already been cleared — and few knew who had done the shoveling.*
>
> *But his contribution to our shul was much, much more. Every weekday morning he learned with his chavrusa, Rabbi Levy. He learned with such chiyus (life), with such*

geshmak! He learned diligently, and one could sense his love of Torah, his reverence for Torah. This affected everyone around him; everyone became uplifted through him.

Shlomie's daughter Tzipora reflected:

When we returned from the levayah in Eretz Yisrael to sit shivah at home, I went upstairs to my parents' bedroom and opened my father's closet. There were all the expensive suits and ties that he had purchased a decade or more earlier, when nice clothing meant something to him. In the last years, he grew and grew spiritually, and these things meant nothing to him. I though of the pasuk, "For upon his death he will not take everything, his splendor will not descend after him."[21] My father had come to this recognition in his lifetime, and now HaKadosh Baruch Hu had taken back his pure neshamah.

At a post-*shivah* gathering his friend Willy Beer said:

He did not know how to do things halfheartedly. We should have learned this from him during his lifetime. Now we must learn this from him after his death.

I feel as if a part of me has gone. Life will never be the same.

I never knew a more devoted husband, father, son, brother, and brother-in-law than Shlomie. He was there for his family, as he was for everyone else.

Shlomie, you must have had more than 24 hours in a day, because you never neglected your family and somehow found the time to help everyone else. We need to learn from you.

You wanted nothing for yourself, not honor, not wealth, not recognition.

---

21. *Tehillim* 49:18.

"I Really Need Him"

AROUND TWO WEEKS AFTER SHLOMIE'S PASSING, A WELL-dressed stranger rang the Gross' doorbell and asked for Shlomie. The family realized that this man did not know that Shlomie had died, and they could not bring themselves to tell him. Finally, the man said, "I really need to speak with him. He gives me money every year before Pesach." The man had lost his source of income a number of years ago, and Shlomie would give him a generous sum each year before Pesach.

Finally, they told him. The man collapsed in a faint.

A *chesed* organization in New York distributes food packages before Pesach. On a designated day, families come to a warehouse to pick up their packages. Last year, the organization received a phone call from one of its regular recipients. "I have a problem," the woman said. "Every year I had a driver who brought me to your place to get my package. But the driver, Mr. Shlomie Gross, died a week after Purim. Could you find me another driver…?"

The day after his passing, an acquaintance mentioned Shlomie's death to his Shabbos host on Long Island. The woman gasped, "Shlomie Gross?" She explained that a few months earlier, she needed to undergo major surgery that was not covered by insurance. She was told to approach Shlomie, who loaned her the entire sum.

A man who was not close to Shlomie was inconsolable. His son asked him, "But you didn't know him well. Why are you so broken?"

"I owe my *parnasah* (livelihood) to him," the father replied.

The Scope of the Loss

EACH PERSON WHO HAD A MEANINGFUL RELATIONSHIP WITH Shlomie in the last 20 years of his life recognized that he was a special person. But it was not until he passed away, when massive crowds of weeping mourners attended his funeral, both in America and in Eretz Yisrael, and personal stories about him were related during the *shivah*, that people began to realize the scope of his greatness.

> Some time ago a family with limited income was preparing for a wedding. One day, the oldest son asked his father, "Ta, what do you think it's going to cost to make this wedding?" His father made a quick calculation and said, "Twenty-five thousand dollars." The son then handed him an envelope with $25,000 and said, "Someone gave this to me to give to you on condition that I would not tell you who he is."
>
> During the shivah for Shlomie, the son revealed to his father his benefactor's identity.

A few weeks after Shlomie's passing, his daughter Tzipora Kaufman, who lives in Jerusalem, called a taxi driver whom she had used in the past. When she entered the car, the driver commented that she had not called him in a while. Just then, she noticed on a wall one of the notices of Shlomie's funeral in Jerusalem. She pointed to it and said, "You see that sign? That was my father. He passed away a few weeks ago, and that's why I haven't been going out much."

"Shlomie Gross from Brooklyn was your father?" the driver asked.

"Yes."

The driver said, "Before I made *aliyah*, I owned a small store on Coney Island Avenue. I sold bagels, danishes, hot drinks … It wasn't much of a living. Your father's office was on Coney Island Avenue and he would come in to the store. He saw how quiet it was, how few customers I had. So he began to come by every morning on the way to work to buy a coffee … a bagel … something to get my day off to a good start."

Surely, there are many stories of his *tzedakah* and *chesed* that will remain hidden forever.

His nephew Avigdor Cyperstein related:

> *Recently, I was sitting at work when a stranger approached me. "I hear that Shlomie Gross was your uncle. I want to tell you what he did for me. I'm in the building supply business, and my business needed a boost. I spoke to some people who told me to speak to Shlomie Gross. I contacted him, and we spoke. The bottom line is that I was a total stranger and he gave me an order that gave my business the boost that it needed."*
>
> *A few minutes later a young man came over to me and said, "Shlomie Gross was your uncle? He was my father's best friend!"*
>
> *I thought to myself, "How can this be? I've never heard of this fellow, and he was my uncle's best friend?"*
>
> *He went on to say that his father was in the construction business and my uncle often got him jobs because he valued his work so much. This may be true, but I think there may have been another factor. My uncle would do anything to help another Jew, and if this man needed work, my uncle was going to find it for him.*

Shlomie's mother-in-law, Mrs. Sarah Cyperstein, said:

> *The last Succos of his life we were together in Eretz Yisrael. One evening he said, "Let's go for a walk in Geulah." We were walking and then I realized that he was nowhere to be seen. He was a block or two behind us, because virtually everyone who passed him — Litvish, Chassidish, Sephardic, kippah serugah — knew him and had stopped to wish him "Gut Yom Tov." He greeted everyone with a smile.*
>
> *He never spoke about how he got to know these people, but it was obvious that he had a relationship with them. It was something amazing — he was such a special person.*

> *Our lives have not been the same since Shlomie passed away. Our tree has fallen. He was so full of life. He always had something new to share with us, whether it was a visit to the gedolim or something else that was happening. He would come back from Eretz Yisrael and talk about the beauty of being there.*
>
> *It's been difficult, but we have bitachon. We are strong, and we go on with our lives to the best of our ability.*

To Go in His Ways

A *BACHUR* RELATED:

> *Shlomie turned my life around. Hashem has made sure that I should think of him often.*
>
> *I learn in Yerushalayim. The walk from my yeshivah to my apartment takes me past Rechov Nechemiah. It is almost a year since he died and the poster announcing Shlomie's levayah is still hanging and has not been covered over by other posters! I have a daily reminder of the man and all that he taught me.*

During the week of *shivah*, the family received a receipt for a $180 donation to the Masbia soup kitchen in Brooklyn with the following note attached:

> *After leaving the house of mourning, we passed Masbia and said, "What would Shlomie Gross do? Could he eat without making sure others eat?" This contribution is in his memory — he inspired us in life and continues to inspire us in death.*

A close friend who flew to Eretz Yisrael for the *hakamas matzeivah* (unveiling) related:

> *After my arrival at Ben Gurion Airport, someone mentioned to me that he had forgotten something on the plane. It was something that could be replaced, but it was*

important to him. He could not return to the plane, however, because he was in a rush to attend a bris. Later, I said to myself, "Right then and there, I had an opportunity to emulate Shlomie, and I wasted it. Had Shlomie been there, without a doubt he would have returned to the plane to retrieve the forgotten item for the other fellow." That was Shlomie. Nothing was too hard or time-consuming if it could benefit someone else.

Another friend related:

This past Sunday, as I was running out of my house to my office to work on our annual dinner, the doorbell rang. A woman was standing there, soliciting tzedakah. My initial reaction was to say, "I'm really sorry, but I'm extremely busy now…"

But then I stopped and said to myself: "What would Shlomie have done?"

For sure, he would have spoken to the woman no matter how busy he was. So I invited her inside, listened to her story, and wrote a check. She pleaded with me for more, and again I said to myself, "Shlomie would for sure give her more…"

A young man related:

Getting to know Shlomie was a life-changing experience. The main thing I learned from him is to love and respect everyone regardless of his station in life.

> *I attended a wedding where one of the guests was obviously a "kid at risk." When Shlomie entered the hall, this boy ran across the room and greeted him like an old friend. Shlomie greeted him in kind, and then took him for a walk.*
>
> *As a division head in camp this past summer, I addressed the camp on Shabbos Chazon and spoke about being selfless. I became emotional as I spoke about Shlomie — who personified selflessness, humility, and true ahavas Yisrael.*
>
> *Not a day goes by that I don't think about him. When I see someone who is down, my first thought is, "What would Shlomie say to lift his spirits?"*

Everywhere, those who knew him seek to emulate him, as someone related:

> *During the week of shivah, I was on line in a kosher supermarket. The first person on line was a young man who struggles to support his family, and the person behind him was a man of means. The first man told the clerk, "Put it on my bill." When his phone number was punched in, the screen showed that his balance was several hundred dollars. When he left the store, the man behind him paid the entire balance. Turning to me, he said, "That's what Shlomie would have done."*
>
> *He gave with his heart, he gave with his soul, but above all — he gave with his smile.*

Let us all become "friends of Shlomie" and think to ourselves, "What would Shlomie have done?"